Inside the
Everyday Lives of
Development
Workers

Inside the Everyday Lives of Development Workers

The Challenges and Futures of Aidland

Edited by
Anne-Meike Fechter and Heather Hindman

Kumarian Press
An Imprint of Stylus Publishing

Inside the Everyday Lives of Development Workers:
The Challenges and Futures of Aidland
Published in 2011 in the United States of America by Kumarian Press,
22883 Quicksilver Drive, Sterling, VA 20166 USA.

The text of this book is set in 11/13 Garamond

Editing and book design by Nicole Hirschman
Proofread by Beth Richards
Index by Robert Swanson

The paper used in this publication meets the minimum requirements of the American National Standard for Information Sciences—Permanence of Paper for Printed
Library Materials, ANSI Z39.48–1984

Library of Congress Cataloging-in-Publication Data

Inside the everyday lives of development workers : the challenges and futures of
    Aidland / edited by Anne-Meike Fechter and Heather Hindman.
        p.   cm.
    Includes bibliographical references and index.
    ISBN 978-1-56549-323-0 (pbk. : alk. paper) — ISBN 978-1-56549-324-7
        (cloth : alk. paper) — ISBN 978-1-56549-388-9 (library ebook) —
        ISBN 978-1-56549-389-6 (consumer ebook)
    1. Nonprofit organizations—Employees—Case studies. 2. Social service—Case
studies. 3. Humanitarian assistance—Social aspects—Case studies. 4. International
relief—Social aspects—Case studies. I. Fechter, Anne-Meike. II. Hindman, Heather.
    HD2769.15.I55   2011
    331.7'6133891—dc22
                                                                    2010043186

Contents

Introduction

Heather Hindman and Anne-Meike Fechter

He appears on the nightly news after a major natural disaster—the aid worker. Speaking into the microphone, a 30-something bearded man recounts the struggles of the noble people to whom he has devoted the past few years of his life. His face haggard by several sleepless nights,

UN Photo/Logan Abassi

he nonetheless appears energetic and hopeful about the daunting task of rebuilding that lies ahead. As he shares with the global news audience the story of his attempts to improve life in this foreign land, he effortlessly switches to some local patois to speak to a nearby child tugging at his sleeve.

This heroic icon is what comes to mind when many people think about aid workers, but he is in the minority of contemporary aid professionals. Left out of the telegenic images are the desk jockeys, completing vast reams of paperwork; the career aid professionals, who struggle to maintain their devotion as jobs are being eliminated; the government professionals serving their time abroad before a desired promotion to a much more comfortable and lucrative job in the headquarters; and the local consultants seeking to transform their role into something more than "cultural experts" on a project. The rugged aid worker stereotype continually clashes with these less-glamorous development laborers, whose motives and lives are often questioned by a world more familiar with the television ideal.

In exploring the everyday lives of aid workers, we, the authors and editors of this book, describe a complex collection of characters and a diverse set of life experiences that bring people to the world of development work. To illustrate the challenges and futures of development, we focus on the world of aid workers rather than on aid policy or development institutions, resulting in a novel set of questions and concerns posed in relation to the laboring aspect of aid work. Too often, scholarship on development is shaped by the ongoing battle between the theories of the academic world and the applied concerns of aid professionals, both of which often neglect the day-to-day experiences of those doing aid work. In the rush to offer either prescriptions or critique, the human actors who transform policy into projects are neglected. Critical appraisals of development often attribute its failures to large-scale ideological concerns, such as neoimperialist agendas or unsustainable approaches, while less-grand influences on project development, from local holidays to retiring department leadership, remain invisible. Rather than presenting a "post-" or "anti-" development point of view, this book calls for an examination of the labor of aid—temporarily putting aside concerns over development's hegemonic character and its tendency to assume a linear understanding of progress—to suggest that the structure of the work itself influences the outcomes of development.

Therefore, this book begins with a goal of collecting ethnographic accounts of aid workers—a social body as worthy of the ethnographic gaze as any other. Without lapsing into new forms of exoticism, we take seriously the idea of a culture of aid work that shapes the world of development professionals as much as other cultures and yet, like all cultures, is rarely singular or simple. The addition of "aid culture" to a conversation about development introduces new concerns brought forth by the implied existence of an aid community, a category made problematic by the injunctions that aid work be focused on the needs of the "other." The everyday problems of doing aid work exist in tension with the persistent demands for benevolence and altruism that dominate aid rhetoric. The failures of development not only occur at the level of theory, history, and hegemony but also emanate from the daily tasks undertaken by development practitioners. Thus it is necessary to pull to the forefront the complex problems that are a part of the daily lives of those on the frontline. Only through investigating the structural impingements and seemingly mundane aspects of the lives of aid workers are the affective dimensions of "Aidland," a term that has captured the interest of development workers themselves as well as of some academics (e.g., Eyben 2006; Denskus 2007), revealed, affective aspects that unavoidably influence the aid product.

Inside the Everyday Lives of Development Workers is thus not a critique of any particular form of development but a call to take seriously aid work as work and as life. Too often, the benevolence presumed to underlie "helping professions" such as development threatens to obscure aid workers' need to consider career logics, work–family balance, and benefits packages as well. Focusing on the laboring aspects of aid work reveals concerns that aid workers share with other contemporary employees. Like many professions, development work is being transformed by processes such as deskilling, outsourcing, and neoliberal approaches to staffing. As some of the chapters in this volume show, the definition of aid work is changing as greater emphasis is put on subcontracting and new kinds of expertise are demanded by new forms of aid. At its most ambitious, *Inside the Everyday Lives of Development Workers* suggests radical reformulation of what have been the presumed boundaries of aid analysis, such as between work and leisure, aid "producers" and "consumers," and the refigures of the ostensible limits of development itself. Debates over the validity of development and its close connections with racial and military hegemonies will continue, yet in turning attention to aid work as work, a new set of neoliberal practices is revealed that threatens to sneak into the world of development through what are claimed as depoliticized "best practices" of employment and efficiency.

Outside the Development Blame Game

We call for the insertion of development workers' lives into studies of aid not merely as a call to examine the unexamined but because we feel that they are part and parcel of the theory of development. Understanding the world of aid workers is central to generating a literature on development that goes beyond accusation and blame, although viewing their lives also produces new avenues for reexamining the processes of development. Rather than seeing human resources programs or the cultural training of aid workers as marginal to the project of aid, we claim that they must be considered as central to aid as more commonly debated issues, such as the changing industry rhetorics around sustainable development or new forms of microfinance. In applied and professional literature on development as well as critical anthropology, aid workers have largely been invisible for a number of reasons, including an interpretation of their work as mere policy implementation and an occlusion of their importance justified by the need to emphasize the suffering of aid recipients rather than aid workers. A perception of aid work as something other than work, such as tourism or charity, means that it is accorded the same scholarly dismissal as forms of leisure or amateur pursuits. In addition, an exclusive emphasis on either philosophies or outcomes of development, rather than processes, directs attention to metropolitan policy practices or retrospective and statistical analysis (and usually critique) of why projects fail. While one might assume the humanist tendencies shared by development practitioners and social science critics would place humans—including aid workers—in the frame of development analysis, they are often left out of the story. While critics and practitioners debate the merits of various approaches to poverty alleviation, underlying processes such as the rise of subcontracting within development and new employment procedures are ignored. The growing importance of business models within aid work and a focus on incremental measures of efficiency are having as much influence on the effectiveness of development as a turn to "community-based development" and yet are often ignored as presumably universal best practices.

Aid Workers as Influential Mediators

The lack of attention to the lives of development workers may stem in part from the understanding of their work as something that merely requires the translation of metropolitan policy into local idiom. Under this understanding, aid work is just a process of "add culture and stir," as aid professionals are called upon to implement the most recent policy agenda. This understanding of aid labor is one that presumes it to be, in the terms of Bruno Latour, intermediary rather than mediating work. This distinction (Latour 2005) indexes the assumptions sometimes made by social science about both human and nonhuman actors—that they are mere conduits or tools to perform a function or play a role in an extant structure. Latour and other actor-network theory scholars use this distinction to highlight the transformative role that things we often take for granted perform and that presumed intermediaries in fact change the world in unpredicted ways. The technology that surrounds us is often thought to be "just a tool," but tools—be they laptops or irrigation consultants—both shape that in which they are engaged and act in unexpected ways, as anyone who has experienced a computer crash can attest. While greater awareness is being directed to the transformations in thinking and sociality caused by "mere tools" such as word processing software and text messaging (Callon 1986; Vaughan 1996; Tufte 2006), similar revelations have yet to be directed to the work of people such as aid workers, who are assumed incorrectly to be mere tools. The individual life situations and motivations of aid workers matter in how their work is accomplished—they rarely act as the mere conduits that some in central offices expect them to—as they are enmeshed in networks that include other aid workers, local interlocutors, and their own families. As greater pressure to attain documentable and externally defined statistical goals is being directed toward aid programs, the invisibility of aid workers in this calculation seems to presume that one is replaceable with another (given appropriate expertise) and that the externalities of families, life courses, and social habits are irrelevant to the performance of their jobs. Central to the very idea of nearly all aid projects is the idea of transformation, and yet the transformative work of the development worker is often denied; instead, the expectation is that the metropolitan policy will (sometimes effectively, sometimes not) be implemented in the field. Until aid workers are taken seriously as mediating actors, the frustration of both policy makers and aid recipients about why projects fail will continue, and both approaches will persist in believing that the other side "just doesn't get it."

The Disappearance of the Aid Professional

One of the most remarkable revelations that appears when one places the work of aid at the center of the focus on development is the relative scarcity of the imagined ideal aid professional as stereotyped in public forums. Like other forms of modern work, linear progress in a single job or even the maintenance of a career throughout a lifetime has become rare. Many of those we spoke with about their aid work identify as engineers, missionaries, or educators rather than as aid workers. While a hydrologist may be working for an aid agency this month, his or her next job might likely be for a private company. This flexible identification with the category "aid worker" is compounded by the prevalence of aid agencies that are reducing their full-time staff in favor of technical subcontracting, hiring short-term experts and outsourcing jobs to private companies. With the rise of specialized nonprofit managers, the labor of development is often allocated by coordinating professionals to temporary volunteers on one hand and outside experts on the other, with the managers themselves providing what limited continuity and oversight exists. Thus while the vision of aid work and the changing philosophies of development are discussed by scholars and central office policy professionals, much of the work of aid has been reduced to a set of technical problems to be solved by experts. What both high modernist projects (Scott 1998) of dam and road building and postdevelopment and community-based projects share is this new corporatism of outsourcing that has fragmented contemporary aid work as a profession. In looking at who is doing the work of aid, we see this process of fragmentation and alienation as an often-overlooked aspect of how aid gets done and suggest that as much as changing development philosophies, this shared business practice is influencing the contemporary pursuit of the goals of development.

The Disjunctures of Audit Culture in Aidland

Evaluations, reports, and assessments are the official language of the aid world, and the production of documentation has become even more important in this era of outsourcing (Power 1994, 1997; Strathern 2000). Written examination and quantification of the many discrete levels and subprojects of any development scheme are demanded by many audiences, not only funders and governments but also oversight agencies and contractors. These evaluations also must stand as calling cards for future business as companies seek to document their efficiency in carrying out the contracted aspect of a project. Thus while nongovernmental organization (NGO) workers have often complained about the onerous burdens imposed by the bureaucracy of documenting success to their superiors as well as potential donors, the fragmentation of aid work has demanded such accounting at many new levels with a single project. Bureaucratic mechanisms and enumerative documentation have long been central to the development project, yet the demands of new forms and scales of aid assessment has also generated new potential for such audits to produce quantitative stories of success that are experienced as failures by various polities involved.

Even as more and more aid workers find their labor devoted to such documentation projects, they see few if any benefits from the process. In official accounts of development projects, documenting successes and failures is central, and while outcomes are attributed to a wide range of influences, the efforts of individual aid workers, or even small teams, are often not prominently noted as causative of a particular outcome. This seems in contrast even to other helping professions; for example, when UK state-school headteachers are individually credited with turning around failing schools, and US school principals financially benefit from "leaving no child behind." Although individual efforts are informally recognized and potentially rewarded through unofficial mechanisms and career progression, the obscuring of individuals from such records seems to suggest a replicablity of roles or that the altruistic labor of aid workers should be exempt from commendation.

With private companies competing in greater numbers for aid money and contracts, organizations and consultants need to constantly document successes to justify their ongoing employment and their comparative value. The flexible labor needs of agencies and protean careers (Hall 1976) are now predominant in the world of development and place new demands on aid workers themselves to document their particular skills and role in producing successful development projects. New careerist motivations are required, as those who are allotting contracts have the ability to ensure a steady flow of interesting and lucrative assignments to workers who can provide data to justify their value to both employers and outside donors. In the era of short-term, project-based aid work, the pressure to be seen to deliver is required to stay employed; thus there are many who find the purported ideal of self-sacrifice associated with aid work in contrast to the market demands for self-promotion. Rhetorics of benevolence and sacrifice for the good of others may find a receptive audience among donors, but when contracts for a new project are being negotiated, agencies are looking for the engineer with the most successful track record, not the one who cares the most. Ignored by both academic studies and their own employers, aid workers are often pulled by a need to laud their own accomplishments to gain employment and then denigrated as bad care workers when they do.

Placing the Study of Aid Within the Anthropology of Work

The very constitution of development work as a form of labor is an important theme in this collection, as many of the chapters observe aid workers' conflicted relationship between heeding the call to engage in forms of sacrifice and emotional labor as part of the caring aspect of aid and keeping their career desires and their own family's financial needs in mind. While feminist scholars have long been cognizant of the uncompensated emotional labor demanded of women (e.g., Hochschild 2003; Foner 1995), aid workers often struggle with similar expectations of uncompensated benevolence—expectations imposed by themselves and others—that are often in conflict with moves to greater rationality, the strengthening of audit cultures, and specialization within development. This tension between the caring side of aid work and the day-to-day financial needs of its practitioners is exacerbated by an unclear boundary between career aid workers and a wider set of those involved in development, such as student volunteers, retirees on working-vacations, and religious groups engaged in outreach. With volunteers working side by side with compensated career aid workers, workplace tensions develop over what is the "right" reason for doing development work and what brings different professionals to the field. These shifts have also displaced some of those previously doing hands-on work with NGOs and government projects, who find themselves moved into fund-raising activities or office work necessary to fulfill bureaucratic demands. Digging more deeply into the everyday practices of aid workers reveals the multitude of responsibilities behind the more publically prominent tasks of feeding babies and teaching literacy. Consultants, technical experts, private subcontractors, and grant writers are increasingly necessary additions to the array of those operating in Aidland, further complicating both the definition of "aid worker" and the perceived motivations and nature of aid work as a profession.

Changes in the profile of the "typical" aid worker have significant effects on the way development work is done. Globalization, in its myriad forms of offshoring, deskilling, and flexibilization, has impacted both aid practitioners and the character of aid work. The involvement of individuals from a broader ethnic and racial spectrum and the increased emphasis on local participation has changed who is doing aid work and where they are performing it, but it has not obviated the accusations of neocolonialism leveled against development work. Instead, this form and aesthetic of diversity among aid workers has often placed the labor of "making progress" into the hands of modernizing local elites with their own history of hierarchies and discriminations. It is only through placing aid work and aid lives in the same frame that one can examine how changes, such as the increased emphasis on technical and management skills in development or the blurring of lines between professional aid work and volunteering, are reshaping the roles taken on by those in development.

Who Are Aid Workers?

In the disjuncture between the altruistic vision of the atomized aid worker of popular imagination and the daily lives of aid professionals across the world, more is at stake in the misrecognition of their labors and demographic profile than merely a mistaken image. The assumption that aid workers fit into a particular stereotype is found not only in public opinion but also in the policies of the aid profession and the anticipation of those with interest in the field. In this book, we frequently employ the convenient shorthand of "aid worker" or "development practitioner" to make a case for their inclusion in a development research agenda. Closer inspection, however, reveals this category as highly complex, if not entirely fictional. Our research suggests that "people who work in aid" make up an extremely varied group, in almost all possible respects. The policies and visions of those who employ aid workers has yet to catch up with the diversity of those in the field, often with deleterious effects on the health, welfare, and happiness of those outside the stereotype.

In the different accounts in this volume, we highlight a few of the lines along which those engaging in aid work distinguish themselves or are distinguished by others. Within the aid community—another term of convenience with its own questionable assumption of homogeneity—one of the most important distinctions is the professional status aid workers claim. The battle between who is an "aid professional" and those who may do similar work, but without such a title being accepted or imposed, determines how their work is valued and compensated, as well as how they envision their futures and their social connections. Yet even this is a site of contestation, insofar as the boundaries between "volunteers" and "professionals" are often intentionally or unintentionally ambiguous. Volunteers participating in government-sponsored aid programs such as the Peace Corps and KOICA (Korean International Cooperation Agency) often do the same work as paid professionals in other organizations. Likewise, entities such as Voluntary Service Overseas run commercial operations offering "voluntourism" adventures to Westerners seeking to have a middleman facilitate their contribution to overseas development. The fact that some volunteers spend more time in a single country than a "professional" aid worker on an assignment and that some international interns may have to pay for their own maintenance while "volunteers" may receive an allowance makes it difficult to differentiate between the two labels based merely on length of stay, kinds of tasks, or compensation. It is also frequently the case that professional aid workers have been volunteers in the past or still act as volunteers outside of their waged positions. Just as the line between development professionals and volunteers blurs, the bounds of the aid worker category become unclear in another direction, as NGOs are delegating tasks once done by direct hires to third-party subcontractors. Thus even large projects may have only one direct employee of the NGO, with the rest of the work being done by short-term experts working directly for large service agencies such as Kellogg, Brown and Root, and Crown Agents. Within a single project there may be parties defined as consultants, volunteers, experts, and tourists, all with very different motivations for participation. The skill sets demanded of the contemporary aid worker also diverge from stereotypical expectations. While the technical proficiencies frequently associated with development, such as in nursing or agricultural engineering, continue to be in demand, many agencies are also looking for a new set of specializations in finance, management, and fund-raising. Many universities are introducing programs in Development Management or the like that specialize in educating students for this new aspect of development work.

The diversity of members of the aid community is further increased by a professional fluidity across both time and space. This means that individuals may move through a range of different job roles and capacities throughout their careers in Aidland or indeed the course of their lives. While starting out as a volunteer or intern, they may gain a fixed-term contract with an aid agency as a junior advisor, which may (or may not) become a permanent contract with the initial employer or a different employer. People may intermittently return to headquarters or change employers; some may choose to be based in their home countries and from then on mainly work as short-term consultants. Even home itself becomes a problematic idea for many aid workers, with many maintaining ties and residences in several locations. While one set of aid professionals carries out a series of assignments that involve a degree of "settling" in one country, staying between two and five years, others work on a project basis with short stays of less than six months in a given country, while yet others decide to remain in a particular place for an extended time period and seek out a series of employers, allowing them to stay in their desired residence.

Ethnicity, geography, race, and mobility (as well as its lack) further complexify understanding the "typical" aid worker. For example, although we refer to "international" aid workers, insofar as these workers' experiences are shaped by different sets of privileges and constraints than those of "local" practitioners, it is often an ambiguous divide made by categories of employment and compensation rather than residence or race, as seen in the accounts of several authors in this volume (especially Verma, Fountain, and Brown). While a large percentage of the development practitioners working in Asia, Africa, and Latin America are white and come from North America, Europe, and Australia, there are also considerable numbers from Japan, South Korea, India, the Philippines, and other Asian countries. In addition, there are Westerners who have taken up citizenship of a country where they have worked in development long term, as well as international aid workers whose parents migrated from so-called developing countries to Europe or the United States in past generations and who are now working in what some see as their home country. This diversity requires that one not assume the "white Western" man of our opening caricature when referring to "international aid workers," although assumptions about the age, gender, sexuality, and singularity of "home" for aid workers persist in the press and structures of employment. Racial and national diversity in aid work was anticipated to ameliorate, if not obviate, the divide between developer and developee, yet many on the ground find that for every hegemony overcome by hiring a different demographic group, new exclusions occur and new sets of prejudice arise (Sassen 2006). With the rise of community-centered development, new fissures and inequities in the romantic ideal of community appear (Joseph 2002). Focusing on the real people behind the aid ideal clarifies their diversity in background and life experience as well as the new problems that occur. The call is thus to recognize diversity not merely as a corrective but also as a move with implications for people's personal lives, professional actions, and local dynamics.

Our mission in this book—to reintegrate the private and public lives of aid workers—stems not only from the revealing philosophical conclusions that such a framing introduces but also from necessity, for it reflects the impossibility of drawing such public–private distinctions in development practice. In a venue where individuals often live away from their home countries for many years and may move across the globe on a regular basis, the assumptions of a nine-to-five job are inapplicable. Thus even as we emphasize the laboring aspect of development, we observe that the world of aid often demands work that exceeds the assumed bounds of more structured careers. Development workers are explicitly plotted into a difficult interstitial position, hired for their ability to bridge a perceived divide between grantor and grantee yet always suspected as potentially "going native" or conversely misunderstanding "local culture." The turn to ethnography and everyday life reveals how daily interactions and individual relations influence international aid workers' practices with regard to issues such as income inequality with peers, home and host racial divides, and understandings of sexuality (e.g., Adams and Pigg 2005). When the critical lens is focused on the world of aid workers, these concerns about family life and emotions come to the fore, and one finds that such concerns are not external to the work of aid but central to their overall effect.

The Uneasy Dialogue Between Anthropology and Development

Anthropological engagement with development has predominantly focused on the analysis of institutions, discourses, and policies rather than on culture or people. The critical development literature of the early 1990s (e.g., Escobar 1995; Ferguson 1990) revealed the structural fissures, teleological presumptions, and neocolonial underpinnings of development as it existed at the time and that continue today. Although these anthropological critiques of development focused on broad structural and political issues, they also included devastating accounts of aid projects, their failures, and the impact on local populations. A recent conversation about the role of ethnography in development has questioned the "monolithic notions of dominance, resistance, hegemonic relations" that it is claimed characterized earlier analysis of the world of aid (Mosse 2004, 645; cf. Crewe and Harrison 1998). Even with this critical awareness, there appear to be endemic problems at the intersection of development and ethnography or, as Tania Li finds, "an ethnographic appreciation of the complexities of rural relations to be antithetical to the position of an expert" (Li 2007, 3). While Li is in this instance pointing to a particular disjuncture between an ethnographic understanding of lives of rural Indonesians and the technical and practical demands of development, we see a more general challenge in this statement—one that suggests that assumptions about development as a form of labor influence what outcomes are possible, as much as if not more than policies and centralized planning. Ethnographic interest in development has seen only the culture of "developees" and the complexities of their relations as worthy of interest, less often according developers themselves similar complexity. Neither anthropology's critical lens on development nor an increased utilization of and respect for ethnography within development itself has been successful in generating a rich story of aid workers. What could be called the "ethnographic turn" in development studies (Hilhorst 2003; Mosse 2005; Lewis and Mosse 2006) often maintains the focus on aid institutions, policies, and projects, with aid workers often viewed only in the role of translators of cosmopolitan policy to local conditions. *Inside the Everyday Lives of Development Workers* sees practitioners themselves not merely as tools in the variable efficacy of aid projects but as an interesting and valuable story in and of themselves.

While international aid workers have not received much attention in scholarly works (for exceptions see Stirrat 2008; Rajak and Stirrat in press), the contradictions and tensions inherent in their lives and labors have been more prominently discussed in popular accounts authored by aid practitioners themselves. A brief glimpse of the everyday world of aid workers was provided by Leonard Frank in his 1986 article titled "The Development Game," where he voiced his concerns about his involvement in what had in his eyes become an "aid industry." The fact that this article was published under a pseudonym highlights the contentious nature of putting the backstage of the aid world on display and a desire by some to maintain a strong border between aid work and anthropological scholarship. A few articles provide a hint of the border-crossing activities of many anthropologists; for example, a short piece by Edward Green (1986) in the *American Anthropologist* on his experiences of being a "short-term consultant in Bangladesh," which produced a debate over the merits of journalistic accounts such as Green's as well as a proposal that such a practitioner's eye view threatens to undermine the more serious problems of poverty that underlie the development agenda (Wallace 1987). The dangers of writing about "doing development" for anthropologists is also seen in David Mosse's account of the policies and processes surrounding a UK-funded, large-scale forestry project in India. In *Cultivating Development: An Ethnography of Aid Policy and Practice*, Mosse (2005) described how writing about his work as a project advisor caused much furor among his employers, who threatened him with legal action, and upset some of his former coworkers on the project, who accused him of professional and personal betrayal. Perhaps it is fear of such responses that has caused many anthropologists active in development to avoid writing about their experiences, even in the age of reflexive anthropology. Tension between academic and applied anthropology makes conversions from practitioner to academic or the reverse risky, particularly for those who lack tenure, reputation, or longevity in their field. Yet the difficult job market in academic anthropology has made such opportunities especially attractive of late. As writings on anthropologists participating in US military operations attest (e.g., González 2009; Price 2009), debates over the ethics of participation can become virulent, especially in realms where moral and political ambiguities are a part of daily life. Although the reflexive and reflective tools of anthropology hold great promise to uncover the murky world of the daily practice of aid work, the involvement of anthropologists themselves in this work—the blurring of "us" and "them"—has often made the informal aspects of aid work invisible. Too often the cultural relativism and sympathy that are a part of the ethics of most anthropologists are withheld when the gaze is placed on the aid worker, a tribe that appears to both repel and threaten many anthropologists. The aid worker is still classed, echoing Malinowski's injunction to avoid the white man (Malinowski 1984, 6), as the barrier to ethnography rather than a source of potential insight.

One response to invisibility of aid workers within scholarly accounts is found in the concept of Aidland. That Aidland, which was introduced as a term of art in the writings of scholars such as its initiator Raymond Apthorpe, has been picked up and used by aid workers suggests that participants find resonance in the suggestion that they are a part of "the development world." For some, it is this identification, as much as nation or employer, that gives them a sense of belonging and continuity wherever they are posted. While Apthorpe (2005) saw this as a description of the way in which aid workers inhabit a separate world with its own time, space, and economics, the term can threaten to downplay the transformative aspects of geographic mobility and the diverse experiences of Aidland. Existing studies of aid workers rarely recognize how the mobility of aid workers fundamentally structures their life course, professional practices, and social relationships. Although useful in capturing a sense of imagined community, as can be seen in the proliferation of websites and blogs produced by aid workers, the concept of Aidland itself can become monolithic, glossing over differences that deserve further scrutiny. The sense of social and professional coherence that it implies may have always been tenuous, and the social, racial, and moral dimensions of difference that are becoming more central further highlight contemporary tensions and distinctions among aid workers. Aid culture, we suggest, can be seen only in the lives of the many aid workers who do (and do not) identify with such a concept.

Stories of Daily Life

The focus on the everyday lives of aid workers revealed several arenas that are neglected by other studies—aspects of the work entailed in making the aid product that come to the fore when practitioners are placed at the center of the study of development. Each of these aspects of aid work requires that one look not merely at policy but also at public perceptions, the personal needs of those engaging in aid work, and the daily conflicts that are a part of any job environment. The focus on aid workers also changes the temporal and spatial scale of investigating development. Investigations that focus on policy tend to assume the time horizons of governments, while those discussing projects begin and end with the cycles of a given program. The demands of a career as an aid professional or even the scope of a "voluntourist" enforce a different perspective on the limits of the project at hand and a diverse set of viewpoints on the final product of a development pursuit. Thus the pieces in this volume capture not only neglected aspects of the world of aid but also a different view on change, engendered by the vision of aid workers themselves. Like many other members of the modern workforce, aid professionals struggle to find meaning and fulfillment in different aspects of their work, and it is often difficult for them to witness the long-term outcomes of their development labors, as career and personal demands press them to move elsewhere.

The first section of this book addresses how aid workers understand and respond to their own and other people's expectations of aid work as charity work that should demand sacrifice on a day-to-day basis. The good intentions often associated with aid work are frequently what draw individuals into this line of work, but there is a dissonance between the ideal of "helping work" that is projected in external depictions of development and the reality of life as an aid professional. Sara de Jong's chapter "False Binaries" looks directly at this disconnect between expectations of altruism and how sacrifice is experienced and understood by aid professionals. De Jong finds a less stringent divide between altruism and selfishness in the minds of the NGO workers she speaks with. What might initially seem a conflict between career and financial motivations and "pure altruism" is experienced by aid workers as a normal part of the job. While aware of the problematic connotations of the hierarchy implied by aid as "helping work," de Jong's subjects seem to be comfortable dwelling in the complex intersection of altruism and egoism.

Thomas Yarrow also finds that the dichotomies assumed by many about aid work are complicated by on-the-ground realities of the need to get things done. Yarrow's study centers on a set of NGOs in Ghana affiliated with the Catholic Church, but it is less Catholicism that draws these aid workers into a moral conflict than diverse understandings of fairness and friendship. While some actors seek to follow what they see as universal best practices and seek to be independent of influence by rejecting the use of "personal relations," many of those Yarrow describes forward a different understanding of legitimacy that stresses the ethical connections that can be obtained only from long-term friendships and reject the formal, institutional pathways common to international NGO expectations. Both Yarrow and de Jong highlight the dissonance between ethics as seen in the metropole and how "right action" is experienced and understood on the ground. Too often, when centrally generated dictums are not followed by local aid professionals, it is assumed that it is because they lack understanding of "the rules" or that they are somehow inherently corrupt. If one focuses on process, rather than policy, a more complex field of morality appears to underpin the work of these aid professionals.

As discussed earlier, one of the most revelatory discoveries of those examining the actual lives of aid workers is the complexity of actors and the shifting hierarchies in the world of aid work. Several chapters of the book attempt to capture the wide range of interactions in Aidland that disturb neat dichotomies such as "donor" and "recipient." Some of this increasing muddiness of what were never clear divisions arises from progressive motivations on the part of development agencies, but often these well-intended moves toward inclusion or diversity have less benevolent effects or are discontinued when they become inconvenient. There are also complexities emergent from the changing world of aid, phenomena that come into being as the former "targets" of aid become practitioners. In Madagascar, Ritu Verma finds a rich example in the intertwined concerns of Malagasay women involved in a program to keep women out of prostitution and the French aid worker charged with teaching them alternative skills, such as cooking and nutrition. She finds significant disconnects as all actors are enjoined to "do gender" in ways that contradict their past experiences and expertise. Though paying attention not just to the official work of the program but also to the lives of the small community of aid workers, Verma finds discontinuities between policy and practice produced by the insular social worlds of the aid workers.

For Philip Fountain, the interchanges among the North American participants in a Mennonite NGO and a diverse set of local actors in Indonesia revolve around the concept of being a "guest." Drawing from both Mennonite ideals and the training programs of the organization, Fountain examines how Westerners brought into this program implement ideas of mutuality to undercut potential forms of hierarchy, but their pursuit of some form of egalitarianism unintentionally undermines the role of local professionals who find it impossible to fulfill positions as either host or guest.

Keith Brown brings an important historical eye to the changing hierarchies and roles of different participants in aid work. While Brown's study uses a civil society project in Macedonia as its frame, it is the human stories of individuals' negotiations of changing policy priorities that is the center of the story. In outlining a complex narrative where categories of "local," "national," and "global" become muddled and strategically implemented, Brown suggests a radical rethinking of the study of NGOs. Brown sees in the human experience of aid workers that the abstraction of Aidland has connections to the local world of implementation, making the processes of development more traceable.

Anne-Meike Fechter's chapter, like several others in the book, explicitly draws on the concept of Aidland to understand the diversity of individuals who are inhabiting this metaphorical space. She explores the worlds of those who are engaged in aid work in Cambodia to present a range of case studies that illustrate concerns shared by the residents of Aidland as well as significant differences between them. In pointing to several moments of interface between different actors involved in contemporary aid practice, we have also neglected many others. The rise in involvement by Asian countries in the global development industry, especially China's growing role in Africa, will further complicate interactions and hierarchy among aid workers and others. Yet it seems unlikely that merely shifting the demographic profile of aid worker or aid beneficiary will bring about the end of hierarchy within development.

Viewing the connection between the professional responsibilities of aid workers and their private lives also foregrounds issues of risk and responsibility that connect the career and family choices of development practitioners. Silke Roth's chapter focuses on aid workers' perceptions of threat and risk that are endured as part of their jobs in aid organizations. What she finds is a diverse set of perceptions of danger and responses to those threats. While employers unevenly deploy techniques to mitigate the danger to their employees, workers themselves often turn to their own strategies of coping or claim that the dangers entailed in the job are mitigated by its benefits.

In Heather Hindman's investigation of a changing aid and diplomatic community in Nepal, she finds a shift in the type of people entering the aid world. The result is a radically new population in the aid community that is produced not by explicit policy dictums but by new understandings of universal best practices and national discourses about "terrorism."

The final piece in the volume brings the discussion full circle to explore how the originator of Aidland reflects on the world of aid professionals in the current era. Raymond Apthorpe finds a large and complex world of aid professionals circulating through Aidland in the twenty-first century but goes further to examine some of the diverse characters in Aidland who often escape the gaze of scholarly analysis of development. In one particularly poignant moment, Apthorpe explores the criticisms and lacuna in his own concept and finds that they in part stem from the mundane realities of living in Aidland—and having or lacking a Land Rover. In reflections on a life in, around, and about the world of development professionals, Apthorpe returns to the importance of people in the processes of aid and the near inevitability of even the best policies having converse, negative effects.

Many recent books proclaim the complete failure of aid (Moyo 2009; Thurow and Kilman 2009; Hubbard and Duggan 2009), yet the aid industry continues and grows. And poverty remains. And the blame game continues. Undoubtedly development policies often fail to help those they are directed toward, and yet considering only the level of discourse and politics neglects the daily work of actually doing aid. Most development practitioners are sincere actors, devoted to their cause. In turning attention to the everyday lives of aid workers, we seek to uncover the space in which transformation happens and the motivations of a group of often-invisible professionals. The illusion of the atomized relief worker was always a stereotype, and its unfitness is growing with time. While this volume has only begun to explore the provocative question put forth by the title of Apthorpe's piece—"Who Is International Aid?"—the value of asking the question seems to become more imperative.

Acknowledgments

The editors would like to thank Jim Lance, not only for being a skilled editor but also for his enthusiasm for the project, his support during the process, and his kindness. This book would not have been possible without him. A Faculty Advancement Award from Northeastern University, as well as grants from the

Economic and Social Science Research Council UK and the South Asia Institute at the University of Texas, allowed the editors the opportunity to craft preliminary ideas for the introduction and put final touches on the manuscript, and the participants in the Sussex Anthropology Seminar, especially Pamela Kea and Ann Whitehead, were gracious hosts for some early conversations about the world of aid workers.

References

Adams, Vincanne, and Stacy Leigh Pigg, eds. 2005. *Sex in development: Science, sexuality and morality in global perspective.* Durham, NC: Duke University Press.

Apthorpe, Raymond. 2005. Postcards from Aidland. Paper presented at the Institute of Development Studies (IDS), Brighton, UK.

Callon, Michel. 1986. Some elements of a sociology of translation: Domestication of the scallops and the fisherman of St. Brieuc Bay. In *Power, action and belief: A new sociology of knowledge?* ed. John Law, 196–223. London: Routledge.

Crewe, Emma, and Elizabeth Harrison. 1998. *Whose development? An ethnography of aid.* New York: Zed Books.

Denskus, Tobias. 2007. What are all these people doing in their offices all day? The challenges of writing-up stories from "post-conflict" Kathmandu. *Journal of Peace, Conflict and Development* 11:1–13.

Escobar, Arturo. 1995. *Encountering development: The making and unmaking of the third world.* Princeton, NJ: Princeton University Press.

Eyben, Rosalind. 2006. Making relationships matter for aid bureaucracies. In *Relationships for aid,* ed. Rosalind Eyben, 43–60. London: Earthscan.

Ferguson, James. 1990. *The anti-politics machine: "Development," depoliticization, and bureaucratic power in Lesotho.* Minneapolis: University of Minnesota Press.

Foner, Nancy. 1995. *The caregiving dilemma: Work in an American nursing home.* Berkeley: University of California Press.

Frank, Leonard. 1986. The development game. *Granta* 20:229–43.

González, Roberto. 2009. *American counterinsurgency: Human science and the human terrain.* Chicago: Prickly Paradigm Press.

Green, Edward C. 1986. A short-term consultancy in Bangladesh. *American Anthropologist* 88 (1): 176–81.

Hall, Douglas T. 1976. *Careers in organizations.* Pacific Palisades, CA: Goodyear.

Hilhorst, Dorothea. 2003. *The real world of NGOs: Discourses, diversity and development.* London: Zed Books.

Hochschild, Arlie. 2003. *The commercialization of intimate life: Notes from home and work.* Berkeley: University of California Press.

Hubbard, R. Glenn, and William Duggan. 2009. *The aid trap: Hard truths about ending poverty.* New York: Columbia Business School.

Joseph, Miranda. 2002. *Against the romance of community.* Minneapolis: University of Minnesota Press.

Latour, Bruno. 2005. *Reassembling the social: An introduction to actor-network-theory.* Oxford: Oxford University Press.

Lewis, David, and David Mosse. 2006. Encountering order and disjuncture: Contemporary anthropological perspectives on the organization of development. *Oxford Development Studies* 34:1–13.

Li, Tania. 2007. *The will to improve: Governmentality, development and the practice of politics.* Durham, NC: Duke University Press.

Malinowski, Brownislaw. 1984. *Argonauts of the Western Pacific.* Prospect Heights, IL: Waveland Press (Orig. pub. 1922.)

Mosse, David. 2004. Is good policy unimplementable? Reflections on the ethnography of aid policy and practice. *Development and Change* 35 (4): 639–71.

———. 2005. *Cultivating development: An ethnographic of aid policy and practice.* Ann Arbor, MI: Pluto Press.

Moyo, Dambisa. 2009. *Dead aid: Why aid is not working and how there is a better way for Africa.* New York: Farrar, Straus and Giroux.

Power, Michael. 1994. *The audit explosion.* London: Demos.

———. 1997. *The audit society: Rituals of verification.* Oxford: Oxford University Press.

Price, David. 2009. Human terrain systems, anthropology and the war in Afghanistan. *Counterpunch.* Retrieved from http://www.counterpunch.org/price12012009.html

Rajak, Dinah, and Roderick Stirrat. In press. Parochial cosmopolitanism and the power of nostalgia. In *Adventures in Aidland,* ed. David Mosse. Oxford: Berghahn Books.

Sassen, Saskia. 2006. *Territory, authority, rights: From medieval to global assemblages.* Princeton, NJ: Princeton University Press.

Scott, James. 1998. *Seeing like a state: How certain schemes to improve the human condition have failed.* New Haven, CT: Yale University Press.

Stirrat, R. L. 2000. Cultures of consultancy. *Critique of Anthropology* 20 (1): 31–46.

Stirrat, Roderick. 2008. Mercenaries, missionaries and misfits: Representations of development personnel. *Critique of Anthropology* 28 (4): 406–25.

Strathern, Marilyn, ed. 2000. *Audit cultures: Anthropological studies in accountability, ethics and the academy.* New York: Routledge.

Thurow, Roger, and Scott Kilman. 2009. *Enough: Why the world's poorest starve in an age of plenty.* New York: Public Affairs.

Tufte, Edward. 2006. *The cognitive style of power: Pitching out corrupts within.* Cheshire, CT: Graphics Press.

Vaughan, Diane. 1996. *The Challenger launch decision: Risky technology, culture, and deviance at NASA.* Chicago: University of Chicago Press.

Wallace, Ben J. 1987. The not so funny short-term consultant in Bangladesh: A comment. *American Anthropologist* 89 (2): 450–52.

2

False Binaries

Altruism and Selfishness in NGO Work

Sara de Jong

Introduction

The work of those active in NGOs has often been associated with altruism. As Silliman (1999, 24) pointed out, in popular discourse NGOs are imagined and idealized as organizations for which people work out of a sense of duty to create social justice, "unmotivated by profit or politics" (cf. Fisher 1997, 442; Lorgen 2002, 292; Hahn and Holzscheiter 2005, 11; Heron 2007, 44). Book titles such as *Agents of Altruism: The Expansion of Humanitarian NGOs in Rwanda and Afghanistan* (West 2002), *The Alms Bazaar: Altruism Under Fire—Non-profit Organizations and International Development* (Smillie 1995), and *The Selfish Altruist: Relief Work in Famine and War* (Vaux 2004) illustrate the connection made between altruism and NGO/IGOs. Furthermore, the latter two book titles provide a glimpse of the critique these organizations are facing regarding their presumed altruism.

In this contribution I analyze notions and practice of altruism and responsibility among women NGO/IGO workers in the global North who work to support women in and from the global South. While altruism is often presented as diametrically opposed to selfishness (e.g., Comte as quoted in Graham 2004, 49; Seglow 2004a), I conceptualize altruism in a way that transcends this binary in order to understand the seemingly contradictory motives of the NGO/IGO workers whom I encountered in my research. Counter to Vaux's assertion that "humanitarianism needs to move towards *pure* altruism" (2004, 7, italics added), I challenge the notions of "pure altruism" versus "impure altruism." I first provide a brief overview of the dominant understandings of altruism and its implications. With the notable exception of work on rescuers of

Jews during the Holocaust (Monroe 1991), much of the literature on altruism, because of the theoretical abstractness (philosophy and economics), the emphasis on experimental settings (psychology) or genes over human beings (biology) deals with disembodied, abstract beings rather than impassioned people and therefore oversimplifies reality with its inherent contradictions. I argue that a reconceptualization of altruism needs to take into account the embodiment of altruism in relation to passions, power, privilege, and ideology. At the same time, the reconceptualization of altruism upsets a simplistic notion that altruism is inherently good and desirable (Glannon and Ross 2002, 69; Seglow 2004b, 145).

In 2007–2008 I conducted 20 interviews with women who worked either on a paid or on a voluntary basis for organizations that either as their core concern or as a subset of a wider remit seek to support women *in* or *from* the global South.[1] The term "in or from the global South" refers both to organizations that have an international presence and "target group" abroad and to those organizations that work on a national level with a target group that (originally) comes from abroad. All of these women were located in the global North, more specifically the United Kingdom, the Netherlands, Denmark, Sweden, Austria, Belgium (Brussels), and Switzerland (Geneva). Most of the relations between the women NGO workers and their target group were articulated across either spatial distance, in the case of organizations based in, for example, Brussels or Geneva (often headquarters of the organization), or spatial proximity, where it was based on the mobility of women from the South as migrants to the global North. The organizations these women worked for ranged in size from smaller to larger organizations in terms of both employees and budget, some of which collaborate with the EU (those based in Brussels) or UN (based in Geneva), while other organizations were active on the national level for women from the global South. The organizations had a wide thematic remit including health, development, sexuality, peace, and immigration.

The interviews addressed relations with clients, beneficiaries, or target groups; how NGO personnel negotiated working at different organizational levels; what was experienced as professionally discouraging; how their own identities played out; where their sense of responsibility came from; and their personal and professional development. The wider research project analyzes how these women NGO workers understand their own work practices and negotiate their roles and their relations with the women they seek to support in the context of feminist and postcolonial critiques, critical development approaches, and the literature on global citizenship/civil society (de Jong 2009).

This research can be placed among the recent, growing body of literature that focuses on the individual experiences of NGO workers (Goudge 2003; Baaz 2005; Charlés 2007; Heron 2007; Cook 2008) in contrast to the earlier organizational focus.

Research participants were found using a combination of "key informant sample" and snowball sampling. In general, I established contact with the research participants over e-mail, and in most cases the interviews were conducted in person either at their offices or elsewhere in cafés or other public spaces.[2] As the research was concerned with the reflections of NGO/IGO workers, the research participants, though selected on the basis of their affiliation with a certain organization, both on their own and on my request, spoke in their personal capacity rather than as representatives of their organization.[3] The anonymity of the research participants was necessary to create a space where the women could be open about their experiences and their reflections on their work practices. The women interviewed have in common that they work for organizations that seek to improve the lives of women from the South and that they share the privilege of being located in the global North. At the same time, my informants are heterogeneous in terms of their nationality, age, ethnicity, and career trajectories. For example, while I met the women at their European "bases," some of the women had non-European (North American or Latin American) national backgrounds. Their experiences, positions, and reflections thus displayed these commonalities and differences.

Understandings of Altruism

As mentioned, altruism is commonly associated with the aid and development work of NGOs: sometimes in positive terms but also in negative terms as in the work of development critics. Traditionally, altruism has been the concern of evolutionary biologists, philosophers, economists, and psychologists. Few studies use the narratives of the supposedly altruistic or nonaltruistic actors as a basis for investigating altruism (cf. Monroe 1991). While I will not provide a comprehensive overview of the literature on altruism here, it is necessary to unpack a number of dominant assumptions about the nature of altruism to subsequently reconceptualize altruism. First, a cursory look reveals that altruism is most frequently presented as the opposite of selfishness and as mutually exclusionary or, as Monroe put it, "as separate, distinct, and inversely-related phenomena" (1991, 399). Auguste Comte, who has been credited with the invention of the term "altruism," already stated that "the chief problem of human life [is] the subordination of egoism to altruism" (quoted in Graham 2004, 49).

The contemporary philosopher Jonathan Seglow equated a lack of altruism with selfishness: "to lack [altruism]—to be selfish—is one of the most common terms of moral condemnation" (2004a, 1). Seglow's statement also points to a second dominant assumption, namely, that altruism is seen as a positive moral value in contrast to the negative value of selfishness (see also Glannon and Ross 2002, 69). The third dominant assumption that follows from the binary understanding of altruism and selfishness is that if it is possible to detect elements of egoism in what would otherwise be regarded as altruistic acts, then these acts are so "contaminated" that they are not "true altruism" anymore. De Wispelaere is exemplary of this kind of reasoning when he divides seemingly altruistic actions into "altruistic" and "quasi-altruistic" ones, the latter referring to those acts that "appear altruistic while in fact being motivated by an 'enlightened' form of self-interest" (2004, 12) (see also Monroe 1991, 402, on "authentic altruism" and Mayo and Tinsley 2008, 3, on "pure" and "impure" altruism). This concern with "unmasking" seemingly altruistic acts relates to the fourth mainstream assumption in discussions on altruism, stemming from the individualistic framework of economics and biology, namely, that human beings are intrinsically selfish. Hence, altruism is commonly presented as a desirable but rare or even nonexistent feature of human beings (for an exception, see Batson and Shaw 1991). In the context of economics, for example, the economists Mayo and Tinsley wrote, "Charitable giving may be thought of as somewhat paradoxical. That is, to the extent that the standard assumption of economic behaviour—self-interest—is abandoned, it may be thought that any form of charitable giving is anomalous" (2008, 3; see also Graham 2004, 49; Seglow 2004b, 145).

Even though every individual field uses different examples—biologists draw on cooperative behavior among animals or human beings, economists on philanthropy, and psychologists and philosophers on helping, volunteering, and rescuing—the idea of altruism as an "other-regarding" behavior is common to all (Seglow 2004a, 2). Batson and Shaw defined altruism, for example, as "a motivational state with the ultimate goal of increasing another's welfare" (1991, 108). Monroe defined altruism as "behaviour intended to benefit another, even when doing so may risk or entail some sacrifice to the welfare of the actor" (1994, 862). Given these definitions of altruism as increasing another's welfare, it is not surprising to see a connection is often made between NGOs, their employees, and altruism. While the term "altruism" is used in literature on development issues and NGOs, there is generally no explicit engagement with the debates from the fields of economics, biology, psychology, and philosophy. Implicitly, however, development literature does share the underlying assumptions about altruism with those academic fields. Even Tony Vaux's important critical engagement with altruism in his book *The Selfish Altruist*, based on his experience as an aid worker at Oxfam, includes assumptions about altruism's binary relation with selfishness (2004, 204), about notions of pure and impure altruism (2004, 60), and about altruism as less natural than selfishness (2004, 115).

From the 1990s, however, despite the growth of the number of NGOs and their apparent success (Pupavac 2006), some cracks started to appear in the optimistic idea of NGOs as "doing good" and as ultimately altruistic (Fisher 1997, 442; Hahn and Holzscheiter 2005, 2). Critics of NGOs, often NGO workers and aid workers themselves, targeted the bureaucratization of NGOs and the (lack of) aid efficacy, which resulted in a crisis of legitimacy (Pupavac 2006). The pervasiveness of the current critical development discourse about altruism and selfishness/careerism in the NGO sector is apparent in the narratives of the research participants.

While I neither hinted that financial or other gains might be a motivation to do the job nor expressed judgment either way in the interview, many of the interviewees responded as if these assumptions had been made, as becomes clear from Lindsey's account. After years of working at the grassroots level, Lindsey is now working for a large intergovernmental organization. Lindsey told me during the interview in her own office,

> The motivation for doing this work [are] . . . my own personal social convictions to equality and to justice . . . , because my motivation for doing this work is not financial, it is not based on professional aspirations, it is really based on a personal commitment to ensuring . . . opportunities for equality for women in various settings.

Lindsey's account, stating specifically that it "is not financial, it is not based on professional aspirations," seems to anticipate a critique of her motivation as selfish and therefore reflects a discourse that is critical of professionalization and careerism. In contrast to this, Helena, a young woman with an educational background in social work who now works on a local level with migrants, in addition to volunteering for another migrant organization, told me,

> I only can do these things, this sounds very egoistic, this sounds selfish, if I get something back from it. With my voluntary job, I learned how to write proposals, project proposals, how to get money for an organization, how to be an own independent foundation so that,

all those things I learned. So in that way, I mainly saw it as helping myself.

While Helena takes the opposite position to Lindsey, her apologetically saying "this sounds very egoistic, this sounds selfish" shows that she is equally conscious of the critical discourse. Ironically, it is Helena who is concerned about sounding selfish, while she refers to a relatively low-status voluntary job, while Lindsey stresses her personal commitment over any careerism in relation to a high-status and relatively well-paid job.

It is interesting to note that in general, theories in philosophy, biology, social psychology, and economics on the one hand and development and NGO literature on the other hand follow the opposite course in their engagement with altruism. Whereas the first started their theories with the assumption that human nature is essentially selfish and struggled to incorporate instances of altruistic behavior, the latter assumed altruism from the outset and were later forced to incorporate selfishness and egoism in their understanding of NGO practices. This can partly be explained by the fact that some of the former theories concern *all* of humanity, whereas the latter concern only a specific group working for an assumed altruistic cause. Many of the former theories, however, similarly concentrate on specific activities, such as donating blood, rescuing Jews, volunteering, or helping strangers. More important, however, is the commonality between the different fields, which is the persistent assumption of the binary relation between altruism and selfishness and the related idea that while altruism is "good," selfishness is a less desirable and appropriate trait.

Although dissecting this common binary understanding of altruism is instructive in understanding some of the responses of the women interviewed—for example, the apologetic phrase "this sounds selfish"—and while using provocative titles as *The Selfish Altruist* are extremely important in opening a discussion on the contradiction and problematic practices in relief work, such binary understanding is ultimately reductionist of the complexities of NGO workers' experiences. Hence, I agree with Monroe's assertion that "the dichotomy traditionally employed oversimplifies reality" (1991, 425) or her more graphic metaphor elsewhere when she stated, "Traditional explanations of altruism resemble a fat lady in a corset: the overall effect may be aesthetically pleasing, but it does fundamental distortion to the underlying reality" (Monroe 1994, 861). Critics of the binary presentation of altruism and selfishness, such as Monroe (1991), propose an alternative understanding of behavior not according to the dichotomy but along a continuum with self-interest on one pole and altruism at the other extreme pole. I go beyond this alternative approach of a continuum and argue that this approach is still ultimately reliant on the problematic assumption that when there is *more altruism*, there is *less selfishness* and vice versa. I suggest here openings suggested by the interview narratives that give scope for a reconceptualization of the term that avoids the binary relation with egoism.

Reconceptualizing Altruism

The first potential space for reconceptualizing is provided through the narrative of Samantha. When I talked to Samantha in the lobby of a hotel in Stockholm, she displayed some doubt concerning the importance of the "right" motivation in relation to the outcome of actions. When I asked her why she cared about others far away, Samantha responded, "Why would I care? Why would I not care? I have energy and every opportunity in life that I can use I guess." After answering this question, she went on: "I assume your next question will be 'Does it make me feel good?' " She noted that she becomes angry and is quite tired of encountering people who "are in it for . . . that they become very 'good people.' " Samantha continued thinking aloud: "I am thinking about that a lot, and maybe that's OK, I have been switching, who cares about the reason . . . if they do the work." When I asked her why it makes her angry, she replied,

> It just annoyed me a bit, because if that's the case, they are not doing enough, the world sucks so . . . and it is not fair sort of to do it for that reason. But they are doing it, so why not? We need more people that do it.

Samantha's observations would be an example of an approach that moves away from evaluating whether the motivation is "right" (altruistic) or "wrong" (selfish) to looking at the outcomes of the work practices. Indeed, whereas the term "altruistic" is sometimes used to refer to motives, at other times it rather refers to (outcome of) actions (Dixon 2008). Combining these two definitions, it is easily conceivable that an action can be *simultaneously* labeled *egoistic* and *altruistic* without posing a contradiction. For example, the actions of an NGO worker can be altruistic in their effect while at the same time be partly motivated by egoistic concerns or vice versa. This approach, which separates motivation from outcome of action, would be one way of understanding how altruism and egoism can be simultaneously combined *without* annulling one another and thereby overcome the commonly assumed binary.

Monica, a young woman who has volunteered for different projects in Asia,[4] similarly oscillates between judging her motivations and judging the

outcomes of her volunteering work when she reflects on her work. She had returned from one of these projects a few months before I spoke to her. Monica
said,

> Is my desire to go and work abroad because I like going to different
> cultures and I want to broaden my work experience? Is what I am do-
> ing in those different countries making any impact or is it incremen-
> tal . . . or is it too arrogant enough to even think that you are making
> a difference? I don't know.

Monica's narrative is suggestive of a range of different issues. On the one
hand, her pondering seems to imply first that even if her motivation to work
abroad is to further her own interests, as long as her actions have a positive
effect on the communities she works with, it is justified for her to volunteer
abroad. On the other hand, however, while she first distinguishes between her
motivation and the outcome of her actions, her last question "is it too arrogant
enough to even think that you are making a difference?" collapses motivation
and action into one. Hence, it becomes clear from Monica's account that it is
not even always tenable to strictly separate motivation and outcome. In addition, Monica's last question hints at the privileges and power differences at
stake when she can consider herself to be in a position to actually make a
difference.

Theorizing about instances of altruism presumes the presence of a person
who is in the position to support, help, or rescue the other person. Indeed
many NGO workers explained their sense of responsibility through referring
to the opportunities they enjoy. For example, Cynthia, who has worked for
about a year for an organization in Geneva on gender equality mechanisms,
said to me,

> Because I have had these opportunities, I would wish that others have
> these opportunities. And one way to do that is to focus on projects
> where I feel that through these processes, at the end of a very, very
> long road and with other projects focusing on all kind of different
> things, there is the opportunity that there will be the possibility that
> these people have these opportunities.

As a young, white, educated woman, Cynthia recognizes the privileges
she enjoys in her position. Barbara's story, without using the term "opportunity," reflects a similar line of thought. A professor in Barbara's university in

the United States involved her and other students in a research project in a hosiery factory in rural area close to the university. When Barbara interviewed the people working there, they told her that they did not have enough money to send their children to university. Barbara, who comes from a similarly privileged background as a white, middle-class, American woman, now works on gender and peace in Geneva after having worked in a postconflict area in the global South. As we had not been able to arrange an interview when I visited Geneva, we had a telephone interview in which she said,

> And my professor made the link to say that these people are all paying taxes and all this tax money is going for my education, so effectively they are paying for me to go to university when they can't pay for their own kids to go. And so, what she said was that because we are given this privilege just by accident of birth, that you have a responsibility to not waste that. . . . Just that idea that it has been an accident of birth that I was given the fortune to grow up in a stable family and go to university and always have enough to eat, it is really just because of where I happened to be born and that not everybody is that lucky. So I can't waste it by doing nothing.

In these explanations of their motivation, a modern version of *noblesse oblige* is at stake, the idea that privilege entails responsibility. This becomes most clear in Cynthia's response to my question whether she feels responsible and whether everyone should feel responsible:

> I don't know, because on the one hand I am still like a struggling student, I certainly don't have an income that makes me able to, I can't engage in philanthropy because I don't have anything to give in a way, other than work really. I suppose it is just a general responsibility that . . . it is difficult to identify because it gets to the questions of "At what threshold do you have enough money or at what threshold are you considered to have opportunities? . . . What stage are you no longer the one in need, and then the one who then can give?"

The idea that privilege entails a responsibility for the welfare of others could easily be categorized as classically altruistic. It is important to note, however, that not only the opportunity to work for an NGO is reliant on a certain privilege but also the work itself has the potential to reinforce privilege. So while doing the work itself was often justified on the basis of a feeling of responsibility because of the opportunities enjoyed in life, not in the least because of the fact that the interviewees were mostly white, educated, and middle class, the work itself also turns out to give opportunities of various kinds. Indeed many of the structures of the NGO world support the selection of the already privileged in NGO positions: the requirements of voluntary and internship experience before getting a fixed contract, the importance of networks and connections, the metropolitan locations of many organizations, and the dominance of the English language and requirements of multilingualism.

Cook (2008), in her research on female volunteers for Voluntary Service Overseas (VSO) in Gilgit, Pakistan, noticed that one reason to take the volunteer placement was to enable career advancement. The women were able to have authority and responsibilities that they would not have had in a job in their home countries (see also Goudge 2003, 9–11, 183). Mary, who is in her late 30s, comes from a small town in Canada and has maintained an international career spanning 12 years, starting when an internship gave her the opportunity to enter the international arena. As the deputy secretary general of a large women's organization, she explained her motivation for her work partly through the opportunities the work had given her:

> Certainly working in a global organization which gives you the opportunity to work on these kind of issues [is motivating] and to have the opportunity to travel to different parts of the world and to have access to, you know, from the community levels to being at the UN, to last week I had dinner with the president of Finland in her palace you know, that is pretty cool, so that's also interesting and motivating.

The benefits received by doing the job do not necessarily have to be financial—and many might say that in NGO work, it is unlikely that the gain is financial—but can vary from having more career opportunities, to traveling, to meeting people. This leads to another approach that leaves space for the compatibility of altruism and selfishness and thereby moves away from notions of pure and impure altruism. As Seglow defined an altruistic act as "further[ing] another person's good at some costs to oneself—or at least a willingness to bear such a cost if required" (2004b, 146), altruism is not necessarily precluding personal gain. In this vein, it is possible for an act to be altruistic when the consequences of that act benefit both the person who performs the act and the person the act is done for. In the context of NGO work, the "costs" someone would be willing to bear could be, for example, accepting a lower salary. That these considerations played a role is evidenced in the following narratives. Hannah has worked for 12 years for the same organization that mostly operates at the European level with women's rights, also starting out as an intern. When I talked to her, she said, "If I felt no responsibility I would not be in this job. I would be in a job where I would be making more money maybe." Iris, who describes herself as a "not very old white woman" from the United States and who works with an organization on peace issues in Brussels, told me during a phone interview, "Because you know what? We are not doing this for monetary gains, you know a lot of people and myself included live what you call 'hand to mouth.' And so we are not doing it for monetary gain, we are doing it because we are following a passion."

When the motivation and outcome of actions are distinguished, it is possible that while NGO workers receive benefits from their work (outcome of their actions), their motivation still remains altruistic. Similarly, the idea that there should be a willingness to bear some costs (not even actual sacrifice) would also give the label of "altruistic" wider application. Most important, however, at the very least, both alternative readings help to go beyond the simple classification of altruistic and selfish behavior and the associated moral judgment and leave space to reflect on the real contradictions and ambivalences of NGO workers' reflections.

Another challenge to the binary conceptualization of altruism and egoism can be found in Helena's account. Her narrative challenged the assumption that work to help others *should* not contain an element of self-interest and rejected the related idea that altruism is necessarily desirable and egoism undesirable. It considers privilege and power relations and hence moves away from the idealized disembodied accounts of altruism. Helena coordinates a buddy project for sex workers and in that role attends the application interviews of prospective "buddies." Helena said,

> If they come to the intake, to the first interview, I also ask them, "Why this group?" and if they say, "I saw a movie on television about trafficking, and I thought, 'Wow, how exciting what happened,'" then I don't think you are a good buddy. But also when they say, "Oh, I really want to help these women," then they really have to convince me that they would be [a good buddy] . . . because it is not equal, but we try to make it as equal as possible this relationship. But actually a lot of women, a lot of volunteers say, "Well, I live in . . . a multicultural city but I don't have any colored person in my social network so I would like to learn from another culture" . . . or "I am also new

[here] . . . so I need to get to know to the city as well, maybe we can explore it together."

Helena displays here an awareness of the way in which some charitable impulses are reliant on the denigration of those helped. Postcolonial feminism has criticized the construction of the poor, victimized, third world subject. Chandra Mohanty, for example, spoke of the construction of the "average third world woman" who "leads an essentially truncated life based on her feminine gender (read: sexually constrained) and being 'third world' (read: ignorant, poor, uneducated, tradition-bound, domestic, family oriented, victimised, etc.)" (1984, 337). In particular, feminist critics of the victims discourse on trafficking (which is also persistent within feminist circles) have spoken out against the victim stereotype. According to Doezema (2001), the trafficked third world woman is not entrusted with her own political voice and is presented as "backward" and in need of rescue by her Western sisters. While it might be counterintuitive, given the current critical discourse against selfishness and instrumentalism in NGO work, in Helena's project those prospective volunteers that motivate their interest in the project solely on an "altruistic" basis (as conventionally understood) are actually deemed unsuitable for the project. Helena acknowledges that the relationship can never be completely equal, but she aspires to make it "as equal as possible." She attempts to establish this maximum level of equality by encouraging volunteers to consider what they can gain themselves from their role as a buddy. Personal gain is presented here as an example to narrow the power gap between the person in need and those supporting. Hence, Helena's example unsettles the idea that personal gain in the helping role is morally questionable and that gaining something automatically widens the gap between the "helper" and those "helped" through increasing privilege. In addition, acknowledging the risk of altruism turning into benevolence, it questions the idea that altruism is inherently desirable and preferable over selfishness.

In addition to being attentive to the power differences between the person "helping" and those "being helped," Helena also points to the potential of identifying similarities between the buddy and the volunteer (e.g., both being new to the city) as a basis for their relationship. This leads to a final alternative way to reconceptualize altruism. When Judith, who has worked for eight years with sex workers for a national migrant organization, talks about her sense of responsibility, the difference between herself and the other is also negated. Judith's passion for her organization and their work surfaced when she took me on a tour around her workplace after the interview, handed me many brochures and articles, and invited me for a film event the organization organized that week.

> JUDITH: With responsibility, I am not sure if I understand this as you mean it; I connect this to feeling so passionate about what I do. I don't know; it is a deep sense of what is fair and what is not fair and of having experienced marginalization myself and of still experiencing it. It is also something that empowers me. And I don't know that I would work in another area, I don't think that working with drugs or so would make me feel so passionately about my work; it is not substitutable.

> INTERVIEWER: It is not just about helping others?

> JUDITH: No! Not at all! No! No, really I don't understand myself as helping others, really, I do not see myself as helping others; as I said the spine of this whole thing is the political. . . . We distance ourselves from social work or these ideas of helping others. It has very much to do with our own lives and situations.

It is important to note that while my research concentrates on those women NGO workers who are located in the global North and the relative privilege they are endowed with through their roles and their locations, it should not be assumed that all the interviewees, or their parents, were born in countries considered part of the prosperous West. Hence, the relationship between those women NGO workers with an immigrant background and the women they supported follows more complex patterns of simultaneous identification and differentiation. In contrast to the white, Western women NGO workers who in the interview accounts quoted previously referred to the opportunities they enjoyed, Judith, for example, shares her Eastern European migrant background with some of the women she supports. Judith's narrative about her work illustrates the relational aspect of her positionality as a woman NGO worker with an immigrant background. While Judith emphasizes time and again that she does not understand her work to be about helping others, which would have been altruistic in the classical sense of "other-regarding" actions, it is too simplistic to summarize her account as one that is merely egoistic. Rather, Judith connects her own experience of marginalization to the structures that marginalize those women whom she seeks to support with her work. Altruism is here based on identification and therefore needs to include the self rather than surpass it. Monroe concluded from accounts of rescuers of

Jews during the Second World War that rescuers "had a perception of self at one with all mankind" (1991, 428).[5] In Churchill and Street's reading of Monroe's study, because of the rescuers' understanding of themselves as connected to others, by rescuing Jews they rescued not only others *but also themselves.* Helping the other and oneself becomes indistinguishable, as "the fear and pain of another becomes his [the altruist's] own fear and pain" (Konarzewski, as quoted in Churchill and Street 2004, 92). In this reading, if selfishness is human beings' natural disposition, altruism is equally "natural" as well.

Many of the narratives, in some way or another, always maintain a theoretical division between the organization in the North and the beneficiaries of their projects. Lindsey, however, challenges that split and described to me very adamantly that the dominant assumption that those groups are neatly separated is wrong:

> I think often you know there is an automatic assumption that when we work on gender that people that are working in gender are not affected by gender relations, which is completely not true. . . . Inevitably the people that I meet along the way who are in what some would consider positions of power in their own communities are still very much affected by gender inequality, still live the norms, roles, and relations that affect everyone and not simply marginalized groups. . . . So for me the women that we work with in that sense are very much also a part of my target audience; it is not only the women that are coming to health centers for services but it is also women who are making decisions as to how these health centers work whether they be members of government, whether they be members of another agency or fellow staff members . . . they are also part of it.

There is a dominant assumption, and one that I arguably also made in the interview with her, that the women who are working in her field are an "emancipated" elite with very different experiences than those "on the ground." Lindsey, however, emphasizes the continuity between the gender struggles of all women wherever they are positioned, in the sense that all face similar structural inequalities or, as she put it, "norms, roles, and relations that affect everyone and not simply marginalized groups." Whereas Lindsey's account is more focused on the idea of partners in the South as a target group, later in the interview Lindsey also spoke of herself and her colleagues in the North as being equally implicated in gender struggles and inequalities. She pointed to the fact that the organization itself, and some of her colleagues, conceive of her and her female colleagues as being outside structures of gender equality. As this extract has real poignancy, it is worth quoting in greater length:

> Going back to something I said before that people assume that those of us that work in international institutions that work on gender equality and women's empowerment, that we don't have to deal with these issues ourselves. That assumption is very, very clear and that has played out, that, for example, once someone asked me to review footage of some film clips that they were planning on showing in last year's international women's year event, which was around ending impunity for violence against women in emergency and conflict settings, and there was no warning that the material I was about to open was very graphic, very difficult, no warning as to what the content would be at all, so that I could choose to open it or that I could not open it. No support provided, no thought. . . . And the fact that that had not been thought through that not only the women but also the men might have gone through something just as traumatic, may have experienced gender-based violence in their own life, whether through physically experiencing it or through supporting someone else through it or finding someone else . . . that that was not thought about, I was quite shocked. And that aspect of my identity, in terms of being not only somebody that works on an issue but somebody that can also have experienced an issue is often ignored. It is difficult because you do not want to be perceived always as people that have gone through something, but I think it is important for institutions [like ours] to think about.

This quote is very powerful in describing the impact of the assumption that the women working for Lindsey's organization are not facing any of the issues they are working on. It shows very clearly why Lindsey feels that the battle she fights for gender equality worldwide really means "at home" and abroad, as it is implied that Lindsey has also experienced gender-based violence herself. Judith's and Lindsey's feeling of responsibility and commitment to others and their awareness of their own implication in these structures are inspired by their feminism and concern with other oppressions. Hence, Lindsey's account and Judith's narrative in addition to challenging the self–other divide at the basis of the selfishness versus altruism discussion also point to the need to consider the role of political commitments and passions in discussions on altruism. More generally, in cases in which there is no clear distinct ideology like feminism inspiring the motivations and actions of NGO workers, psychological explanations that understand empathy as the capacity to relate the self to the other (Krebs 1991) can account for the blurring of the lines between self and other and the subsequent erasure of the clear distinction between altruism and selfishness. This then runs counter to Vaux's assertion that "in order to understand the person in need and his or her full social, economic and political context, *we need to obliterate our own self*" (2004, 7, italics added). Hence, it is more constructive to understand Judith's, Lindsey's, and others' reflections from an intersectional approach that pays attention to one's positioning in relation to those one supports, "impell[ing] new ways of thinking about *complexity and multiplicity in power relations as well as emotional investments*" (Brah and Phoenix 2004, 82, italics added) rather than categorizing work practices according to the altruism versus egoism binary.

Conclusion

In this chapter I have explored what I called the "false binary" of altruism and selfishness in relation to the reflections of women NGO/IGO workers who support women in or from the global South. While traditionally NGO/IGO work has been associated with altruism, in recent years the presumed (lack of) altruism of NGO workers has increasingly been the subject of criticism. In relation to the NGOs more generally, and in the women's movement in particular, there is a critique of the increased professionalization of NGOs and the associated careerism of the employees, which is seen to be incompatible with altruistic values (Lang 1997, 115; Alvarez 1998; Menon 2004; de Alwis 2009). The narratives of the women NGO workers clearly show an awareness of this discourse, through either supporting it, challenging it, or justifying their position in response.

A survey of the literature on altruism shows that altruism is generally understood in a binary with selfishness, in which the first is considered desirable but rare and the latter is considered common but immoral and undesirable. Related to these main suppositions is the notion that when egoism contaminates seemingly altruistic acts, they become impurely altruistic. I have argued that while the incompatibility of altruism and egoism is commonly assumed, it does not reflect the complexities of practice, as many of those theories seem to rely on images of disembodied abstract beings rather than impassioned people. Hence, I have argued for the need to reconceive altruism in ways that will provide spaces for a more nuanced reading of the relation between altruism and selfishness. The reconceptualizations I have proposed both move away from the rigid moral judgments associated with altruism and selfishness, respectively, and take into account the passions and ideologies of real people. I have explored the possibility of the simultaneous presence of altruism and selfishness by delving deeper into seemingly contradictory situations in which the motivation could be seen as selfish and the outcome as altruistic, and vice versa. In this context, I have presented some examples of a kind of *noblesse oblige*, where seemingly altruistic motives, albeit based on privilege, lead also to the *reinforcement* of those privileges in terms of advancing one's career, travelling, and widening professional networks. The second alternative approach allows personal gain as long as the altruist is willing to bear costs (see Seglow 2004b). This conceptualization could be applied to career-minded NGO workers who at the same time are prepared to sacrifice other gains, such as financial ones. I have argued that both these alternative approaches go beyond the simple classification of altruism and selfishness and therefore consider the ambivalences and contradictions of NGO work. A third way to rethink altruism has been suggested on the basis of reflections of a volunteer coordinator who encourages "selfish" or "instrumental" motivations for carrying out volunteering work. This challenges the assumption that pure altruistic motives are necessarily preferable. Arguably, NGO workers or volunteers driven by "selfish" motives are on a more equal level with those they seek to assist, as the latter are not dependent on their "benevolence," which is an important consideration in light of the critique of the "third world women as victims discourse." The final reconceptualization considered understanding the self as connected to others in a common humanity (see Churchill and Street 2004) or as subject to similar gender (or other oppressive) norms and values in the case of feminist work. In this approach, as self and other are connected, selfishness and altruism cannot be clearly separated either, and more attention needs to be paid to the embodied relations between people. I have argued in this chapter that if we want to understand the actions and motivations of NGO workers as embodied, passionate beings, we need to leave behind the common assumptions associated with altruism. This means transcending the egoism–altruism binary, its associated moral judgments, and the idea that the selfishness is more natural than the altruism. It also implies complicating the notion that seemingly altruistic acts with traces of selfishness are "contaminated" or "inauthentic." Rather than attempting to label practices altruistic or selfish, we need to liberate ourselves of the shackles of this binary and instead critically investigate *under which conditions* altruism takes place. In a structurally unequal world, this means interrogating the personal gains, power relations, opportunities and privileges, and political and emotional investments at stake.

Notes

1. Most of the organizations could be classed as nongovernmental organizations (NGOs); on their websites, however, a few organizations rather self-described as platform, charity, nonprofit organizations or networks. Some of the organizations were intergovernmental organizations (IGOs). These latter organizations were not NGOs in the strict sense of the term; if one follows Hilhorst's definition of an NGO as "doing good for the development of others," however, a definition that she called the "most common use" of the term "NGO," it is easy to see the relevant commonality of the women interviewed (2003, 7).

2. Relevant organizations have been identified through Internet research and the use of Internet databases of global women organizations (http://www.distel.ca/womlist/womlist .html—I hereby want to express my gratitude to Denise Osted for voluntarily compiling the global list of women's organizations, which proved an invaluable source), through women umbrella organizations in the United Kingdom (e.g., http://www.wrc.org.uk/ and http://www .womeninlondon.org.uk/wrc.htm), and on the basis of information from mailings from similar organizations.

3. I agreed with all the research participants to not use their real names and to ensure that when their quotes were used, they are not connected to their organization. Hence, all names and some details have been changed. Inevitably, the need for confidentiality implied that compromises had to be made in terms of contextualizing the women's reflections. Comparable studies with a similar focus on individual reflections as data (Heron 2007; Goudge 2003; Cook 2008; Hopgood 2006) have taken a similar approach to this issue. In Hopgood's study of Amnesty International, for example, he stated, "Some readers might find the lack of context about the speakers off-putting. I can only sympathize and say that this was unavoidable" (2006, viii). As the informants were often nonnative English speakers, in some cases the interview quotes were slightly altered to make them read more smoothly.

4. Monica is an exception in the research sample since, in contrast to all the other research participants who were located in the global North for their work, she was located in the global South for the duration of the projects.

5. In her study, Monroe differentiated between the philanthropists and entrepreneurs whom she studied and the war rescuers by stating that the first tend to act to support only local causes or people they know or feel a connection to while the latter also act for "unknown people far away" (1991, 423). As she argued that "rescuers" feel a connection to humanity in its entirety, however, the distinction is actually weakened, as it can be argued that similar to philanthropists and entrepreneurs, rescuers help those they feel connected to; they only feel a connection to a wider scope of people.

References

Alvarez, Sonia E. 1998. Latin American feminisms 'go global': Trends of the 1990s and challenges for the new millennium. In *Cultures of politics: Politics of cultures: Re-visioning Latin American social movements*, ed. S.E. Alvarez, E. Daginino, and A. Escobar. Oxford: Westview Press.

Baaz, Maria Eriksson. 2005. *The paternalism of partnership: A postcolonial reading of identity in development aid*. London: Zed Books.

Batson, C. Daniel, and Laura L. Shaw. 1991. Evidence for altruism: Toward a pluralism of prosocial motives. *Psychological Inquiry* 2 (2): 107–22.

Brah, Avtar, and Ann Phoenix. 2004. Ain't I a woman? Revisiting intersectionality. *Journal of International Women's Studies* 5 (3): 75–86.

Charlés, Laurie L. 2007. *Intimate colonialism: Head, heart and body in West African development work.* Walnut Creek, CA: Left Coast Press.

Churchill, Robert Paul, and Erin Street. 2004. Is there a paradox of altruism? In *The ethics of altruism*, ed. J. Seglow, 89–106. London: Frank Cass.

Cook, Nancy. 2008. *Gender, identity and imperialism: Women development workers in Pakistan.* Houndmills, UK: Palgrave Macmillan.

de Alwis, Malathi. 2009. Interrogating the "political": Feminist peace activism in Sri Lanka. *Feminist Review* 91:81–93.

de Jong, Sarah. 2009. Constructive complicity enacted? The reflections of women NGO and IGO workers on their practices. *Journal for Intercultural Studies* 30:387–402.

de Wispelaere, Jurgen. 2004. Altruism, impartiality and moral demands. In *The ethics of altruism*, ed. J. Seglow, 9–33. London: Frank Cass.

Dixon, Thomas. 2008. *The invention of altruism: Making moral meanings in Victorian Britain.* Oxford: Oxford University Press.

Doezema, Jo. 2001. Ouch! Western feminists' "wounded attachment" to the "third world prostitute." *Feminist Review* 67:16–38.

Fisher, William F. 1997. Doing good? The politics and antipolitics of NGO practices. *Annual Review of Anthropology* 26:439–64.

Glannon, W., and L.F. Ross. 2002. Are doctors altruistic? Symposium "Heroes—or just doing their job?" *Journal of Medical Ethics* 28:68–69.

Goudge, Paulette. 2003. *The power of whiteness: Racism in third world development and aid.* London: Lawrence and Wishart.

Graham, Keith. 2004. Altruism, self-interest and the indistinctness of persons. In *The ethics of altruism*, ed. J. Seglow, 51–69. London: Frank Cass.

Hahn, Kristina, and Anna Holzscheiter. 2005. The ambivalence of advocacy: International NGOs and their discursive power of attributing identities. Paper presented at the Global International Studies conference "Bringing International Studies Together," Bilgi University, Istanbul, August 24–27.

Heron, Barbara. 2007. *Desire for development: Whiteness, gender and the helping imperative.* Waterloo, Canada: Wilfred Laurier University Press.

Hilhorst, Dorothea. 2003. *The real world of NGOs: Discourses, diversity and development.* London: Zed Books.

Hopgood, Stephen. 2006. *Keepers of the flame: Understanding Amnesty International.* London: Cornell University Press.

Krebs, Dennis L. 1991. Altruism and egoism: A false dichotomy. *Psychological Inquiry* 2:137–39.

Lang, Sabine. 1997. The NGOisation of feminism: Institutionalisation and institution building within the German women's movements. In *Transitions, environments, translations: Feminism in international politics*, ed. C. Kaplan, J. Wallach Scott, and D. Keates, 101–20. London: Routledge.

Lorgen, Christy C. 2002. The case of indigenous NGOs in Uganda's health sector. In *Group behaviour and development: Is the market destroying cooperation?* ed. J. Heyer, F. Stewart, and R. Thorp, 291–306. Oxford: Oxford University Press.

Mayo, John W., and Catherine H. Tinsley. 2008. Warm glow and charitable giving: Why the wealthy do not give more to charity. *Journal of Economic Psychology* 30:3.

Menon, Nivedita. 2004. *Feminist politics beyond the law.* Urbana: Permanent Black University of Illinois Press.

Mohanty, Chandra. 1984. Under Western eyes: Feminist scholarship and colonial discourses. *Boundary 2* 12 (3): 333–59.

Monroe, Kristen. 1991. John Donne's people: Explaining differences between rational actors and altruists through cognitive framework. *Journal of Politics* 53 (2): 394–433.

———. 1994. A fat lady in a corset: Altruism and social theory. *American Journal of Political Science* 38 (4): 861–93.

Pupavac, Vanessa. 2006. Humanitarian politics and the rise of international disaster psychology. In *Handbook of international disaster psychology*, 15–34. Westport, CT: Praeger.

Seglow, Jonathan. 2004a. The ethics of altruism: Introduction. In *The ethics of altruism*, ed. J. Seglow, 1–8. London: Frank Cass.

———. 2004b. Altruism and freedom. In *The ethics of altruism*, ed. J. Seglow, 145–62. London: Frank Cass.

Silliman, Jael. 1999. Expanding civil society: Shrinking political spaces—The case of women's nongovernmental organisations. *Social Politics* 6:23–53.

Smillie, Ian. 1995. *The Alms Bazaar: Altruism under fire—Non-profit organisations and international development.* London: Intermediate Technology Publications.

Vaux, Tony. 2004. *The selfish altruist: Relief work in famine and war.* London: Earthscan.

West, Katarina. 2002. *Agents of altruism: The expansion of humanitarian NGOs in Rwanda and Afghanistan.* Aldershot, UK: Ashgate.

3

Maintaining Independence

The Moral Ambiguities of Personal Relations Among Ghanaian Development Workers

Thomas Yarrow

Lucas and I are on our way to the headquarters of the NGO he has just set up in one of the rapidly expanding suburbs of Ghana's capital, Accra.[1] We pick our way slowly along the heavily rutted road in his large red pickup, and he starts to tell me more about his new NGO. For some time now the New Patriotic Party has been pursuing a policy of water privatization. His NGO is going to protest against this policy. With a steely sense of purpose, he outlines the inequities that will result from the "neoliberal travesty" this will unleash and the measures his organization will take to try to stop the policy. Lucas, in his early 50s, is dressed in a local batik smock that seems purposefully chosen to understate the power and influence he wields as a public figure of considerable repute. Like many others in Ghana's NGO movement, he spent much of his youth engaged in socialist political movements—activities that led him into exile and subsequently prison. The ideological legacy of these engagements is clear in the orientation of the NGO he now runs. What I have also come to realize through over a year of ethnographic research among Ghanaian NGO workers is the ongoing significance of the personal relations that developed alongside these political engagements. As Lucas explicitly puts it to me, "The mobilization we did in the '80s remains relevant to Ghanaian politics today. There's hardly any town I've been to where I am not able to identify somebody who was a student during those days and that took part in those actions." For Lucas, as for many Ghanaian NGO workers, personal relationships were thus seen as the very means by which civil society could function effectively, enabling consensus to be built and allowing resources to be effectively marshaled so as to hold the government, donors, and powerful organizations to account.

Lucas's story is a personal one, yet it highlights wider themes. For Rudolf, as for other NGO workers, personal relations were imagined as a resource to be tapped: they provided the basis for formal collaborations between organizations with the NGO sector and enabled NGO workers to enlist the help of people outside of it. Similarly they were important in enabling access to funds and resources. In this sense being an effective NGO worker depended on being "connected"; pursuing a particular set of aims or ideas depended on knowing the people who can make this happen—and knowing how and when to use them. NGO workers at times acknowledge that such connections can work against the common good, leading to charges of nepotism and corruption. Yet my argument in this chapter is that by contrast to prevailing donor discourses of "good governance," Ghanaian NGO workers' understandings of "personal relations" foreground the importance of relations that are not formally transparent or accountable. Seen in this light, personal relations provided a key means by which NGOs were able to enact the values for which they stood. Rather than compromising the independence of organizations, as prevailing arguments might lead us to believe, personal relations were key to upholding the ideological autonomy of NGOs in the face of various threats from government and donors. My suggestion is not that such informal relations constitute an alternative to formal institutional procedure but rather that these are mutually implicated forms of practice and that the existence of the former need not undermine the latter.

While the relations I focus on originate in the historically specific context of activism in Ghana, the tensions articulated in relation to these find wider resonance both in Africa (e.g., Pommerolle 2005) and further afield (e.g., Abelmann 1996). My broader argument is that while personal relations may indeed compromise organizational processes and public interest, the fact such relations are not *formally* accountable does not mean that these are not accountable. Indeed the moral and ethical debates that arise in relation to such relations themselves constitute informal checks and balances.

While this chapter draws selectively from existing anthropological accounts of development, it departs from the central tenets of the postdevelopment impulse in certain key respects. In the wake of landmark works by Ferguson (1994) and Escobar (1995), anthropologists have broadly imagined development practice to be driven by disguise and have correspondingly imagined their task to be the critical unmasking of the processes that underlie the surface representations of various development discourses. Through rendering development as "discourse," anthropologists have tended to focus on these issues at an abstract level, portraying development as an ethically problematic enterprise (Crush 1995; Escobar 1995; Hobart 1993). By contrast this account attempts to move beyond these abstract critiques (cf. Quarles Van Ufford and Giri 2003) by foregrounding development workers' own discussions of the various dilemmas they face. The chapter builds on recent work suggesting that the prevailing forms of deconstructive critique that have framed social scientific understandings of development over the past two decades (e.g., Crush 1995; Escobar 1995; Grillo and Stirrat 1997; Hobart 1993; e.g., Sachs 1992; Wright 1994) have tended to preclude a more nuanced account of the ideologies and actions of particular development practitioners (Lewis and Mosse 2006; Li Murray 2007; Mosse 2005; Mosse and Lewis 2005; Olivier de Sardan 2005; Yarrow 2008b, 2008c; Yarrow and Venkatesan forthcoming).

Personal Relations and Social Aspirations

During the past three decades, increasing donor funding has led to the proliferation of NGOs claiming to speak in the name of the public good. In 1988 Africa as a whole had between 8,000 and 9,000 formally recognized NGOs; by 2006 there were 98,928 in South Africa alone (Igoe and Kelsall 2005). In 1960 the number of officially registered NGOs in Ghana was estimated at around 10 (Amanor, Denkabe, and Wellard 1993). By 1991 this figure had increased to 350, and by 1999, when the last official count was made, the figure had grown to over 1,300 (GAPVOD/ISODEC 1999). As in the world more generally, the proliferation of NGOs has taken place as a response to state retrenchment that has accompanied the neoliberal reforms of the past three decades, as well as through international donor policies aimed at promoting "good governance" through the strengthening of "civil society." Explicitly drawing on the work of Habermas, such discourses frame civil society as a space between kinship and the state. The legitimacy of NGOs, as components of civil society, is therefore seen as a matter of the independence from both these domains. Promotion of the public good is seen to involve detachment from narrow self-interest. Against these idealized visions of civil society, recent critiques have highlighted how in practice ideas of civil society are often used to legitimate the selfish pursuit of economic and political gain. In Africa the persistence of various forms of "neopatrimonial" relationships has been widely imagined as antithetical to the development of an independent civil society (Bayart 1986, 1993; Chabal and Daloz 1999; Ekeh 1975). In particular it has been argued that the articulation of common concerns and interests is compromised by personal interests pursued through informal networks of personal relations (e.g., Gyimah-Boadi 1994). In a related way scholars have highlighted the role of informal relationships in undermining NGO independence from the state (e.g., Fowler 1991).

Although this critique forms an important corrective to normative donor narratives, it unhelpfully assumes an antipathy between personal relations and public interest. As du Gay (2000) argued, this view is based on a number of foundational Western separations that oppose, among other things, reason and emotion, pleasure and duty, public and private. Against this, he suggested the need for a contextual understanding of the way in which people negotiate different relations:

> Rather than requiring the eradication of all personal feelings and their replacement with "soulless instrumentalism," bureaucratic conduct only engenders a specific antipathy towards those relations that open up the possibility of corruption, through . . . the improper exercise of personal patronage . . . indulging incompetence or by betraying confidences. (du Gay 2000, 56)

In this vein my own analysis looks at how particular "personal relations" are seen to uphold or compromise various forms of ideological and organizational detachment (Dorman 2005; Pommerolle 2005). While the concept of "personal relations" has tended to be afforded a self-evident analytic and empirical status, this is unsettled by an ethnographic consideration of ways in which actors variously define and understand the concept. Thus my analysis does not afford these relationships a reality beyond the terms in which people explicitly talk about them. My argument is not simply that people debate the role of personal relations but that these debates challenge the status of such relations as objectively existing entities. In most of the contexts to which I refer, however, the "personal" status of such relations emerges through a broad contrast to formally defined practices (Lea 2002; Riles 2001).

This chapter draws on ethnographic fieldwork undertaken among a range of NGOs but focuses on one of these, Catholics for Action (CFA).[2] Through oral history narratives of the organization's development, I explore the role, meaning, and significance of various kinds of interpersonal relations. Although such relations are by definition personal, these narratives shed light on wider understandings of friendship as an "ideological" and hence noncorrupting relation. In the latter part of the chapter, I consider the significance of such friendships in the context of wider debates about the contemporary NGO sector in Ghana.

Catholics for Action

CFA is a small community development NGO, located in a modest office in a squat concrete building off the main Accra–Kumasi road. The organization was founded in the early 1980s at a time in which a range of other significant national NGOs were founded. Although the emergence of these organizations can be related to wider donor policies and to the NGO explosion (Igoe and Kelsall 2005) that took place globally, it is also important to locate the emergence of these organizations in relation to forms of political activism that arose during this period in the context of Ghana. In common with a range of other organizations that have since become prominent within the Ghanaian NGO movement, CFA founders supported the "popular" coup that brought Jerry Rawlings to power in 1981 and saw their own activities contributing to the "socialist revolution" he initially sought to achieve. While relatively few in number, many of those initially involved in the organization have since gone on to play important roles as subsequent founders of some of the country's largest NGOs and as important public figures in various other spheres. Thus the organization has been central to the development of a network of people, whose personal relations have in many cases outlived their involvement with CFA.

Funded mostly by international Catholic agencies, the organization attempts to use the gospel as the basis for concrete actions to help the "poor and oppressed." Specifically the organization has sought to accomplish this through a variety of activities including undertaking small-scale community projects and various advocacy initiatives. Founded in 1981 by a small group of Catholic students centered around the University of Science and Technology in Ghana's second-largest city, Kumasi, the organization was set up with the aim of putting into practice the teachings of liberation theologists. As a brochure produced by the organization explained, the aim was "to live out the radical message of the gospel, epitomized in the liberation of the poor and oppressed." During interviews with founder members of the organization, these ideologies were further elaborated. Significantly these ideologies were seen not simply as the basis for the organization but also as the basis for the interpersonal relations that developed between them.

Thomas, one of the eight founder members of CFA, left some time ago when funding difficulties made it impossible for him to remain involved. He now works as a marketing manager for the international drinks firm, Guinness.

At his suggestion I interviewed him one afternoon in the plush surrounds of the Novotel hotel. As we sat chatting over Cokes at the side of the pool, expats lay sprawled on sun loungers as a group of young Ghanaians splashed boisterously around a beach ball. Gesturing vaguely at the surrounding scene, he contrasted the evident wealth of Accra's contemporary elites with the experiences of poverty and hardship that led him and others to want to set about changing things for the better. In the 1970s, he explained, mass corruption led to a situation in which the conditions of the poorest members of society were increasingly unacceptable. For him, as for other CFA founders, the teachings of liberation theologists provided a way of understanding this inequality and a moral imperative to act on them. In this context he located the organization's formation in the central importance of using the gospel to bring about social and political change:

> There was a new consciousness of using Christianity not as a church thing but as a community thing, as a society thing, as a political tool. Not a political tool in the sense of just political leadership but for political change, to effect the national economy—everything.

More generally CFA members described the importance they attached to the "action, reflection, action" methodology used in their study groups. Being influenced by the teachings of Paulo Freire and Bishop Romero, they stressed that the idea was not simply to discuss issues but to use reflections as the basis for action.

Albert, another of the CFA founder members, left the organization some time ago to set up his own NGO but remains committed to the ideologies that originally led to the organization's inception. An imposing man in both stature and demeanor, he now runs one of the country's leading community development organizations, focusing on projects promoting the rights of children. I talked to him in the NGO's headquarters, where he connected CFA's approach to the one he continues to take: "The idea was that you intervened and God supported you. It was not just about talking but also about doing things." Later he described how attempts were made to implement community projects and to use these as a way of *conscientising* villagers about inequalities between the rich and the poor.[3] He recounted how a project undertaken in a village near Kumasi enabled them to go beyond the theorizing and thinking of their study sessions:

> We were toying with Paulo Freire's idea of pedagogy for the poor. One of the words that leapt out from his writings was *conscientisa-*

tion. I remember we went to the village and worked with the local community. It was basically an attempt to help these people put up a structure—a clinic or something—but it was an attempt by us to put into practice some of the things we had learnt.

More generally CFA members saw the organization as a means to go beyond ideas and rhetoric and put the teachings of the gospel "into practice." Ideology was not opposed to action but provided a stimulus to social change. As elucidated below, it was in this context that personal relations became instrumentally useful. Friendships were based on the need to act and provided the means by which this became possible.

Friends and Brothers

Relationships within the group were imagined to have a number of particular qualities encapsulated in the term "friendship." During this period ethnic and tribal differences were widely regarded as socially and politically divisive and the basis for various corrupt and nepotistic relations. Members of CFA came from various ethnic groups including Ewe (who at the time constituted much of the support for Rawlings's regime under the Provisional National Defence Committee) and Akan (the main stronghold of support for a more conservative tradition of politics). Against perceived differences in terms of ethnicity, family background, and class, CFA members considered themselves to be connected by their common beliefs. Their profound faith was said to give rise to long-standing friendships. George, the only founder member still working for the organization, explained, "Because our views were so similar, it was easy for us to get together and have fun. And as we continued to have fun, the bonds became stronger." Thus he described how the group formed an "open brotherhood" in which relationships were intimate and enduring: "If you went round to friends, you knew without being told that you had an invitation to eat—that helped to cement the bonds a lot. We had parties, but it was not like you would get a big sound system and invite a lot: it was more like a family gathering."

While the group was often described as small and intimate, friendships within it were understood to be "national" in scope, connecting people from all over the country and from different social backgrounds. Many of those who were active in the formation of CFA had previously known one another through involvement in other Catholic organizations, such as the Young Christian Students (YCS). These provided the basis for personal relations that were important in bringing CFA members together. Although Gabriel himself was not involved in the CFA, he got to know many of its founders in the context of this wider movement. While talking to him in the offices of the international NGO he now works for, he explained their significance: "We'd meet every year in the holiday for work camps, for congresses, for meetings . . . and this is at the national level. So there was a lot of synergy, and that is what built the solidarity and fellowship." In describing such relations as "national," CFA members drew attention to the ethnic composition of the group, seeing parallels between their own ethnic diversity and the ethnic diversity of the nation.

Such friendships were therefore imagined as national in scope. They were also imagined as *nationalistic*, contributing to the development of a properly functioning state. Martin, now in his late 40s, left the organization in the mid-1980s, when work on his PhD made it difficult to remain actively engaged. Unlike many of the other founders, he came from a poor family in a rural part of the country and was able to attend university only through a scholarship. Echoing sentiments expressed by a number of the others, he related the social diversity of the group to the "universality" of their outlook. Correspondingly he contrasted it with the tribalism and corruption that was widespread at the time.

Through describing their relationships in terms of friendship, CFA members actively sought to downplay the importance of these other kinds of affiliations. In this sense they were seen as exemplary, contributing to a country in which *what* you knew, rather than *who* you knew, counted. Gabriel, a national leader of YCS in the mid-1980s, contrasted the relationships existing within the Catholic Youth with those that predominated in the country more generally:

> The corruption was unprecedented. You could only do what you wanted depending on who you knew: which part of Ghana you were from made a difference. But we came from across the country, and that created a space for us to look at one another not in terms of tribe or in terms of geography. . . . We gathered around common aspirations that went beyond the boundaries of ethnicity and class.

Relations within the group were regarded as open and meritocratic, defined in terms of ideals and aspirations rather than along more ostensibly exclusive criteria of social and cultural membership. The legitimacy of such relations derives from their imagined basis in "the common good," as defined against the more parochial underpinnings of relations of ethnicity and kinship (cf. Bissell 1999).

Such friendships were often described as a novel and even unprecedented in the context of the period. By highlighting the "mass corruption" of the 1970s, CFA members drew attention to a state in which the use of connections along the lines of kinship and ethnicity was rife. The corrupt nature of these relations was related to their use for personal gain, in nepotistically favoring family and hence in undermining the wider public good. Against this, they highlighted their own distinctiveness from one another, seeing their connections as ideological rather than deriving from inviolable connections of kinship or ethnicity. By contrast to relations based on kinship or ethnicity, friendship was premised on a conception of people as originally distinct (see also Bell and Coleman 1999; Carrier 1999; Paine 1999; Rezende 1999). In this sense intellectual engagement was considered possible only through detachment from other, potentially compromising relations.

Friendship was understood as a relation that made this possible. While CFA members stressed the ideological foundation of such relations, they nonetheless spoke of their capacity to ground disagreement and debate. In this vein it was often held that "because we are friends we can disagree." As such, they spoke of a capacity to detach the "personal" from the "ideological." In other words, ideological disagreement is a particular kind of detachment that friendship allows for.

The independence of friends was related to the idea that such relationships were voluntary and open to negotiation. While some members described the persistence of friendships made through their involvement in CFA in the early '80s, this persistence was itself seen to be a matter of choice. Now in his late 40s, Tony worked as one of the first paid coordinators for CFA during the early 1980s. In the late '80s, he left to help set up his own NGO. For some time I lived with Tony and his family in Kumasi. During this time I came to see the enduring importance of friendships forged through this historical period. Many of the CFA members continue to live locally. Despite now working in different organizations, many continue to collaborate professionally. Some also continue to see each other socially. On one occasion I asked how he accounted for this enduring importance, and he highlighted the enduring ideological connections:

> We still are together, we still challenge each other. We don't always see eye to eye, but those you don't see too much eye to eye with, you don't carry on with.

If friendship is premised on shared ideals, then by the same token these could be severed by disagreements. Thus members described how they maintained relationships with those in the group with whom they continued to share an ideological connection, while disputes or differences of opinion led people to drift apart.

Many of the understandings of friendship that CFA members articulate bear striking similarities to what Carrier (1999) referred to as the ideal Western form. Friendship is a specific way of thinking about affective relations. It depends on a notion of a "self" seen to exist independently of external constraints of alliance, faction, and patronage and free from self-interest; it is imagined to be based on affection and sentiment; and it is therefore seen to arise on the basis of common interests and values rather than social or class distinctions. Yet if such ideas of friendship echo those encountered in other Western contexts, there is a specificity to the context in which they are articulated, which prompts a degree of self-consciousness about what friendship is and is not. In claiming to associate as friends, CFA members explicitly see themselves in distinction to the perceived norms of society. In this context, the autonomous "self" is not an a priori given but a positive achievement that entails not only a commitment to ideology but, as a corollary, the nonrecognition of the significance of other relational forms (cf. Reed 2003).

Friendship and Adversarial Culture

Similar ideas of friendship were more widely expressed by so-called pioneers of the NGO movement—those, now mostly in their 40s and 50s, who set up the first national NGOs in the 1980s (Yarrow 2008a). In common with CFA members, many of these also had backgrounds in the so-called Young Catholic Movement. Other NGO pioneers traced their roots to socialist political activism that emerged during the late 1970s and early 1980s around a range of organizations including the June the Fourth Movement and New Democratic Movement.

Now in his mid-40s, Mawuli was active in the New Democratic Movement during the early 1980s, while studying law at the University of Ghana in Legon. He now works for an international human rights NGO. Speaking to me in the organization's headquarters in the leafy Accra suburb of Legon, he outlined to me how his activism developed through ideological currents encountered during his youth. Being a socialist, he initially supported the broadly socialist Rawlings government that came to power via a military coup in 1981. As the regime became increasingly authoritarian, however, he became more outspoken in his criticism against it. In the late 1980s, he exiled himself to the United Kingdom from where he continued to protest against the government. With the formal return to democracy in 1992, and increasing funding for NGOs, he returned to the country to help set up the human rights NGO he now codirects. Questioned about the broader significance of the interpersonal relations that developed during this period, he acknowledged their continued strategic importance in terms of the functioning of the contemporary NGO sector. In contesting my suggestion that such relations were potentially nepotistic or corrupting, he highlighted their ideological basis. For him, such relations constituted the means for addressing some "simple but profound problems" relating to ongoing social inequalities in the country.

While he maintained friendships developed through his political engagement during the early '80s, relationships his current NGO relied on were based "purely on a shared vision of how Ghana should develop." He went on to explain, "We went into the movement only for political purposes. I got to know them as friends because I became politically connected with them. So I would go to their houses and have a drink. Before I was part of the movement, I wouldn't go to their houses to have a drink." Hence, the "personal" relationship derives from the "political" relationship. People without prior relationships and from different ethnic and class backgrounds came together in the context of a shared ideology. Because such friendships have their basis in shared ideology or shared politics, they are seen to persist only so long as ideological similarities remain:

> You go into political movements as an intense personal commitment and a *fierce* commitment to do something. So your bonding is also very fierce. But precisely because you went there for personal commitment, you also have the fiercest fallings-out. When you fall out, you fall out because you are fighting about your dreams. So friendships made out of the process of politics get exploded when the politics explode.

More generally NGO pioneers echoed these sentiments, describing how the political turbulence of the country had its counterpart in the turbulent nature of such interpersonal relations. Shifts taking place at the level of personal relations proceeded from the dynamics of shifts taking place between organizations and factions of national politics. Former political activists now working in the NGO sector talked of the ways in which the ideas and dreams of the '80s were shattered by Rawlings's betrayal of the revolution and the values it stood for. The ideological disputes around this period were often related to the "factionalism" that resulted and the termination of long-standing relationships. In these understandings friendship is regarded as a personal relationship that does not compromise the independence of the values and beliefs of individuals, being built on the basis of ideals.

Debating Independence

The instrumental possibilities of such personal relations and friendships were often described in positive terms as facilitating various forms of ideological and institutional autonomy. During the 1980s an authoritarian political culture developed in which formal opposition became impossible. During this period funding for both national and international NGOs increased. In the context of neoliberal reform and accompanying state retrenchment, NGOs became increasingly important in fulfilling various welfare functions. While service NGOs were generally tolerated, government criticism was not. As Peter, one of the CFA founders, explained, "Things were very fluid, and you had to be able to build a network in order to get your ideas across." In this context he related how friendships were often instrumental in the formation of coalitions that were less prone to persecution. In the context in which formal means of opposition were closed off, NGO workers described how civil society went "underground," becoming increasingly dependent on a set of relations that were largely invisible to the state.

In the contemporary situation, friendships were also seen as important means by which independence from government could be maintained. In this vein, relationships deriving from social and political activism of the 1980s were seen to be pragmatically important in creating formal alliances and networks and disseminating ideas. A former political activist now directing a Ghanaian NGO thus told me, "If you want to get things across to the media, you can easily identify [friends] who are working for the media and see what support you can get from them in terms of airing things that are of national concern that you can't get out any other way. These connections are very important." Personal connections, in other words, were regarded as legitimate to the extent that they were seen to enable advocacy that was in the broader public interest.

A similar logic underpinned the idea that personal relations and contacts were legitimate as a means of maintaining independence from donors. On one occasion I interviewed the director of one of the country's leading advocacy NGOs. A former member of the socialist New Democratic Movement in the early 1990s and an active member of the student movement, he described the importance of relations forged through these engagements in the context of the work he does today. He explained,

> I now find some of my colleagues in quite a number of sectors who are outspoken and supportive speaking less and less because they don't want to upset funders. . . . I know this NGO, I know they are supportive of me but officially they are neutral, or they may even be saying things against what I am doing. But at a personal realm when they meet me they say, "You go on" and even give me information that I may not know.

In a situation in which donor agendas are imagined to suppress dissent, personal relations make the existence of alternative perspectives possible. If the existence of a "public" presumes the existence of autonomous individuals and interests, then in the face of state oppression and donor attempts to co-opt development agendas, personal relations are seen as the very condition of civil society autonomy.

Despite the acknowledged virtue of such relations, however, they were also sometimes regarded as problematic, having the potential to distort organizational goals and indeed the very existence of an effective civil society. Among NGO pioneers the use of friends and contacts was sometimes debated. Reflecting on work of CFA during the 1980s, Albert, one of the CFA founders, related the fact that a number of members of the organization had personal relations to government ministers, to the effectiveness of the organization. From his perspective this made it easier to advocate for the views they believed in and therefore to bring about the kinds of social change they hoped for:

> We'd go to the minister and say, "This is what you said, but you are not doing it. Why not?" Because we had some access to the state, some access to higher government, they were scared.

Yet other CFA founders played down the significance of such connections either through denying their existence or through claiming that they did not use them. Contrasting their approach with the widespread nepotism and corruption at the time, Martin explained to me, "We had independent minds; we did everything the way we thought it should be done." For him, "independence" meant using "formal mechanisms" and hence eschewing a more particular set of personal relations. Indeed, as somebody from a relatively humble background, he saw his "lack of connections" as a positive virtue.

Similar criticisms were also leveled by younger NGO workers who sometimes suggested that the older generation of NGO pioneers constituted an "old boys network." From their perspective, long-standing relationships developed through social and political activism during the 1980s were seen to have the capacity to close down debate as friends side with one another regardless of their ideological beliefs. Similarly it was sometimes claimed that such relations were used to gain employment or funding. In this vein, the ideology of the older generation of NGO pioneers was sometimes construed as a "charade," masking self-interest and the pursuit of personal gain.

Now in his mid-50s, Emmanuel engaged in activism during his youth, being an active member of the student movement and later the socialist June Fourth Movement. His activism led to imprisonment and later exile. Following the formal restoration of democracy, he returned to the country and now works as a development consultant. Although being friends with many of those now at the forefront of the NGO movement, he was also highly critical of the negative effect that such relations can have. Talking to me over a lunch of *fufu* at an upmarket Accra chop-bar, he explained,

> Africans like to connect with who they know. Where they come from. Kinship is very important. When they organize, they tend to bring along who they know, and a lot of these formations shape the way NGOs organize. Even in terms of modern governance structures there is an illusion of independent institutionally organized structure. But if you go deeper, you find a network of relations that either go back to the past, a shared history of experience, or are basically from university.

From this perspective, the problems of Ghanaian civil society were seen as part of a more general "African" problem. Rather than emergent features of social life, the existence of specific kinds of personal relations are thus seen as facts *about* Africa.

Conclusion: The Ambiguities of Friendship

Anthropological theories have tended to regard organizational procedure as a detached form of practice, by contrast to the purportedly more concrete and specific workings of personal relations. In this vein bureaucracy can be seen positively as upholding egalitarianism (e.g., du Gay 2000), accountability, and fairness or negatively as promoting soulless instrumentalism and indifference (e.g., Herzfeld 1992). On the other hand, patronage can be seen positively as the means by which order is obtained in an otherwise lawless world (e.g., Bayart 1993) or alternatively as a pathology of society—the means by which collective goals are subordinated to individual or parochial interests (e.g., Chabal and Daloz 1999; Price 1975).

Ghanaian NGO workers' understandings of friendship complicate this opposition. As I hope to have shown, these interweave *both* detachment and engagement. For these actors, personal relationships are not straightforwardly opposed to their stated goal of organizational autonomy. Rather the former enable the latter. Various NGO actors recognize that personal relations may at times compromise the kinds of independence and detachment they strive for. This does not entail a necessary antipathy between these, however.

Some time ago, Cohen (1981) pertinently argued that no society can be organized along purely rational bureaucratic lines. In the context of a study of Sierra Leonean creoles, he showed how public organizations—and those that claim to speak in the name of the public good—inevitably depend on extensive informal dealings, secrecy, and concealment. Yet although necessarily invisible from public view, such covert coordination nonetheless conforms to unwritten rules, norms, and beliefs. These ensure that while friendships may be regarded as personal in the sense that they arise on the basis of deeply held beliefs and give rise to a range of emotional attachments, they are not *necessarily* used to pursue personal gain. Indeed Ghanaian NGO workers often used such informal mechanisms to pursue visions of social and economic development, even at the expense of their own personal interest (Yarrow 2008a) and often at the risk of considerable personal danger.

These understandings complicate prevailing donor and policy discourses of "good governance" in which personal relations have been broadly equated with personal interest and hence corruption. Although Ghanaian NGO workers also see the potential for personal relations to work in this way, they also highlight their more positive role in upholding ideological visions at odds with those of donors and the government and hence in maintaining ideological and organizational independence.

Given that the informal nature of such relations constitutes the very condition of possibility, there is clearly no sense in which their promotion could ever be a meaningful policy objective for international donors or governments. Recognizing the importance of these relations, however, does make the case against the overdetermination of policies that close down the space in which such relations operate and emerge. In particular I would suggest that the normative valorization of transparency undermines the effectiveness of relations that are not formally and hence institutionally visible. At best these initiatives provide a way of redescribing relations that already exist in more acceptable terms to an external audience of donors and international NGOs; at worst the pursuit of formal transparency and accountability runs the risk of undermining the very forms of relationship practically required to bring these about.

Acknowledgments

The initial idea for this chapter developed during my PhD and was stimulated in part by the observations of Marilyn Strathern and Sue Benson. Research was funded by the Economic and Social Research Council. I wrote this chapter with the generous support of a Leverhulme Early Career Fellowship.

Notes

1. This chapter was written in the ethnographic present of 2003, when the bulk of research for the chapter was undertaken.
2. This and all personal names referred to in this chapter are pseudonyms.
3. The term derives from liberation theology. CFA members described it as an unveiling of social reality that precipitated and enabled social action.

References

Abelmann, Nancy. 1996. *Echoes of the past, epics of dissent: A South Korean social movement.* Berkeley and Los Angeles: University of California Press.

Amanor, Kojo, Aloytius Denkabe, and Kate Wellard. 1993. Ghana: Country overview. In *Nongovernmental organizations and the state in Africa*, ed. K. Wellard and J.G. Copestake, 183–94. London and New York: Routledge.

Bayart, Jean-Francois. 1986. Civil society in Africa. In *Political domination in Africa*, ed. P. Chabal, 109–25. Cambridge: Cambridge University Press.

———. 1993. *The state in Africa: The politics of the belly.* London: Longman.

Bell, Sandra, and Simon Coleman. 1999. The anthropology of friendship: Enduring themes and future possibilities. In *The anthropology of friendship*, ed. S. Bell and S. Coleman, 1–19. Oxford and New York: Berg.

Bissell, William. 1999. Colonial constructions: Historicizing debates on civil society in Africa. In *Civil society and the political imagination in Africa: Critical perspectives*, ed. J. Comaroff and J. Comaroff, 124–60. Chicago: Chicago University Press.

Carrier, J.G. 1999. People who can be friends: Selves and social relationships. In *The anthropology of friendship*, ed. S. Bell and S. Coleman, 21–38. Oxford and New York: Berg.

Chabal, Patrick, and Jean-Pascal Daloz. 1999. *Africa works: Disorder as political instrument.* Oxford: James Currey.

Cohen, Abner. 1981. *The politics of elite culture.* London: University of California Press.

Crush, J. 1995. *Power of development.* London and New York: Routledge.

Dorman, Sara Rich. 2005. Studying democritization in Africa: A cast study of human rights NGOs in Zimbabwe. In *Between a rock and a hard place: African NGOs, donors and the state*, ed. J. Igoe and T. Kelsall, 35–59. Durham, NC: Carolina Academic Press.

du Gay, Paul. 2000. *In praise of bureaucracy: Weber, organization, ethics*. London, Thousand Oaks, and New Delhi: Sage.

Ekeh, Peter P. 1975. Colonialism and the two publics in Africa: A theoretical statement. *Comparative Studies in Society and History* 17:91–112.

Escobar, Arturo. 1995. *Encountering development: The making and unmaking of the third world*. Princeton, NJ: Princeton University Press.

Ferguson, James. 1994. *The anti-politics machine: "Development," depoliticisation, and bureaucratic power in Lesotho*. Minneapolis and London: University of Minnesota Press.

Fowler, Alan. 1991. The role of NGOs in changing state-society relations: Perspectives from eastern and southern Africa. *Development Policy Review* 9:53–84.

GAPVOD/ISODEC. 1999. *Directory of non-governmental organisations in Ghana*. Accra: Authors.

Grillo, R. D., and R. L. Stirrat, eds. 1997. *Discourses of development: Anthropological perspectives*. Oxford and New York: Berg.

Gyimah-Boadi, E. 1994. Associational life, civil society and democratisation in Ghana. In *Civil society and the state in Africa*, ed. J. Harbeson, N. Chazan, and D. Rothchild, 125–48. Boulder, CO: Lynne Reinner.

Herzfeld, Michael. 1992. *The social production of indifference: Exploring the symbolic roots of Western bureaucracy*. Chicago and London: University of Chicago Press.

Hobart, Mark. 1993. *An anthropological critique of development: The growth of ignorance*. London and New York: Routledge.

Igoe, Jim, and Tim Kelsall. 2005. Introduction: Between a rock and a hard place. In *Between a rock and a hard place: African NGOs, donors and the state*, ed. J. Igoe and T. Kelsall, 1–33. Durham, NC: Carolina Academic Press.

Lea, Teresa S. 2002. Between the pen and the paperwork: A native ethnography of learning to govern indigenous health in the northern territory. PhD diss., University of Sidney.

Lewis, David, and David Mosse. 2006. Theoretical approaches to brokerage and translation in development. In *Development brokers and translators: The ethnography of aid and agencies*, ed. D. Lewis and D. Mosse, 1–27. Bloomfield, CT: Kumarian Press.

Li Murray, Tania. 2007. *The will to improve: Governmentality, development and the practice of politics*. Durham and London: Duke University Press.

Mosse, David. 2005. *Cultivating development: An ethnography of aid policy and practice*. London: Pluto Press.

Mosse, David, and David Lewis. 2005. *The aid effect: Giving and governing in international development*. London: Pluto Press.

Olivier de Sardan, Jean-Pierre. 2005. *Anthropology and development: Understanding contemporary social change*. London and New York: Zed Books.

Paine, R. 1999. Friendship: The hazards of an ideal relationship. In *The anthropology of friendship*, ed. S. Bell and S. Coleman, 39–58. Oxford and New York: Berg.

Pommerolle, Marie-Emmanuelle. 2005. Leader in the human rights sector: The paradoxical institutionalisation of a Kenyan NGO. In *Between a rock and a hard place: African NGOs, donors and the state*, ed. J. Igoe and T. Kelsall, 93–113. Durham, NC: Carolina Academic Press.

Price, Robert. 1975. *Society and bureaucracy in contemporary Ghana*. Berkeley, Los Angeles, and London: University of California Press.

Quarles Van Ufford, Philip, and Anta Kumar Giri. 2003. *A moral critique of development: In search of global responsibilities.* London and New York: Routledge.

Reed, Adam. 2003. *Papua New Guinea's last place: Experiences of constraint in post-colonial prison.* New York and Oxford: Berhahn Books.

Rezende, Claudia Barcellos. 1999. Building affinity through friendship. In *The anthropology of friendship*, ed. S. Bell and S. Coleman, 79–97. Oxford and New York: Berg.

Riles, Annelise. 2001. *The network inside out.* Ann Arbor: University of Michigan Press.

Sachs, Wolfgang. 1992. *The development dictionary: A guide to knowledge as power.* London: Zed Books.

Wright, Susan, ed. 1994. *Anthropology of organizations.* New York: Routledge.

Yarrow, Thomas. 2008a. Life/history: Personal narratives of development in Ghana. *Africa* 78:334–58.

———. 2008b. Negotiating difference: Discourses of indigenous knowledge and development in Ghana. *Political and Legal Anthropology Review* 31:224–42.

———. 2008c. Paired opposites: Dualism in development and anthropology. *Critique of Anthropology* 28:426–44.

Yarrow, Thomas, and Soumhya Venkatesan. Forthcoming. *Differentiating development: Beyond an anthropology of critique.* Berghahn.

4

Intercultural Encounters, Colonial Continuities and Contemporary Disconnects in Rural Aid

An Ethnography of Development Practitioners in Madagascar

Ritu Verma

Development practitioners are complex social beings who live and work within a particular "culture" that exists regardless of the country where they are deploying development from. At the same time, it is difficult to pin down exactly what the culture of development practitioners is, as it is neither an established immigrant community, nor a nomadic culture, nor a diaspora, nor a community in exile. Perhaps the best way to describe development is as a "free-floating," transportable, mobile, and transient culture (Verma 2007, 2009)—although it is not tied to any one country or region, it is easily transported and transplanted in any "developing" country context (Ferguson 1994). In Madagascar, it is made up of both foreign expatriates from all over the world, including volunteers and experienced development practitioners, and mostly elite Malagasy women and men.[1] Regardless of national origins, the culture of development practitioners is characterized by a high degree of hypermobility. This transportability owes itself to the propensity of development practitioners to move from country to country, as they negotiate with development organizations and agencies on a contract-to-contract, project-to-project, country-to-country, and sometimes organization-to-organization basis (Verma 2009, unpublished). If they remain within the practice of international development, their mobility increases over time, as they move from "hardship" postings such as volunteering in the "bush" to more lucrative postings in the capitals of countries. Unlike anthropologists, who spend large amounts of time in specific field sites or on context-specific issues, development practitioners regularly cross geographical space, with little regard to cultural differences, spending an average of two years in a posting (Verma 2009, unpublished). During this time, they may also change their sectoral focus over the life of their careers to fit into various postings, organizational strategies, and donor demands.

Bruno Latour and Steve Woolgar suggested in their groundbreaking work *Laboratory Life* (Latour and Woolgar 1979) that similar to "an intrepid explorer of the Ivory Coast" who studies the belief systems or the processes of production of a particular sociocultural group by living and studying among them, the role of the anthropologist is to make descriptive and analytical observations about activities and sociopolitical relations regarding a particular scientific setting (Latour and Woolgar 1979, 28). They reasoned that while we have detailed knowledge about "the myths and circumcision rituals of exotic tribes, we remain relatively ignorant of the details of equivalent activity among tribes of scientists, whose work is heralded as having startling or at least extremely significant effects on our civilization" (p. 17). And while we may have knowledge about the external effects of science on society, our understanding of the complex internal networks, processes, and knowledge of scientific activity remains undeveloped (Latour and Woolgar 1979). On the basis of this conceptualization and methodological approach, they studied the social world of a microbiology laboratory, describing in detail the way in which social and political processes shape the way scientific knowledge is produced. With this pioneering work, a new subfield of anthropology, the anthropology of science, was born. Since then, other anthropologists have built on this concept and further documented and analyzed the complex working worlds of scientists, including Latour himself (1987, 1993, 1996), as well as Haraway (1988, 1991), Martin (1994, 1997), Knorr-Cetina (1981, 1999), and others who have carried out overview works on the subject (Keeley and Scoones 1999; Shrum 1988). Until recently, however, the focus of much of this work has primarily been on work relations and environments within scientific settings and laboratories. Little research has been carried out on the social lives, cultural practices, diverse perspectives, and personal experiences of a particular group of scientists and practitioners working in the industry of international development—the "traditional" stuff of anthropologists.

This chapter is about a particular domain of scientists, namely, development practitioners, who play a key role in the deployment of development in many parts of the world but yet, until recently, whose lives have been hidden from view from much of social and anthropological analysis. This omission is remarkable given that they shape and have a significant impact on the way development affects people and their environments. When anthropologists and social scientists have turned their attention to development practitioners in the past, it was done in a way that separated their working and social worlds and often ignored their social lives altogether in terms of ethnographic analysis. This was somehow seen as a "no-go" zone and not constitutive of the study of development. In recent years, the study of development has taken a critical turn. Dissatisfied with only the analysis and deconstruction of development project texts and ethnography of those being "targeted" for development as explanatory of the effects of development, a new field of anthropology is emerging that turns its attention to those women and men who are doing the actual "targeting."

As part of this emerging field, this chapter is part of a larger study focusing on the lives of development practitioners working on rural development aid projects in the Central Highlands of Madagascar (Verma 2009, unpublished). In particular, it focuses on a "women's project" that development practitioners regard as a way of improving women's lives and nutrition through the introduction of "new and improved" cooking methods. It examines the effects of the project from the perspective of the rural women being targeted by the intervention, but, what is more significant, it explores the lived realities of the development practitioners themselves and the effects of development on their social and work lives and practices. Dimensions of culture, context, status, identity, and mobility, as well as norms and social and gender relations, are explored in terms of the creation of "islands" and understanding continuities from colonial pasts. I argue that sociocultural dimensions and preferences are important in understanding wider relations and practices of development and how they shape development interventions, encounters, and effects. This chapter argues that development disconnects more often characterize development encounters than meaningful interface. The construction of social and cultural worlds plays as much of a role in determining this dynamic as do the strategies development practitioners engage to mitigate the blast radius of impact of deploying development.

Theoretical Points of Departure: Contextualizing Aidland

Ferguson (1994, 254) suggested that what is perhaps most important about development projects is not so much the regular failures of projects to meet their objectives but their unintended effects. Critical anthropologists of development have been concerned about the larger, more complex political spaces that are often beyond direct observation and constituted in "off-stage speeches, gestures and practices that confirm, contradict or inflect" the dominant ideologies of power relations (Scott 1990, 4) but that nonetheless shape development. Norman Long argued that the objective is to gain an "ethnographic understanding of the 'social life' of development projects—from conceptualization to realization—as well as the responses and lived experiences of the variously located and affected social actors" (2001, 14–15), and this is done through the analysis of interfaces of development encounters. Earlier work based on this approach focused on the complex lives of rural women and men and what development affected and meant for them in a particular location (Ferguson 1994; Fairhead and Leach 1996; Carney and Watts 1990; Moore 1993; Long and Long 1992; Mackenzie 1995; Pottier 2003; to name but a few). In some cases, the working dilemmas of development practitioners were also explored (e.g., de Vries 1997; Arce 1989). Development practitioners are the drivers of the development machine. Yet if we consider Stirrat's argument that "we probably know more about the missionaries and colonial civil servants of the 19th and early 20th centuries than we do about contemporary development workers" (2008, 407), then we are missing detailed knowledge of a significant domain of actors who play a critical role in shaping political–economic and social dynamics in countries such as Madagascar. We remain in the dark regarding the social lives, cultural practices, and lived experiences of development practitioners and the way this shapes development.

In addressing the gaps in earlier studies of development,[2] a new ethnographic field of inquiry has emerged in recent years: the anthropology of development practice, or Aidland. This new type of ethnography of development focuses on development practitioners and demonstrates that the practice of development projects and policy is inseparable from the social realm (Verma 2007, 2009, unpublished). Several studies in this genre have emerged over the past decade or so. First, there are those studies that focus on development practitioners as the subject of ethnographic inquiry but are contained within the context of a development project. In other words, the focus is on the social relations of development practitioners within the context of a specific development project, organization, or program only, such as that of Mosse (2005), Hilhorst (2003), de Vries (1997), Goetz (2001), Grammig (2002), McKinnon (2007), and Arce (1989). Second, there are those who push the ethnographic boundaries further by looking at social relations in their own right, including those outside of working hours and outside development projects, programs, and organizations (and in some cases, including the social relations within projects, programs, and organizations). They include the work of Hindman (2002, this volume), Shrestha (2006), Fechter (2007, this volume), and Verma (2006a, 2006b, 2007, 2009, 2010, unpublished).

This chapter represents a third subfield that gives equal ethnographic weight to the social and professional relations of development practitioners but expands the analysis further by simultaneously undertaking a similar analysis of working and social lives of rural farmers as the targets of development. It aims to juxtapose and explore the interfaces and disconnects in meaning, practice, and engagement as these two worlds come together or bypass each other in the name of development (Verma 2009, unpublished). It is based on the idea that international development is as much about the people who are being "developed" as it is about those who are doing the "developing." While I elaborate the broader study elsewhere (Verma 2009, unpublished), this chapter focuses on the development interface and the social and working lives of development practitioners.[3] This focus is a deliberate choice: given that power relations and access to development resources often privilege development practitioners, it might be worth considering that the lives of development beneficiaries are of equal, if not greater, importance in explaining the disconnects that characterize development projects and nonetheless impact the lives of those they are meant to develop. This may be as significant in Madagascar (this chapter) as in any other part of the so-called developing world.

Development Misencounters: "Selling Doughnuts Instead of Their Bodies"

Madagascar has been subject to numerous types of interventions over many centuries. Over time, it was subject to intense attempts at religious conversion, slavery, colonization, and conquest from Europe, as well as slavery and conquest within its own borders. It is rich in resources, both natural and biological, and is home to a diversity of rich cultures, varied climates, biodiversity, and stunning landscapes. It is not surprising that Madagascar draws travelers, visitors who succeed the interventions of the early settlers, conquering colonialists, converting missionaries, and, recently, development practitioners. Indeed, in the contemporary context, the great red island hosts a large number of development projects, programs, and practitioners from all over the world aimed at combating what is viewed by some as a "bleak picture" and its long-suffering battle with "absolute poverty . . . high population growth, intensive deforestation and soil erosion, declines in soil fertility, declines in health status (particularly among children), and political and social turmoil" (USAID 2000, 1).

During my fieldwork situated in one rural area in the province of Fianarantsoa—as well as multiple-sited locations from this extremity to the central locations of the development machine (Foucault 1980) in the provincial and the country's capital—I studied several development projects aimed at improving farmers' lives. These ranged from dam rehabilitation, irrigation infrastructure upgrading, and improvements in rice cultivation to "improving" women's lives by controlling their reproduction and sexuality. These spheres of development, however, were not the only things on the development menu. Other aspects of farmers' lives that needed developing were women's cooking methods, human nutrition, household budgets, and access to microcredit. In addition, repetitive interventions undertaken by several different and successive development practitioners during my fieldwork included the ever-popular mission to formalize women into groups and prevent them from high-risk activities such as prostitution (Verma 2009, unpublished). In this chapter, I focus on the way Lilianne,[4] a French volunteer living in a major rural town called Ambiraika[5] in the Betsileo Highlands, perceives "women's issues" and subsequently deploys a series of "women's projects," including one aimed at improving the way women cook through a series of trainings aimed at improving women's and their families' nutrition.

The projects are initially engaged with the Young Prostitutes Women's Group living at the periphery of the large weekly cattle market in Ambiraika and later with women from another nearby village. Lilianne explained why she targets this particular group:

> The objective was for the women to have something to sell. . . . We tell them instead of selling their bodies, we tell them about things that are more original than what they are doing. . . . We try to support their efforts in doing well with the vegetables that they're growing already and to do new ones. They don't always know how it will enter into their food patterns. So we try to make them taste it in advance, to show them original things, and at the same time [show them] the nutritional aspects, and what it can give the children. . . . So we try to do this with products that are really in the village. . . . That's to say, flour, oil, salt, vegetables, and all the things they can get in the village, that they can furnish it themselves. And [with] all the things that they already have in the house, [such as] firewood, charcoal, plates, and their time, their ears, and their hands.

At first glance, the thinking behind the training seems straightforward: a simple intervention introducing new, modern methods of cooking that will simultaneously improve women's and their families' nutrition at the same time.

During the training aimed at improving cooking methods, women enjoy the sessions greatly, and there is a festive atmosphere in the air. This is evident during the first cooking demonstration, as many more women show up to the session than are members in the group involved in the trainings. The atmosphere is lively, and some members get slightly drunk on locally brewed *toka-gache* (potent local liquor distilled from rice). The day is seen as an afternoon off from the heavy and time-consuming activities that make up a woman's day, such as collecting water and wood, tending children, washing clothes, cooking, working in home gardens and rice fields, selling *mofos* (fried local doughnuts made from flour) at the weekly cattle market, and so on. It is a time for festivity, to socialize, to drink some *toka-gache*, and to be exposed to something out of the ordinary—complete with two *vahazas* (foreigners like Lilianne and myself), Madame Louise (a Malagasy public servant from the ministry of social services), and special food not eaten on a daily basis. But the most telling results are revealed long after the training is over, as I interviewed women on the content of the trainings and the applicability of it to their everyday lives.

Despite the festive atmosphere during the session itself, the result of the training is poor. One reason is that some of the ingredients used in the recipes, such as cooking oil, meat, eggs, and flour, are not affordable to most women on a daily basis. While Lilianne uses the ingredients on a daily basis in her own kitchen, rural women tend to use them only during festive holidays. Over and above the unaffordable price, the ingredients are unavailable for purchase in rural villages and must be bought in the nearby rural town. Given the special ingredients, the meals have the potential of being prepared and eaten only during holiday events and celebrations. Another reason why the cuisine is not taken up is the daily food preferences, which are deeply embedded in Betsileo ancestral, cultural, and social relations. For instance, two of the recipes used in the trainings include vegetables such as pumpkins, which are aimed at improving farmers' nutrition but are not used on a daily basis by rural farmers. Rather, these types of vegetables are considered cash crops to be sold in the weekly market to feed urban appetites. Furthermore, development practitioners and foreign visitors to the area often express astonishment that Betsileo farmers eat rice three times a day. Rice is the main dish and is normally accompanied by a small amount of leafy green vegetables on the side, if and when available. Few farmers can afford to eat meat, bread, or *mofos*, as they are reserved for special occasions such as national holidays, weddings, funerals, and *famadihana* (the returning of the dead, a festive ceremony involving removing the reshrouding of recently deceased ancestors). Although this adherence to certain meal preferences is similar to the propensity of Americans and some Europeans to eat wheat-based products three times a day (bread, pasta, cereal, etc.), from the perspective of development practitioners, the habit of eating rice three times a day is seen as illogical and unhealthy and, therefore, in need of changing and improvement. While an unbalanced rice-based diet may have nutritional deficiencies because of its high starch content (especially when it is not accompanied by vegetables), such reasoning ignores the importance of rice as a vital link to the ancestors and the value placed on rice as the most important crop and livelihood practice—even over and above *zebu* (cattle) (Verma 2009, unpublished). In addition, during periods of famine, rice stocks tend to be depleted, and most people are unable to eat three meals a day. They are reduced to eating "poverty" crops such as cassava and maize.[6] Besides being unaffordable and not reflecting daily eating preferences, the French volunteer's "improved cooking methods" also require a great deal of planning and time, but time is a precious resource for most rural Betsileo farmers and most especially for women, who face intense labor demands on a daily basis. This renders the potential of the recipes being integrated into daily life unlikely. None of this surprising, as the recipes have been pulled out by Lilianne from an outdated cookbook borrowed from a local library in the town of Fianarantsoa, printed in the 1960s in France, and do not reflect Betsileo farmers' tastes, budgets, lifestyles, time constraints, and cultural food preferences.

Although deployed with the best of intentions, this type of women's project is simplistic and relies on undertheorized assumptions about the category "woman" rather than on women's relations of power, gender division of labor, decision making, and access to resources. Repeating patterns from the women-in-development era, and similar to women's projects in other parts of Sub-Saharan Africa (Verma 2001), "doing gender" is seen as something straightforward, not requiring any previous training, skills, knowledge, or experience. Similar to women's projects in other parts of Africa, the only skill needed is the belief in development and that poor rural women need to be pulled out of patterns of poverty, traditional practices, and high-risk behavior.

Indeed, the new cooking methods are not taken up by the Young Prostitutes Women's Group or by women in the other villages. While Lilianne has the best of intentions and is confident about the success of her training, she is also oblivious to their inappropriateness in the context of women's everyday lives. From her side of the interface, she is frustrated by their failure and relegates it to lack of motivation by the women. From the other side of the interface, the trainings are a day of festivity but not something that can be realistically used in the women's everyday lives. Beyond a critique of the training's failure to meet the objectives of development practitioners, it is important to ask how it is possible for development practitioners to be so far off the mark, despite the fact that they are in a unique position for most development practitioners, as they live in close proximity to the farmers. To answer this question, it is necessary to investigate the lived worlds of the French volunteers by exploring work and social aspects of intercultural encounters outside the immediate development interface situation.

Development Practitioners as a Unique Tribe of Actors

Lilianne is in her late 20s and trained as an agricultural engineer in France. This posting in Madagascar is her first professional experience, apart from a six-month internship after graduating from university. After traveling abroad for the first time in Senegal, she felt inspired and wanted to return to Africa to work and travel. The French Volunteering Programme proved to be the best avenue to get work experience abroad, especially for a young graduate with no prior professional or international development experience. When Lilianne first came to Madagascar, she was posted in a small village on the eastern coast of Madagascar, until the project ran out of money. Because of the village's remoteness, humid climate, and lack of transportation and communication with the outside world, she felt unhappy living there. She asked the head office in Antananarivo for a transfer and was transferred to Ambiraika, along with her boyfriend, Christophe, who managed to obtain a job as a French volunteer with the same agency after coming initially to Madagascar as a tourist to visit her.

She lives in the rural town with Christophe in a two-story house provided to them by the mayor's office. It is part of what volunteers in the large rural town call the "Melrose Place" housing complex where Charles, another French volunteer, and Mark, an American volunteer, also live and work. Christophe and Lilianne have a modern Betsileo three-bedroom house, with one bedroom converted into a living room; another into an office complete with a computer, telephone, and Internet access; and another serving as a bedroom. They also have running water, access to electricity, and an outhouse that has been partially adapted to Western needs. Although they live next door to Mark, their standard of living is quite different from his. This is because French volunteers are paid more, have access to more development resources such as a "setting up" allowance and project funds, and earn several times more than the approximately 200 US dollars per month that their American colleagues earn.

Although French volunteers do not live a privileged expat life and earn far less than many development practitioners in the capital of the country, they can afford amenities such as stereos, computers, and televisions. Lilianne, Christophe, and their team have access to imported French mountain bikes and a motorbike, and Charles (who works on a separate tourism project) has a small truck. Having a means of transportation makes both their work and their social lives easier, and it is indispensable for visiting remote villages, as well as leisure and tourist sites and other development practitioners. Having a fully equipped kitchen with a fridge, oven, and stove allows the couple to prepare meals they are accustomed to. Lilianne does most of the cooking for the couple, and this includes preparing homemade bread, jams, and flavored rums. Weekly trips to the provincial capital city of Fianarantsoa and periodic trips to Antananarivo and other cities also provide a means of gaining access to imported goods such as French cheese, condiments, and cooking ingredients difficult to find in the small rural town.

Lilianne's boyfriend, Christophe, has formal training as a winemaker. They both work with two Malagasy counterparts, Alphonsine, who recently graduated as a hydraulic and environmental specialist, and Rakoto, who is a technical agricultural specialist. The focus of their projects in the area, as defined by their Swiss donor and French volunteering organization, is agriculture, irrigation, women's projects, and income-generation activities. Despite the fact that Lilianne is officially the coordinator of the project, has been in Madagascar longer than Christophe, has more experience in Africa, and is trained as an agricultural engineer, she is in charge of women's projects, while Christophe, the winemaker, carries out agricultural projects. Neither of them has any training in international development.

Lilianne and Christophe spend a great deal of time together, not only as work colleagues but also as girlfriend and boyfriend in a long-term relationship. There are many difficulties in this arrangement, a situation that is exacerbated by the fact that their office is also located in their house. Unlike everyday life in France where one's professional life is well demarcated and bounded from one's personal life (unless one works from home or engages in household and child-rearing work), both social and work worlds regularly collide on a daily basis. As Lilianne related, "It's unpractical. Although we live well, it's not like that all the time. [It was OK] for a year or so. There are people [*rural farmers and trainers*] who come to see us all the time. Even on Sundays. It's hard." The small town they live in is one hour away by car from the provincial capital and approximately 10 hours from Antananarivo. With fewer than a dozen expats living in town, and despite daily interaction with farmers and local officials, their general feeling is one of alienation, isolation, and the sense that they are living in a fishbowl where they are constantly being observed and speculated about. Indeed, as discussed further later, the fishbowl syndrome is something that many volunteers and development practitioners complain about. For Lilianne and Christophe, in addition to living and working together in extremely close quarters, it makes life as a couple especially difficult.

Having a normal social life has been difficult for Lilianne. Most of her friends in the rural town are work-related colleagues. She explained, "I never worked with a boyfriend. When you are in your familiar surroundings [in France], there are lots of things, more friends, and hobbies. Here . . . there are not a lot of things to do. We try to do some things different, but it's really hard. That's why we really needed to separate our [social] activities; he goes to cultural centre and gives lectures, he plays football. I try to see other people, Madame Louise. Rakoto too. In the beginning, we used to go running together too! [*Laughs.*] Also, the effects of being in a foreign country also affect us." There are other issues as well, mostly to do with the vulnerable position of expat women as a result of the high instances of married expat men engaging in extramarital relations. She explained,

> The temptations are everywhere. In Tulear [*a popular coastal tourist destination*] or Antananarivo, [there are] beautiful women. You just have to call. But here, if there are only three, it's still a temptation. I don't know. It's still hard [for men] to resist when you are solicited 10 times a day. When the guy knows they are prostitutes, it's not as tempting. . . . It's really something I don't like to think about, because there are already so many destabilizing things here. And you are already fragile between being a couple, between work . . . you will break your head thinking of these things.

Christophe perceives that Lilianne is "too dependent" on him. Patriarchal and patronizing attitudes toward women like Lilianne—from farmers as well as from Christophe—play a role in determining Lilianne's role in the project and the relationship. In addition, gender power relations between Christophe and Lilianne within the social relations of their intimate relationship, as well as their work relationship, privilege Christophe as a man within both French and Betsileo gender discourses and practices. They help to explain why Lilianne does not put into practice her training as an agricultural engineer in agricultural projects within the volunteer's project but instead blindly attempts to implement a series of highly problematic and ill-designed women's projects—simply because she is a woman. As Christophe remarked, "If you are woman, it is good to work with women." This reasoning helps to determine Lilianne's work focus on women's projects that center on household activities, while ignoring Betsileo women's central engagement in rice cultivation, agriculture, and other productive activities that are also inseparable from what is considered as the household.

Similar to Lilianne, Christophe experiences problems and remarks about the mixing of work and personal lives:

> In France, you have the couple's life, because in the morning they go to work and in the evenings, they meet again, but for us, it's 100 percent of the time and it's really difficult. . . . You don't have your own space. . . . If you work alone, you fix your own limits. . . . In the couple for sure, you have lows and highs . . . it's a double whammy—you have the culture shock and plus you have your couple's life . . . not all the time, but you have rough patches. It's really harder.

Five months after speaking these words, and toward the end of my fieldwork, Lilianne and Christophe ended their three-year relationship. The stresses of working and living together in a small fishbowl environment proved to be difficult and eventually wore down their relationship. Lilianne moved next door, where she and Christophe lived as neighbors while sharing a common office, kitchen, and outhouse. Lilianne's assignment ended shortly thereafter, at which point she moved back to France, where she was dating another former French volunteer who also worked in Madagascar. Christophe stayed in Ambiraika for another year afterward before taking another assignment in the south of Madagascar, where he now works for an international NGO and lives with his new Malagasy wife.

"Islands" Within the Great Red Island: Development Culture and Social Relations

The social and work lives of development practitioners reveal critical dimensions about development in practice. They also provide insights about the way decisions made in social lives shape the way development is deployed. Such analysis also helps us to explore elements of culture, work, status, identity, hypermobility, and social lives, highlighting and contextualizing development encounters and disconnects that occur within the development interventions described here and elsewhere.

As argued at the beginning of this chapter, development practitioners are part of a particular culture that is free-floating, transportable, mobile, and transient across contexts. Their hypermobility is shaped by the bureaucratic imperatives of their development organizations and donors, including frequent moves across countries, sectors, and hierarchies as practitioners move up the professional ladder from rites-of-passage "hardship" postings in rural areas. Many practitioners followed this trend within this study, including Christophe, who began as a winemaker in France and, without any previous development training, attempted to work with farmers in sectors such as rice cultivation, beekeeping, aquaculture, and so on in the Central Highlands of Madagascar. He later moved on to working on issues of food security in the southern region of Madagascar, changing once again his sectoral and geographic focus, as well as his social status.

The social and professional status and identity of development practitioners are dynamic. Sometimes, development practitioners move as "bachelors," while at other times they move with their spouses, families, or partners—and sometimes these spouses and partners also change from posting to posting. Over time, I have followed the life trajectories of several practitioners from this study (which began in 2001), noting their many moves and changes in status from one part of the globe to another. In the development intervention described earlier, Lilianne returned to France where she is now dating another ex-Madagascar volunteer, and Christophe remained in Ambiraika for another year before moving to another region in the south of Madagascar with a new Malagasy wife. Both are early in their career trajectories, and their status may change again. Development practitioners at the beginning of their careers are less able to negotiate more lucrative postings. Similar to Christophe and Lilianne, they often end up in remote areas under hardship postings until they can acquire the expertise necessary to develop their careers further as their family and professional needs become more demanding and, therefore, negotiate for postings in urban spaces.

It is worth considering the dynamics of this free-floating culture and its implications on the social and emotional lives of development practitioners. Hypermobility, short-termism, and contractualism are driven by development bureaucracies that define themselves around time-bounded short-term projects and programs (Verma 2009, unpublished). The development apparatus, premised on development projects, programs, and policies, changes on a regular basis to accord with the two- to five-year funding cycles that themselves vary by the organization, agency, or donor providing aid. Another factor limiting the time spent in any given country is that many development organizations view in-depth knowledge, intimacy, and established relationships in any given context as countering the delivery of development projects and programs. This is based on the logic that practitioners may lose their objectivity and become biased as a result of long-term exposure to different cultures, societies, and contexts.[7] It normally takes at least two years, however, for any practitioner to begin to understand the complexity of issues in any given context. In this vein, Christophe reflected, "It is now after the end of two years that I understand really the problems here. Maybe in the third year, maybe I'll understand even better . . . it's at the end of two years that I know more than all the months I've passed here already." Given that most projects and contracts are normally two to three years long, it not surprising to see the various disconnects arising in the practice and deployment of development.

This raises some interesting issues about the unique social worlds of development practitioners. Similar to their colonial counterparts, many development practitioners create "islands" or "bubbles" as they seek to carry out their mandates within shifting contexts while recreating social worlds that are similar from one context to the next. These are characterized by particular bounded social spaces, networks, events, and rites of passage, which are interrelated to working lives in the development industry. In countries such as Madagascar, this means islands are created on the island, within which intense networks are formed, reproducing nostalgic notions of "home" that are influenced by colonial ways of life. For many development practitioners in this study, the most valuable social relations tended to be with other development practitioners, including intimate partners, friends, colleagues, and casual sexual liaisons. For instance, as described earlier, Lilianne and Christophe created islands in Ambiraika. Often, on weekends and holidays, they hosted at their Melrose Place compound other volunteers or visiting French friends, organizing parties, sleepovers, dinners, and local excursions. The fact that they had a house in a safe compound where they could comfortably provide French-style cuisine, use of Western amenities and technologies, and hospitality also attracted many of their friends from France, who might have otherwise thought twice about spending time in the "bush." Intense social relations with other expats helped to counter feelings of vulnerability and alienation but also reinforced social barriers of misunderstanding with Betsileo farmers, as discussed later.

Long-term relationships with spouses and partners can be a stabilizing force for expat development practitioners within a context where they encounter feelings of vulnerability and alienation in foreign contexts. Lilianne, for example, reflected on the culture shock Christophe and she experienced living in an alien context and the way their relationship mitigated feelings of dislocation: "Whatever you experience, whatever you are shocked by, whatever you are feeling, it is really hard to explain it by letter or by telephone [to friends and family in France]. To be able to share that, it's really enormous. He's a person that I can always talk to about this. . . . It is really a strong experience that we share." As in the case of Christophe and Lilianne, the intensity of working and living together in a fishbowl setting can also become overwhelming and erode long-term relationships to a point that it breaks them apart.

Similar to colonial hardship postings, posts in rural areas are often assigned to development practitioners who are early in their career trajectories and/or life cycle positioning. At the bottom rung of the development ladder, they are normally young expatriates and volunteers, practitioners who are trying to break into the development industry through "rites of passage" jobs. Working in the bush is seen as too isolating, too local, and too small scale. As young and inexperienced development practitioners pay their dues, gain professional experience and knowledge, increase their social status, and form their own families, other needs prevail, such as access to formal education and medical care for their children and the need for greater remuneration, access to development resources, and professional status. Hence, "over time, and over the course of the career of a development practitioner, there is a discernable shift from rural postings to urban-based jobs closer to centers of power and influence from where development is deployed, and where access to social services, amenities and networks are greater. Perhaps more importantly, this shift reflects both work as well as social needs" (Verma 2009, 53).

As Hindman (2002, this volume) also noted in Nepal, some norms of behavior of development in Madagascar highly resemble colonial practices. The colonial community considered itself a community in "exile" (albeit sometimes a transient one) and created its own social world in the image of home. In the contemporary context, as Lilianne and Christophe illustrate, this requires particular amenities, furnishings, and technologies. Although less available in rural contexts, services and social spaces, such as international schools, hospitals, recreational clubs, emergency evacuation assistance, diplomatic services and certain hotels, restaurants, and social clubs dating back to the colonial period, continue to attract expatriate and elite clients as continuing symbols of modernity. Hence, exclusive social spaces and networks forged during colonial imposition continue to provide "retreats" and "escape mechanisms" for development practitioners seeking to normalize their transient, disruptive, and hypermobile lifestyles with the reproduction of more familiar spaces and norms of behavior. Some remnants of this continue to exist in small rural towns such as Ambiraika where fewer than a dozen expat development practitioners live and work but continue to frequent spaces such as the town hall, local restaurants, local tourist attractions, and an old colonial hotel that was a popular tourist destination for French women and men during the colonial period. Work life continues to be intimately connected to social life, as development practitioners socialize with other development practitioners and expatriates after hours and on weekends. Urban cities are especially attractive in terms of providing space and opportunities for such socializing. Not so coincidentally, it is also where the central locations of power and the development apparatus are located. Frequent visits to or living in urban spaces provide social and career advantages for development practitioners but also can exacerbate the strains and difficulties of maintaining interpersonal relationships in foreign settings.

Disconnects in Aidland

While social spaces, networks, and urban biases in development highlight the tenacious continuities of colonial pasts into present-day contexts, they simultaneously and inadvertently create disconnects in contemporary times in other ways. Here, disconnects refer to gaps and lack of meaningful interface, interaction, communication, understanding, connection, and congruent meaning between domains of people, individuals, or what Knorr-Cetina (1981) defined as epistemic cultures (Verma 2009, unpublished).[8] Disconnects are defined as distantiations, discontinuities, disjunctures, and dislocations (Verma 2009, unpublished) that occur in development contexts around the world and contribute to the persistent failures of development projects and programs to meet their intended goals and outcomes. Hence, what is intended ends up looking very different than what actually happens.

The creation of islands means that development practitioners are distantiated by several degrees of separation from the people they are meant to develop. Urban bias within development work and social lives add fuel to the separation. Rural field sites are vast geographic distances from the central locations of development; in this study, distances ranged from 60 to 70 kilometers between village locations to the provincial capital and approximately 450 kilometers between village locations to the capital of the country. The distances are not only geographic, however, but also social and cultural. Social choices are biased toward the reproduction of Western lifestyles, and this is as true in urban spaces as it is in rural ones such as Ambiraika. Development practitioners in rural areas may attempt to bridge cultural differences in their work relations to varying degrees, while in their personal lives, they tend to buffer, isolate, and cocoon themselves from the social and cultural worlds of rural women and men. To cope with feelings of isolation, practitioners mostly adhere to Western and European modes of household furnishing, utensils, appliances, dress, habit, food, social relations, and, in particular, cooking methods. They also engage and seek social relations with other development practitioners, and this helps to counter feelings of vulnerability. Visits to, from, and between development practitioners as well as the maintenance of long-distance relations with home and urban centers are made possible by technological resources such as computers, the Internet, mobile phones, and telephone lines that are accessible by expatriates even in rural areas. Through these resources they can access news from home and stay connected with family and friends. These same social and technological resources, however, help to create islands between them and rural farmers—islands that mitigate feelings of vulnerability and isolation for development practitioners but within which practitioners such as Christophe and Lilianne find themselves paradoxically marooned and dealing with insular social and working lives.

This culture of development—including social norms of behavior, household practices, and gender relations imported from France, which fortify these islands—eventually collides with Bestileo norms, social and gender relations, and environments, creating fissures and disconnects. For instance, norms of behavior, gender relations, and household practices, including French cooking methods, are both part of their everyday social lives and deployed as development interventions, without consideration to the Betsileo context and existing practices and preferences. These skills are prescribed to combat poverty and high-risk behaviors of a group of women that development practitioners have problematically designated as "prostitutes" (Verma unpublished). Most interestingly, for a project that is aimed at women, context-specific gender analysis, issues, and relations are not reflected on or analyzed in any depth. Many of these issues are also exacerbated by, are related to, and influence the bureaucratic imperatives, professionalism, and apparatus of development (Verma unpublished).

Disjunctures in the way practitioners socialize often have little to do with the Malagasy women and men they are there to develop, except in cases where they become sexual objects, conjugal partners, or friends. The islands or fishbowls in which development practitioners live can be viewed from the outside, and they are also places from which to view the world (Verma 2009, unpublished). They are places where one can remain hidden, protected, and sheltered but also sites that create barriers that inhibit other encounters from taking place (Verma 2009, unpublished). In describing NGO field workers in Nepal, Shrestha (2006, 208) suggested that they "did not seek to 'blur boundaries' between themselves and the people among whom they worked: they did not adapt local dress, eating habits, dwelling form, or local titles . . . benefactors were unlikely to ever return to project areas once the project was over. Rather, field workers sought to transcend the difference that they, and management, through the spatial and social organization of the NGO, had worked to create through a series of strategies aimed at 'bracketing' differences." Hence, development practitioners did not "so much seek to translate incommensurable worlds as prevent these worlds from 'mixing' . . . they did not seek to bridge or broker these disjunctures, as suggested by notions of bridging (Arce and Long, 1992), or 'translation' . . . rather, NGO workers sought to maintain and reproduce these disjunctures" (Shrestha 2006, 213).

For development practitioners living and working in rural areas, an important coping strategy is, as Shrestha reflected, "not just the translation of separate worlds, but also, to borrow from Latour (1996), the work of 'purification': keeping distinct the world of beneficiaries, the 'particularistic', 'tradition bound', 'non-modern', and the world of benefactors, 'the progressive', 'universalistic' and 'modern'" (2006, 213). Most often, the tendency to cope with the disconnects through the creation of separate and disjunctured and discontinuous worlds overrides altruistic intentions to bridge differences in culture (Verma 2009, unpublished).

Conclusions

The idea of "tribes" from Latour's work has resonated deeply in the study that informs this chapter. It involves viewing development practitioners and scientists as a tribe of people with their own activities, processes of production, sociopolitical relations (Latour and Woolgar 1979), norms, hierarchies, rites of passage, and gender relations—in effect, their own culture. The notion of viewing development practitioners as a tribe is provocative. I engage it in a problematized way in this chapter, engaging in it as a metaphor only and in quotation marks. It allows a way to bring culture and social relations—the stuff of anthropology—back into the field of analysis. My research findings show that in reality, sociocultural relations cannot be viewed in isolation and are inseparable from the deployment of development.

The deployment of development cannot be disassociated from different domains of knowledge, cultural differences, divergent understandings, and

asymmetric power relations. Given that development practitioners are privileged in terms of power, their own constructions of knowledge and meanings
within their own social and work lives overshadow rural Malagasy women's
and men's meanings, understanding, and needs. The latter tend to get marginalized and ignored, despite the best intentions of development experts, so
that projects remain "from the outside" and disconnected from the realities on
the ground. This is as true for development practitioners living in urban areas
as it is for those living in rural ones. The construction of social islands creates
distantiations, disjunctures, and discontinuities that work against congruent
interfaces. Hence, intended objectives rarely match outcomes, and development projects continue to fail on a regular basis. These disconnects are not
just about development projects, programs, and organizations, however; they
are also generated from the vast differences in the social lives of development
practitioners from those people they are meant to develop.

It is also worth considering the side effects and the blast radius of impact
generated because of the hypermobile, transient, and dislocated lifestyles that
characterize the lives of development practitioners in Aidland. A highly mobile way of life creates many vulnerabilities for development practitioners as
they encounter feelings of isolation, alienation, and nonbelonging, as Shrestha
(2006) and Stirrat (2008) also noted in other contexts. The loneliness, instabil-
ity, and isolation of moving from country to country while living in fishbowls
or islands gives rise to high rates of depression, divorce, stress disorders, break-
downs, other psychological problems, and so on (Foyle 2006). For this reason, coping strategies that compensate for such disruptions, such as forming
intense and intimate social networks and creating a home, however transient,
with material comforts and memorabilia symbolic of development practitioners' former lives, become a matter of emotional survival. Most development
practitioners prefer to live in urban spaces, where they feel less desperate, alien-
ated, and isolated from comforts and amenities they are accustomed to. This
means that there is a high degree of distantiated urban bias in social decisions
regarding where development practitioners choose to work and live and therefore where they deploy development from (Foyle 2006). It is also worth considering that these are perhaps not just choices but part of an earlier pattern
of colonial and development interventions that structured development (Foyle
2006). As Hindman suggested in analyzing American development in Nepal
in the 1950s, many of the institutions, contract details, housing, amenities,
and social relationships and tensions were all part of the establishment of development presence and procedures influencing the structure of development
work, if not the work itself, and are still in place today (2002, 126, and this

volume). They generate deep urban biases and sometimes produce very little interest on the part of development practitioners in "venturing out into the villages" (2002, 123).

When development practitioners do venture into villages, they do so in ways that create barriers and islands between themselves and those they are meant to develop. These barriers are fostered as much by (mis)assumptions about work and career paths as by the social coping strategies practitioners create, both of which nonetheless shape the deployment of development. Doing "development" and "gender" is seen as not requiring any previous skills, experience, or training, facilitating the deployment of young volunteers who are trained to become experts in a type of laboratory setting where farmers are involuntarily "experiments" and "steep learning curves" (Verma 2009, unpublished). Another insight is found in the assumptions in the practice of development about social and gender dynamics that allow an agronomist to blindly undertake "women's projects" merely because she is a woman, which simultaneously neglect Betsileo meanings of rice and understandings of rice cultivation as outside the domain of women. Thus it continues to be assumed that doing gender in development does not require any particular analytical skills, knowledge, or expertise. Contrarily, gender analysis can be just as complex as the most scientific problem, if not more so. Instead, it is often considered merely an add-on, a box to check off, a simple problem that can be easily solved through the imposition of technical solutions and modern methods (Verma 2001, 249–50). Here, analysis is often conflated with including a woman, and while being gender aware may be important for political action and mobilization of resources, it is not enough to meaningfully carry out women's projects or to understand the lived realities of women, such as their cooking methods, income-generating activities, and social and sexual practices (see Verma 2009, unpublished).

These dynamics shed light on our understandings of the work and social worlds of development practitioners and add nuances to our understanding of the disconnects between development projects and their unintended consequences and failed outcomes. When anthropologists attempt to "study up" within the context of development projects, policies, and organizations, however, as Mosse (2005, 2006) and Hilhorst (2003) have done, many issues and unintended controversies arise. Most of these issues have to do with differential relations of power, whereby ethnographic findings are contested by development practitioners and sometimes lead to a rupture in relations and broken "rules of fair play" with people they engage in research with (Mosse 2005, xi; cf. Sridhar 2005). In the case of Mosse (2005, 2006), development practitioners strongly disagreed with his representations, and Hilhorst (2003) similarly experienced critiques of her ethnography by the NGO staff she was writing about. Although these critiques raise conceptual questions about power relations and critical methodological concerns about anthropologists engaging in ethnographic studies of development organizations and projects, they also challenge the rigid divide that conventionally exists between what is considered work and social in the everyday lives of development practitioners. What this new type of ethnography of development practitioners and practice demonstrates is that rather than a rigid divide, the reality is more fluid whereby social and cultural lives shape the way action and decisions are made in work spheres. They are inextricably intertwined domains that play powerfully together in determining the way development is deployed and, most important, the way it regularly fails to achieve its intended goals.

Acknowledgments

This chapter is based on a larger study as part of doctoral research in anthropology (Verma 2009) at the School of Oriental and African Studies (SOAS) and was made possible by the UK Overseas Research Scholarship (ORS), the SOAS Research Student Fellowship, the University of London Central Research Fund Award, the ASA/Radcliffe Brown Trust Award, and the Canadian Centennial Women's Scholarship.

Notes

1. During the fieldwork for this study, I encountered approximately 36 different nationalities of development practitioners, ranging from countries as diverse as Haiti and Australia.

2. For further discussion about the gaps and fissures in the anthropology of development, see Verma (2009, unpublished).

3. This chapter is based on fieldwork and multisited ethnography in the Central Highlands of Madagascar from 2001 to 2003.

4. The names used for Lilianne and other development practitioners described in this chapter are pseudonyms to help ensure anonymity and confidentiality.

5. The name used for the town of Ambiraika is a pseudonym to help ensure anonymity and confidentiality of the research participants involved.

6. Interestingly, in other parts of Sub-Saharan Africa, cassava and maize are considered staple crops and the preferred choice for daily meals and are also imbedded in cultural norms and preferences.

7. Interestingly, this is diametrically opposed to the logic of anthropological and social scientific inquiry, which demands rigor, depth, and presence in one context.

8. Epistemic cultures are composed of persons who share roughly the same sources and modes of knowledge (Knorr-Cetina 1981).

References

Arce, A. 1989. The social construction of agrarian development: A case study of producer–bureaucrat relations in an irrigation unit in western Mexico. In *Encounters at the interface: A perspective on social discontinuities in rural development*, ed. N. Long, 11–51. Wageningen, the Netherlands: The Agricultural University.

Arce, A., and N. Long. 1992. The dynamics of knowledge: Interfaces between bureaucrats and peasants. In *Battlefields of knowledge: The interlocking theory and practice in social research and development*, ed. N. Long and A. Long, 211–46. London and New York: Routledge.

Carney, Judith, and Michael Watts. 1990. Manufacturing dissent: Work, gender and the politics of meaning in a peasant society. *Africa* 60 (2): 207–41.

de Vries, Pieter. 1997. *Unruly clients in the Atlantic zone of Costa Rica: A study of how bureaucrats try and fail to transform gatekeepers, communists and preachers into ideal beneficiaries*. Amsterdam: Centre for Latin American Research and Documentation.

Fairhead, James, and Melissa Leach. 1996. *Misreading the African landscape*. Cambridge: Cambridge University Press.

Fechter, Anne-Meike. 2007. From "incorporated wives" to "expat girls": A new generation of expatriate women? In *Gender and family among transnational professionals*, ed. A. Coles and A.M. Fechter, 193–210. London and New York: Routledge.

Ferguson, James. 1994. *The anti-politics machine: "Development," depoliticization, and bureaucratic power in Lesotho*. Minneapolis: University of Minnesota Press.

Foucault, Michel. 1980. *Power/knowledge: Selected interviews and other writings 1972–1977*. Brighton, UK: Harvester Press.

Foyle, Marjory. 2006. Preventing expatriate depression. Paper presented at Development People: Professional Identities and Social Lives, Fourth Workshop on Globally Mobile Professionals, International Gender Studies Centre, University of Oxford, Oxford, UK.

Goetz, Anne Marie. 2001. *Women development workers: Implementing rural credit programmes in Bangladesh*. London: Sage.

Grammig, Thomas. 2002. *Technological knowledge and development: Observing aid projects and processes*. Routledge Studies in Development and Society. New York and London: Routledge.

Haraway, Donna. 1988. Situated knowledges: The science question in feminism and the privilege of partial perspective. *Feminist Studies* 14 (4): 575–99.

———. 1991. *Simians, cyborgs and women: The reinvention of nature*. New York and London: Routledge.

Hilhorst, Dorothea. 2003. *The real world of NGOs: Discourses, diversity and development*. London and New York: Zed Books.

Hindman, Heather. 2002. The everyday life of American development in Nepal. *Studies in Nepali History and Society* 7 (1): 99–136.

Keeley, James, and Ian Scoones. 1999. *Understanding environmental policy processes: A review*. Working Paper 89. Brighton, UK: Institute of Development Studies.

Knorr-Cetina, Karin. 1981. *The manufacture of knowledge: An essay on the constructivist and contextual nature of science*. Oxford: Pergamon Press.

———. 1999. *Epistemic cultures: How the sciences make knowledge*. Cambridge: Harvard University Press.

Latour, Bruno. 1987. *Science in action: How to follow scientists and engineers through society*. Milton Keynes, UK: Open University Press.

————. 1993. *We have never been modern*. Hemel Hempstead: Harvester.

————. 1996. *Aramis or the love of technology*. Cambridge and London: Harvard University Press.

Latour, Bruno, and Steve Woolgar. 1979. *Laboratory life: The social construction of scientific facts*. Princeton, NJ: Princeton University Press.

Long, Norman. 2001. *Development sociology: Actor perspectives*. London and New York: Routledge.

Long, Norman, and Ann Long, eds. 1992. *Battlefields of knowledge: The interlocking theory and practice in social research and development*. London and New York: Routledge.

Mackenzie, Fiona. 1995. "A farm is like a child who cannot be left unguarded": Gender, land and labour in Central Province, Kenya. *IDS Bulletin* 26 (1): 17–23.

Martin, Emily. 1994. *Flexible bodies: Tracing immunity in American culture from the days of polio to the age of AIDS*. Boston: Beacon.

————. 1997. Anthropology and the cultural study of science: From citadels to string figures. In *Anthropological locations: Boundaries and grounds for a field science*, ed. A. Gupta and J. Ferguson, 131–46. Los Angeles and Berkeley: University of California Press.

McKinnon, Katharine. 2007. Postdevelopment, professionalism, and the politics of participation. *Annals of the Association of American Geographers* 97 (4): 772–85.

Moore, D. 1993. Contesting terrain in Zimbabwe's eastern highlands: Political ecology, ethnography and peasant resource struggles. *Economic Geography* 69:380–401.

Mosse, David. 2005. *Cultivating development: An ethnography of aid policy and practice*. London and Ann Arbor: Pluto Press.

————. 2006. Anti-social anthropology? Objectivity, objection, and the ethnography of public policy and professional communities. *Journal of the Royal Anthropological Institute* 12:935–56.

Pottier, Johan. 2003. Negotiating local knowledge: An introduction. In *Negotiating local knowledge: Power and identity in development*, ed. J. Pottier, A. Bicker, and P. Sillitoe, 1–29. London: Pluto Press.

Scott, James. 1990. *Domination and the arts of resistance: Hidden transcripts*. New Haven and London: Yale University Press.

Shrestha, Celayne. 2006. They can't mix like we can: Bracketing differences and the professionalization of NGOs in Nepal. In *Development brokers and translators: The ethnography of aid and agencies*, ed. D. Mosse and D. Lewis, 195–216. Bloomfield, CT: Kumarian Press.

Shrum, Wesley. 1988. Review essay: The labyrinth of science. *American Journal of Sociology* 94 (2): 396–403.

Sridhar, Devi. 2005. Ethics and development: Some concerns with David Mosse's "Cultivating Development." *Anthropology Today* 21 (6): 17–19.

Stirrat, R.L. 2008. Mercenaries, missionaries and misfits: Representations of development personnel. *Critique of Anthropology* 28 (4): 406–25.

USAID. 2000. *Madagascar overview*. http://www.usaid.gov.

Verma, Ritu. 2001. *Gender, land and livelihoods in East Africa: Through farmers' eyes*. Ottawa, Canada: IDRC.

————. 2006a. Life in a "fishbowl": At work and at play in the development machine. Paper presented at Development People: Professional Identities and Social Lives, Fourth Workshop on Globally Mobile Professionals, International Gender Studies Centre, University of Oxford.

———. 2006b. Development disjuncture: The power of multi-sited ethnography in exploring divergent relations of power, culture and environmental cosmologies in the Central Highlands of Madagascar. Paper presented at the ASA Panel on Methodological Approaches to Cosmopolitanism, ASA annual meeting, Keele.

———. 2007. At work and at play in the "fishbowl": Gender relations and social reproduction among development expatriates in Madagascar. In *Gender and family among transnational professionals*, ed. A. Coles and A.M. Fechter, 171–91. London and New York: Routledge.

———. 2009. Culture, power and disconnect in the Central Highlands of Madagascar. PhD diss., School of Oriental and African Studies, London.

———. 2010. A view from inside the development machine: Culture, power and development disconnect in Madagascar. Paper presented at CASID, Panel on Putting Culture in Development, Montreal, Canada.

———. Unpublished. Inside the development machine: Culture, power and disconnect in the Central Highlands of Madagascar.

5

Orienting Guesthood in the Mennonite Central Committee, Indonesia

Philip Fountain

Drinking Tea With the Locals

While researching the Mennonite Central Committee (MCC), a middle-sized transnational NGO, I frequently came across a recurring image that was invoked to express the normative ideal of expatriate field service with the organization. This ideal was expressed to me in a variety of ways but generally included the following: an MCCer sitting down in a mud hut in Africa drinking tea with the locals. This image often implicitly, and sometimes quite explicitly, served as an ideological backdrop for MCC's work in Indonesia; it is a prominent and influential organizational myth. Three issues arise from this image that constitute key themes of this chapter.

First, drinking tea, or local equivalent, highlights the ideal of a noncoercive and profoundly relational approach to international service with MCC. Drinking tea is less about doing something *for* those living in mud huts, and thereby exercising one's power on or over them, than about engaging *with* them and receiving from them. While assistance in its various forms is never entirely discarded, the notion of drinking tea does dislodge such concrete acts of "aid" from the position as the sole or even ultimate goal. In this chapter I argue that concerted attempts are made within MCC to encourage self-reflexivity and to displace the privileged positions of its North American service workers. This displacing was considered the necessary precondition for being able and willing to "drink tea."

The second and third points form an apparent paradox that lies at the heart of my argument. On the one hand "drinking tea" is a logic of association, suggestive of warm relationships involving reciprocity and friendship. It also expresses an ideal of expatriate MCCers living with and alongside the locals, speaking the vernacular, and taking time to bond with them. However, and this is the third point, the very concept of "the locals" relies on a logic of disassociation. It situates the expatriate MCCers as those who are serving not-in-their-own-place; as foreigners they are located away from home. Expatriate MCCers carry out their work within the politics of these competing logics.

MCC is a North American NGO that works in over 50 countries around the world. A substantial literature on MCC exists (see Graber Miller 1996; Kreider and Goossen 1988; Kreider and Mathies 1996; Marr 2003; Yoder, Redekop, and Jantzi 2004; Unruh 1952), though it has received only intermittent attention outside of Mennonite contexts (a recent exception is Dicklitch and Rice 2004). The argument made here is based on ethnographic research on MCC conducted in Indonesia and also more briefly the United States and Canada.[1] This multisited fieldwork enabled the exploration of the transnational connectivities (Tsing 2005) that enmesh the organization. Such an approach is valuable for organizations that, by their very nature, span diverse spatial and cultural contexts. Through the fieldwork I sought to respond to Mosse's challenge to ask not so much whether "but rather *how* development works" (2005, 2, emphasis in original). A significant part of how MCC works is informed by religiosity. MCC in Indonesia is properly understood as a cultural outlier of a specific North American ethno-religious peoplehood. This religious tradition deeply informs how MCC imagines and practices its work. This research therefore builds on emerging interest in the intersections of religion and development (see Bornstein 2003; Clarke and Jennings 2008; Quarles van Ufford and Schoffeleers 1988; and Ter Haar and Ellis 2006). I argue that the normative myth of drinking tea with the locals is part of a religiously inflected ideology of guesthood that, though not uncontested (cf. Hilhorst 2003, 23–24), provides a distinctive imagining for MCCers in their work in Indonesia.

It is useful to see guesthood as a parallel term to a cluster of other "buzz-words" (Cornwall and Brock 2005) currently popular in development discourse. Among the most prominent terms in this new vocabulary are "empowerment" (Kilby 2006), "participation" (Cooke and Kothari 2001), and "partnership" (Lewis 1998; Morse and McNamara 2006). These terms are aimed at various targets, imply different intended effects, and are accompanied by their own technologies of implementation. What they all share with guesthood, however, is their deployment to negate or counteract potential or actual accusations of the coercive use of power in international development. The context in which development organizations now operate is increasingly beset by pervasive critiques from within academia and beyond that question the legitimacy of development interventions and highlight negative effects. The goodness of NGOs (Fisher 1997) cannot simply be taken for granted. While guesthood has a very different history and comes out of a particular identity and theology (and is on the margins of mainstream development discourse), it is also an organizational-level response to this same context of pervasive critique. The articulation of guesthood serves as both justification of and normative ideal for MCC's work.

Notions of "guest" and its correlate "host" have had little resonance in the literature on the anthropology of development. This is in direct contrast to anthropological studies of tourism where they have long been key words used by ethnographers (cf. Smith 1989). McNaughton (2006) critiqued, however, the limitations of a host–guest framework on the grounds that the implied dichotomy predetermines the ways in which researchers approach the study of tourism relationships. Likewise, I argue that blanket application of a host–guest paradigm (implying a rigid dichotomous understanding of actor involvement) is unhelpful to the study of development processes. When those within development organizations or on the "receiving" end of development programs use such language, however, anthropologists need to pay attention to the situated "cultural logic" (Erb 2000) or "moral framework" (Selwyn 2000) at work. MCC's guesthood ideology is such a framework that locates expatriate MCCers as "guests" in relationship to both "home" and "hosts" in particular ways.[2]

In this chapter I first explore the ways guesthood is articulated and disciplined within expatriate workers through specific orientation events. I highlight here the paradox of simultaneous and competing logics of association and disassociation that ensue from attempts to behave as guests. This paradox runs parallel to a case analyzed by Bornstein (2001, 595) in which NGO projects "simultaneously transcend difference and exacerbate it." I then present two biographical narratives to examine the ways in which the logics of (dis)association work out in the everyday lives of MCCers.

Displacing Privilege: Orientation in Akron, Pennsylvania

The starting point for my analysis is to examine specific orientation events in MCC. Organizational orientations are rich spaces for analysis. They are events in which organizational seniors represent the goals and mission of their organization to newcomers. Communication is carefully framed and crafted though sometimes also highly contested. Such events can be seen too as an initiation ritual or rite of passage (Turner 1979). They are markers of points of entry or changes in role or responsibility. Because orientation rituals are primarily designed for internal communication, they represent a potentially very different mode of discourse about an organization from those communications produced for public consumption.

The first orientation I analyze took place in MCC's binational headquarters in tiny Akron, Pennsylvania. The location of MCC in this rural town seems at first quite peculiar. Most major international NGOs situate their head offices for accessibility to major transport nodes and proximity to corridors of power. To understand the location of MCC in Akron, we must ask to whom is it accessible and to which corridors it is proximate? Akron is in the midst of "Pennsylvania Dutch" country, long a heartland of a distinctive North American "ethno-religious tradition" (Bush 1998) or "peoplehood" (Loewen 2008; Nolt 1999; Winland 1993). Urry (2006, 6) described the implications of "peoplehood" in these terms:

> By "peoplehood" I mean the particular Mennonite sense of identity based on their faith and sense of being and belonging. Core features of what it means to be a people of faith are often expressed in their confessions of faith and include adult baptism, nonresistance, and remaining separated from "the world." . . . Belonging is centered on a strong sense of social community founded on the interconnections of people through descent, both from founding ancestors and the historical experiences of the people of faith and often also through the genealogical descent of the community's members. The popular concept of "ethnicity" does not quite capture this sense of being and belonging, which is informed by a culture of faith rather than faith in culture.

During my fieldwork with MCC, I imagined that I was carrying out an organizational ethnography (cf. Bornstein 2003; Crewe and Harrison 1998; Hilhorst 2003; Fox 1998; Mosse 2005). It was disconcerting therefore to be frequently told that I had been misinformed, that MCC was not in fact an organization at all. It was rather a "peoplehood movement" of the North American Mennonite and Brethren in Christ churches. This same sense was articulated on the very first day of the orientation I attended in Akron. In a session providing an overview of MCC, the presenter posed the question, "Who owns

MCC?" The first and primary answer was that in MCC the Mennonite and Brethren in Christ churches in Canada and the United States were known as "the constituency." She went on to say that these churches "created MCC," they "support MCC," and as a result "they own us." MCC literature likewise articulates a sense of MCC being a "part of the Mennonite and Brethren in Christ church family" (Mennonite Central Committee 2007, 26), as "sponsored by" those churches (Mennonite Central Committee 2009, 2), as "representing" them (Zehr 1996, 1), or simply as "a church organization" of the Anabaptist-Mennonite tradition (Mennonite Central Committee n.d.). Despite MCC having worked continuously in Indonesia since 1948, and therefore being among the longest-running international NGOs in the country, it remains organizationally, legally, and, in its workers self-identification, indelibly a part of this North American peoplehood. According to one MCCer, "It's in our DNA to be North American."

The orientation I attended in Akron took place over a two-week period in July 2008. In attendance were international "service workers" about to embark for various parts of the world and also, though only for the first week, new staff starting work in Canada and the United States. The vast majority of the attendees came from North America. International service workers are all volunteers and so for the duration of their service receive no salary and have only their living requirements covered by MCC. Three or more such orientations take place each year, often with between 40 and 60 participants in each.

Prior to discussing various activities that took place in this orientation, I want to note a key absence. There were no workshops or training sessions in community development tools such as participatory rural appraisal, logical framework analysis, or monitoring and evaluation systems. The reason for this is that few MCC service workers use these mainstream development techniques in their work. Assignments that awaited this group of orientees included a diverse range of occupations including hostess of a retreat center, university lecturer, and English-language teacher. These do not fit classic development industry position profiles. While MCC classifies its work under the three general headings of relief, community development, and peace building, each of these terms is subordinate to the broader notion of "service." Service is a key word (Wierzbicka 1997) in North American Mennonite society, being both ubiquitous and prominent in Mennonite publications. It resonates deeply with much Mennonite theology. The lack of learning about mainstream development tools in this orientation results from the limited influence industry norms have over the creation of assignments for MCC workers.

During this orientation a "Theology of Service and Peacemaking" session was led by experienced MCC staff. The session took place on the fourth day. After staff introduced the topic, all the participants were split into groups and asked to go outside onto the grassy lawn to undertake an "unofficial power survey." Questions were called out by the leader, and depending on one's response, participants would step forward, stay still, or step backward, embodying their answer. It was explained that while the survey was not exhaustive, the exercise was designed to address issues of "structural inequality" and "power imbalances" in US and Canadian society. For example, on the topic of gender, men were asked to step forward and women backward to highlight the privileges of being gendered male. Various other categories were raised, including race/ethnicity, formal education, physical ability, sexuality, and country of citizenship. Once the survey was completed, participants were invited to discuss their feelings and whether they would change any of the categories. According to a handout, the purpose of the exercise was to recognize that "power is not distributed equally. When we are aware, we can be accountable and use the power we have responsibly."

This exercise was immediately followed by a parallel activity that highlighted "relational values." This experiment was designed, according to the handout, "to emphasize sensitivity to relationships that are mutual and respectful, and to build global awareness and community." Although this activity was much the same as the previous exercise, this time issues were weighted differently. For example, in the gender category women were asked to step forward and men backward, as this "reflects the reality that women have traditionally nurtured relationships that are more mutual rather than competitive and hierarchical." Additional categories were added, including language skills (more than one language—step forward), car ownership (step back for each vehicle; step forward for using public transport), the ethnic diversity of one's church and/or neighborhood (diverse—step forward; homogenous—step back), and so on. Unsurprisingly, the spread of participants was a near mirror image of the previous exercise.

This activity occupied a couple of hours of orientation time. It was not, however, the only such exercise. In a session provocatively titled "Sex, Lies and the Global Economy," participants were invited by a different facilitator to fill in an "economic privilege grid" to provide an indicator of relative advantage as a result of family history, upbringing, ethnicity, opportunities, and so on. Having filled in some 104 separate questions and allotted ourselves positive or negative scores, we lined up in a row from the highest scorer (most privileged) to the lowest. Again, in an entirely different session on "Anti-Racism Awareness," participants (largely of European descent) watched a video that explored "white privilege" and engaged in discussion of its contents. A handout even addressed "Why Servanthood Is Bad" (McKnight 1989) through deconstructing professionalized provision of services—such as done by most NGOs—to argue instead for greater emphasis on community-based mutual care.

I avoid questions of whether these sessions adequately address the complexities of power to instead explore why such activities were part of the MCC orientation process. Collectively they amounted to a sustained critique of power privilege. The goal was to facilitate self-reflexivity about participants' privileged backgrounds and displace this inherited power. The activities were a communal ritualized corporeal confession designed to inspire a modified conception of the self. They were a sustained negation of potential inclinations toward a messianic complex. That is, the Akron orientation sought a displacement of privilege so as to create space for a noncoercive engagement. The dynamics here rest on the assumption that noncoercion is the first and foremost condition for guesthood. Accordingly, it is necessary that MCC's guest candidates are encouraged to be aware of their privileged backgrounds so that they may assume the desired noncoercive stance. This emphasis on noncoercion shares close connections with the traditional concern of Mennonite theologians to emphasize nonresistance and simplicity as privileged forms of Mennonite engagements with power.

Locating Expatriate Guests: Orientations in Central Java, Indonesia

> As guests in Indonesia, we can't just criticize things here. But I can criticize the [American and Christian] international school that my children attend. I bottle it [my criticisms] up and let it out on the international school.
>
> **—MCC Rep during an orientation session for newly arrived service workers**

In addition to a predeparture orientation expatriate volunteers in MCC Indonesia also participate in an orientation after their arrival in country. This introduces orientees to MCC's work in Indonesia and the Indonesian context. The responsibility for the postarrival orientations remained with the MCC Representatives (MCC Reps), the most senior level of management within each field context. In Indonesia the MCC Reps had always been North American.[3]

MCC's programs in different countries and regions are characterized by considerable heterogeneity. MCC Indonesia, I was frequently told, is quite distinct from MCC's work in other contexts in terms of program implementation as well as in more "cultural" concerns such as leadership structure, group dynamics, and team interactions. One distinction of MCC Indonesia was that most of the international volunteers, up to about 30 at any one time, worked in education. During their stay they were seconded to local schools or universities to work as members of those institutions' staff teams.[4] Although education secondments took place in other MCC programs, the focus this sector received in Indonesia was unusual. Unlike in some other contexts, MCC Indonesia had no operational programs. Instead, in addition to seconding workers, MCC's programmatic activities were run entirely through local Indonesian organizations. These partnerships involved financial transfers and other forms of assistance. MCC Indonesia's idiosyncrasy was apparent too in the way in which orientations were run.

In Indonesia the MCC Reps, an American couple in their 40s who were unusual in the extensive duration of their field service with the organization, had considerable experience in designing and implementing orientations for new expatriate staff. In this section I focus on two orientation sessions. Each took place over two days. The first program was specifically for four participants of MCC's Service and Learning Together (SALT) program, an 11-month exchange for young adult North Americans. The SALT assignment includes three core components: living with an Indonesian host family, participating in a local church, and working in a local organization. SALTers had a weeklong orientation in Akron prior to arriving in Indonesia. The second orientation I discuss was attended by eight recently arrived MCC expatriate service workers who had previously participated in an orientation similar to that described earlier. Those in this particular group were considerably older than the SALTers, and some had previous experience with MCC in other contexts. Both groups had yet to start their assignments; most were tasked with teaching English as a second language in high schools (*Sekolah Menengah Pertama* or *Sekolah Menengah Atas*) or lecturing in various disciplines in Indonesian universities.

When I inquired with the MCC Reps about their approach to orienting new staff, I was given a booklet by Brewster and Brewster (1980) titled *Bonding, and the Missionary Task* published by the Summer Institute of Linguistics (SIL).[5] While this came from a non-MCC source and its recommendations were adopted selectively, it nevertheless communicated certain influential philosophies. It was often given to expatriates before or immediately after their arrival in Indonesia. Critical of the "foray approach" (p. 22), the Brewsters argued that "bonding"—intimate relationships "at a very deep level" (p. 28) between expatriate missionary and locals—as well as a sense of "belonging" to the new culture and people are vital for the missionary task. The booklet focuses on strategies of how this can be achieved, including a strong emphasis on attaining fluency in the local language. Concomitant to this developing bilingualism, the missionary should also develop a new bicultural identity. The text outlines the "imprinting" theory developed by naturalists to explain why immediately after hatching, ducklings, in a heightened state of alertness and ready for relational commitment, would attach themselves to the present scientist instead of the absent mother duck. According to the Brewsters, missionaries going through the process of entering a new culture are similarly ready for imprinting. It is critical, they argued, that during this initial period, missionaries therefore bond with the right people, "the local people" (p. 4). This initial experience will enable the newcomer to learn about insiders' attitudes and society as well as consider "adopting [their lifestyle] for himself [sic] and his own family" (p. 7).

During the orientation for the SALT volunteers, the MCC Reps dismissed the gendered language of the booklet as anachronistic. More significant, they indicated their discomfort with the "missionary" terminology employed. Certainly, while the term "mission" is heavily contested within wider Christian discourse, most MCCers in Indonesia actively distanced themselves from engaging in evangelistic activities. The "bonding" the Brewsters advocate, however, was clearly also the sort of relationship that the MCC Reps hoped expatriate volunteers would assume with Indonesians. This ideal was broadly shared among many expatriate MCCers in Indonesia and is a key component of the "drinking tea with the locals" myth.

The MCC Reps also explained to the SALTers that after their structured language learning had finished and before they were sent to their assignments, the SALTers would receive mobile phones. These were intended primarily for safety purposes and communication with the MCC team rather than to communicate with friends and family back home. The justification for this was that they were encouraged to bond with their local host family, church community, and colleagues and look to them for emotional care rather than rely solely on distant supporters. This point was made forcefully in this orientation because the issue had grown significantly in preceding years. Since mobile phones had become cheaper to use and Internet phone conversations had become possible, communication with people back home had become increasingly frequent. Some SALTers had talked with family almost every day. That some communication would take place was regarded as natural and encouraged by the MCC

Reps. The norm of seeking emotionally fulfilling relationships with Indonesians, however, was promoted as ideal.

While the temptation of reliance on support from home was often present, another tendency was to attempt to operate as an atomized individual. SALTers were also advised that "we come as Westerners to this place wanting to be self-sufficient. But it is good to be vulnerable [with our hosts]." Similarly, certain topics were avoided during orientation, such as contemporary Indonesian politics, so that the SALTers would learn about politics "through Indonesian eyes" rather than from a Western perspective. Through encouragement and advice, as well as through intentional absences, SALTers were counseled to learn primarily from their Indonesian hosts.

The focus on bonding was also expressed in the orientation for service workers framed through the concept of "relationships." About halfway through this orientation session, an MCC Rep asked whether anyone could remember the content of the discussion on MCC's values that had taken place during their Akron orientation. No one could. The MCC Rep then reminded the group of the priority given in MCC to the value of relationships. This value, it was explained, provided the justification for MCC in bringing North American volunteers to Indonesia. It wasn't that Indonesia lacked skills (and was therefore somehow deficient) or that MCC had solutions to Indonesian problems (and so brought in foreign "experts") but rather to facilitate "exchange" and for "building relationships." Furthermore, it was important for MCC's partners in Indonesia that MCC wasn't simply an organization "across the ocean, writing letters" but rather that "we are here as the face of MCC."

Ideologically, the Brewsters' philosophy of entering a new culture clearly provided justification for two specific practices that were applied in orienting new MCCers. The first was the practice of staying with an Indonesian host family in the first week in Indonesia. This immersion experience in a local home was held out as an ideal for service workers. Much effort was made to ensure that these homestay experiences were neither too comfortable nor too awkward for new arrivals. Often these initial experiences were looked back on with considerable pleasure or at least with good humor. The opposite response, however, was also possible. One couple who had a weeklong homestay in Eastern Indonesia came back to Central Java for language study exhausted from the rustic conditions. To make matters worse, one had contracted malaria during the homestay, which further dampened their enthusiasm for the experience.

The second orientation practice that connected closely with the Brewsters' booklet was the emphasis on language learning. During my fieldwork in Indonesia, all new MCCers studied at the same small language school in Central Java run by a young Javanese man and his staff. For service workers on three-year terms in Indonesia, at least three months were spent in full-time language study. Because of the shorter stay, SALT participants were allocated six weeks. Most had no Indonesian language skills before arriving in Indonesia, and therefore gaining full proficiency in that time was difficult. Nevertheless, it gave sufficient foundation for many MCCers to eventually become fluent in Indonesian. In the SALT orientation, an MCC Rep justified the language-learning process by pointing out that "your ability to have relationships in Indonesia is based on language."

Fechter (2007) argued in her recent book *Transnational Lives*, an analysis of corporate expatriates in Jakarta, that expatriates structure their interactions with Indonesians through powerful and pervasive boundary constructions. With myriad separations, expatriates distance themselves from Indonesians. What is remarkable about MCC's ideology of guesthood analyzed in these orientations is how starkly this contrasts with Fechter's observation of sharp differentiation; the norms and intentions of MCC are profoundly different from those of "normal" expatriates in Indonesia. MCC discourse consistently encouraged "bonding," immersion experiences, and language learning among expatriate staff to bridge cultural divides. MCC discourse also sought to dissuade them from senses of superiority. Unsurprisingly, therefore, myths of the "lazy native" or the "expat expert" (pp. 154–55), which Fechter saw as pervasive among corporate expatriates, were completely absent among MCCers. A sense of being a "victim" (p. 3) was also rare. Revealingly too, the sorts of metaphors that Fechter found in frequent use in Jakarta—the expatriate "bubble," "frontier," "bunker," "ghetto," "hot house," and "Disneyland" (pp. 150–54)— were never expressed in my discussions and interviews with expatriate MCCers. They were, rather, encouraged to live up to the ideal of "drinking tea with the locals," a metaphor with profoundly different implications.

The quote at the start of this section, however, provides hints that a more complex dynamic is at work. The expatriate MCCers express their withdrawal from criticizing Indonesian actors as a consequence of being "guests." Here there is intentional distancing from Indonesian contexts; a kind of separation *is* drawn. It is not the case that opinions are unformed but that they are withheld, "bottled up." According to the cultural logic at work here, guests should not criticize. They should behave in a manner appropriate for those who are just visiting. This withholding directly contrasts the relationship with the American international school their children attended. As a result of assuming a nonguest identity, of being "at home," the MCCer engages in a proactive politics of influence. That is, guesthood also operates as a disassociative impulse. By refraining from criticism, a medium that articulates belonging, the ontology of foreignness is reinforced.

Accordingly, many MCCers frequently commented on perceived North American Mennonite "failings," noted disappointments and occasionally considerable anger with MCC as an institution, and engaged with their home country's national politics. Simultaneously, they refrained from critiquing perceived failings in Indonesia and sought to avoid involvement in Indonesian political processes. This bifurcated politics is based on MCCers assuming specific relationships with others in negotiating a dichotomized world of home–away, insider–outsider, and host–guest. While the stated goal was to bridge these divides through bonding, the attempt to bridge the gaps in a noncoercive manner also reinscribes those very distinctions. So on the one hand, guesthood facilitates a powerful logic of association with Indonesia and Indonesians with the normative myth of "*drinking tea* with the locals" facilitating an intimate sense of bonding as the organizational ideal. On the other hand, guesthood facilitates a sense of differentiation with "*the locals*" in the tea-drinking myth situated as other. A sense of demarcation therefore remains, though it is complex in its ambiguity. Guesthood is simultaneously associative and disassociative.

Living Guesthood: (Dis)Association in Practice

I now explore the biographical narratives of two MCCers: a North American Mennonite who volunteered in Indonesia as a service worker and a Javanese member of MCC's staff who worked in the province of Aceh.[6] The orientation sessions discussed previously were attended almost exclusively by expatriate MCCers. Of course, few international NGOs rely only on expatriate workers; this is especially so in MCC, with its three-year term operating as normal for service workers. MCC's Indonesian staff have long played a vital role, readily acknowledged by expatriate colleagues, in enabling MCC to conduct its work.

In presenting these two biographies, I illustrate the effects that MCC's ideology of guesthood has in everyday lived experience. While guesthood is grounded in and propelled by an attempt to displace expatriate MCCers' privilege, it is also the source of a very different sort of displacing. If MCC is a North American Mennonite peoplehood movement, what are the implications of this for local staff? I argue that the powerful dynamics of guesthood reinscribe the distinctions that bonding sought to bridge by excluding Indonesian staff from full belonging in MCC. The irony is that this might be an unintended consequence of a noncoercive approach to development. Through comparison between these two biographies, I seek to further illuminate the effects and paradoxes of guesthood.

Frank Kauffman, in his 20s, was born in Africa while his American parents served with a Mennonite mission agency. His family name is a well-known Swiss German Mennonite name. Numerous relatives, including his parents, are deeply involved in Mennonite church institutions. He studied in Mennonite schools and attended an Anabaptist-affiliated college, where he met Daphne, his wife. After Frank completed a master's degree in English literature and taught briefly at a community college, he and Daphne volunteered for overseas service with MCC. They chose placements in Indonesia as their preference because the position description specified that they would be teaching in a Christian university in Central Java. Like most North Americans, they knew little about Indonesia before arriving in the country.

Both attended the orientation in Akron, Pennsylvania, and Frank mostly appreciated the content, though when I talked about it with him a few years later, he found it difficult to recall much in detail. The various activities, despite blurring together, he considered appropriate and meaningful. Upon arrival in Central Java, they were greeted at the airport by a Javanese family, who hosted them for the first week. Though communication was limited, Frank enjoyed wandering around to catch a sense of the city that he would live in for the next four years. He also read a lot of novels. He appreciated this first taste of Indonesia and much later would still occasionally visit his host family.

Frank and Daphne's in-country orientation took place over a weekend. Though brief, he regarded it as sufficient. He had come to learn about Indonesia not from expatriates but rather from Indonesians. Three weeks after arriving in Indonesia, they had both started teaching assignments at their university. This was considered unusually short but was not resented. Again, Frank explained that he had come to build friendships with Indonesians and was glad that he was able to do so without delay. They soon began intensive language learning, working with a Javanese tutor. After a few months this language study continued on an ad hoc basis for several more months. Although Frank taught all his classes in English (as requested by the university), he became fluent in Indonesian and used it regularly in most of his relationships with Indonesians.

At the time that I first began my fieldwork in early 2007, there was considerable conversation among MCCers about building a stronger MCC community in Indonesia. Frank didn't consider this necessary. Although he enjoyed friendships with other MCCers, he considered his university colleagues as his "primary community" in Indonesia. Although Frank lived in the same town as the MCC Indonesia office, he rarely visited and thought he had limited knowledge of its daily affairs. The two annual countrywide gatherings of MCCers were important events but were considered an interlude from his everyday relationships. Likewise, while he regularly played basketball at the nearby international school with other expatriates, the friendships he made there remained marginal to his everyday life. Frank and Daphne attended an Indonesian Mennonite church in which the services and sermons were entirely in Indonesian. Despite feeling a disconnect between his own spirituality and the church's ritual practice, he attended every Sunday anyway.

Frank understood that one reason he was valued and appreciated at his university was his status as a native speaker of English. For governmental accreditation purposes, English departments benefit greatly if they have a native speaker as a faculty member. Each time government officials came through the department, Frank would be on the list to meet with them. Frank initially was asked by his department to teach English-language courses. This did not excite him. He had been under the impression that he would take up a position teaching literature rather than language per se. This disjuncture between his expectations and the department's priorities was disconcerting. Over time, however, he managed to shift progressively over to teaching more from his interests and training. Frank did not manage any staff in the department, and his supervisor was Indonesian. He participated along with colleagues in staff meetings. This participation increased with his developing language skills and his knowledge of the context.

As arranged by the MCC Reps, Frank and Daphne's house and visas were provided by the university. MCC provided all other living expenses, however, including food, holidays (which they occasionally took in Bali), a motorbike (of the low-cc variety colloquially known as a *bebek*), health care, and also a domestic worker (*pembantu*). At first Frank found the relationship with the *pembantu* awkward, as it seemed layered with class and hierarchy dynamics. He was particularly uncomfortable when she cleaned in the same room where he was working or relaxing. Also Javanese customs of deferral to social superiors, offered through visual cues and verbal exchange, was something he hadn't expected or wanted. Frank and Daphne tried at first to treat their *pembantu* as a member of the family and have lunch with her on a regular basis. They would often chat in Indonesian with her and express an interest in her family. Although Frank thought their friendliness was appreciated, he also thought she was uncomfortable with attempts to flatten or dissolve the hierarchy. Frank justified hiring a *pembantu* as providing someone with employment, and they paid her at higher rates than other expatriates and Indonesians they knew. When Frank and Daphne had their first child in Indonesia, delivered in a local hospital and given an Indonesian middle name, however, they found their *pembantu's* help invaluable in managing their house and assisting with child care.

Frank and Daphne regularly wrote newsletters home to supporters to explain their work and provide updates. On one occasion they mentioned that they missed eating good chocolate, and a few weeks later they were inundated with chocolate sent from the United States. Frank also kept up with family on the phone and, once they installed broadband in their home, over the Internet. He paid close attention to American politics and was a passionate Obama supporter. Members of both Frank and Daphne's family visited them in Indonesia. After two years in Indonesia, Frank and Daphne decided that they would extend their initial three-year commitment to four years. This gave them the chance to take "home leave" for two months back in the United States, which they spent largely in Pennsylvania between the houses of both sets of parents. They had numerous speaking engagements during this time with Mennonite churches and schools during which they told stories of their time in Indonesia and sought to provide a glimpse into Indonesian life worlds. On occasions this was a National Geographic–type description of some of the flora, fauna, cultures, and religions of the archipelago.

Frank felt some ambiguity due to working as both a lecturer in his university and an MCC service worker. On the one hand, this was experienced as disjuncture. For example, Frank expressed disconnect between what he had been told since childhood about MCC's identity—"development, relief, and peace building"—and his role of teaching English literature, which he saw as distantly or tenuously connected with these goals. He sought to lessen this disconnect by associating more closely with his university than with MCC. On the other hand, Frank also discussed with me how the process of being a service worker in MCC gave him a sense of ownership and belonging to the organization. By working with MCC, he made it *his* organization. Although his secondment meant that he didn't work directly within MCC organizational structures, and although he felt removed from MCC Indonesia's office routines, he still frequently became animated about some of the large-scale changes taking place in the organization.

When Frank and Daphne finished their service with MCC, they returned home to Pennsylvania. Again they did a round of itinerant speaking during which they spoke at numerous Mennonite churches, schools, and community events. They have started attending Daphne's parents' Mennonite church and remain open to further involvement with MCC as supporters. Frank is now partway through his doctoral studies and is considering undertaking field research in Indonesia for his thesis. Although the four years in Indonesia were seen as a defining experience, he was glad to leave Indonesia when he did and be back home, close to family and features of life in Pennsylvania. Though the effects of his experience would continue to shape his identity, the geographical separation was also a temporal demarcation indicating an ending to that season of his life. Having been a guest in Indonesia for four years, Frank had come back home to both the United States and the Mennonite peoplehood.

In the following narrative of Paulus, I highlight points of comparison with Frank's experience of working with MCC. Paulus is a Javanese man in his 30s. He was brought up in a tough neighborhood in Semarang, Central Java. During the notorious "Petrus" operations in the 1980s, in which the Indonesian government commissioned extrajudicial assassinations of suspected criminals (*preman*), a number of Paulus's neighbors were targeted and executed. Paulus told me that his neighborhood had such a bad reputation that even police were afraid to go there. Still he managed to gain a good education and was able to move away from this disadvantaged situation. Paulus's family members were part of one of the Indonesian Mennonite churches (*Gereja Kristen Muria Indonesia*), and he grew up in the church.

Paulus worked as a graphic designer and eventually set up his own business. He had an entrepreneurial streak and was good at his work. For a few years in the late 1990s, he was hired by his church's Synod office and through this connection heard about MCC's International Visitor Exchange Program (IVEP), which runs parallel to the SALT program discussed previously. He applied for the program and was surprised when he was accepted into it. Paulus spent a year in Canada with IVEP (mid-2000 to mid-2001), his first significant personal connection with MCC and North American Mennonites. He greatly enjoyed his stay in rural Ontario. Socially it was very fulfilling, as he interacted with both Canadians and other fellow IVEP participants from all over the world. His work experience also furnished him with an opportunity to learn a variety of new skills, and his English-language skills improved considerably. He also said that during his time in North America, he learned what it really meant to be a Mennonite.

Upon returning home to Java, Paulus continued working in graphic design. In December 2004, when the Indian Ocean tsunami devastated coastal Aceh, he talked with friends about the possibility of going there to help. The opportunity to do so opened up in January 2005 when his church office was called by MCC asking if they knew of anyone willing to work in MCC's newly established Aceh programs. The church office suggested Paulus. At this time Aceh was like a battlefield, and many Indonesians were unwilling to work there. When Paulus was called and offered the chance to join the MCC team there, he was given two hours to consider the offer because of time pressures. He decided to take it up given his flexibility stemming from being self-employed and not yet married. The next day he was on a flight to Jakarta for meetings with other NGOs, and by early February he was in Aceh. Initially he committed to just one month, but this kept being extended. Paulus worked in the MCC office there from the start of MCC's work in Aceh till the Aceh office closed down in 2008.

During the early months of the relief work, there were five management transitions in the Aceh office—each new manager was from North America—and a similar high turnover of short-term expatriate staff. This situation eventually stabilized with more permanent appointments. Paulus's early tasks included looking after the logistics of housing, transport, and food for the rest of the Aceh MCC team. This initial role soon shifted to partnership liaison. He had no job description, however, and was unclear what his responsibilities were. During his time in Aceh, he carried out a wide range of tasks. His work in administration and partnership liaison was fairly typical of the roles given to local staff in the organization; they worked as key brokers and translators (Mosse and Lewis 2006) between MCC and partners. Unlike some Indonesian friends in other NGOs, he had no specific background in the field and received little formal training from MCC to do his job, although some supervisors worked closely with him in various tasks. Paulus never received an orientation to working with MCC, neither in Indonesia nor in North America. While the high-pressured nature of the tsunami response was part of the reason, the lack of an orientation was considered normal among Indonesian staff.

When Paulus arrived in Aceh, he felt like a complete stranger. He didn't know the Acehnese language, had limited transportation, and felt that many Acehnese resented the presence of Javanese. He had to learn entirely new customs and cultural norms and tried to pick up some language. He felt ambiguous in his status in MCC too. For although he was Indonesian, he felt, like the North American MCCers with him, like an expatriate, a foreign visitor. Like them too he was a volunteer rather than salaried. His work was often similar to that of his colleagues, regardless of their country of origin. For the first eight months of his work in Aceh, he also worked and slept in a single house with all the other MCCers, which created a certain communal equity among the team. This ambiguity—Was Paulus a local or expatriate staff member?—however, was resolved through two processes. First, after three months Paulus shifted from voluntary status to paid employment. This reinforced the traditional distinctions in the organization between expatriate volunteer service worker and local salaried staff. The pay levels for local staff were considered generous. Second, as mentioned previously, Paulus's role became increasingly clarified as a partner liaison. Again, this role was traditionally held by local staff and demarcated him from most of the expatriate volunteers who were increasingly seconded to other local organizations. Consequently, Paulus was reinscribed as a local staff member, while his feelings of being out of place in Aceh continued.

Another important change of identity simultaneously took place. Paulus became increasingly aware that the organization "exists for North Americans." He came to this awareness through learning of his place within the organization. While he was initially involved in making decisions on the work in Aceh, change in supervisors meant the tasks given to him changed too. At one point he said, "We [*local staff*] are ground people. We don't know what is going on upstairs with the politics and decision making." Over time he felt like he had an increasingly limited role in decisions being made. He also felt like he rarely received all the information he needed. This sense of MCC being not his organization was particularly apparent to him during the two annual gatherings of the whole MCC team, during which he felt the discussions often revolved around interests and concerns of the North American staff rather than the issues that he was dealing with. I never heard Paulus express a sense of ownership over MCC.

Paulus met his Indonesian wife in Aceh; she also worked for an international NGO. They married and soon after had their first child while still based in Aceh. At the end of three years of operation, the MCC Aceh office closed down. Paulus and his wife subsequently moved to the capital, Jakarta, where he returned to entrepreneurial graphic design work. He looked back on his experience with MCC quite positively and thought that it had freed him from fear (*ketakutan*) by exposing him to previously unconsidered opportunities and by helping expand his imagination for what he thought was possible in terms of both vocation and his own personal abilities. He appreciated his time with MCC, but it was for only a certain period of time.

These two biographical narratives illustrate the paradoxical (dis)associative impulses of MCC's ideology of guesthood. Frank's relationship with his host institution epitomizes the goal of MCCers in prioritizing relationships with their Indonesian colleagues and neighbors. The deeper these relationships, the more they were celebrated by other MCCers. These relationships, however, were spatially and temporally bounded. Discussions of "home leave" and returning "home" as well as ongoing accountability to and communication with "home" continued to inscribe a sense of separateness. Indonesia was "away." In Indonesia Frank understood himself as a foreign guest. Frank came from the North American Mennonite peoplehood and returned there on the conclusion of his term of service. Furthermore, the awkwardness of relating to the *pembantu* illustrates the dynamics involved in the attempt to be noncoercive. When the Javanese helper adopted a subservient position in her role, this caused discomfort and necessitated attempts to diminish the hierarchical power relations. That these attempts were eventually unsuccessful could be read as an acceptance that Frank's own framework should not be forced on the lives of the Indonesians he interacted with. These illustrate the behavior of a "good guest."

While Frank, like almost all expatriate service workers, was seconded to an Indonesian organization for the duration of his service, Paulus, like all Indonesian staff, was directly employed by and worked within the structures of MCC. It seemed to Paulus that identity in Aceh and MCC was at first quite ambiguous as to whether he was a foreigner or a local staff member. This was eventually resolved, however, with Paulus increasingly being ascribed by other MCCers the latter identity. His growing understanding of MCC as a North American organization also showed a sense of distance from it. As an Indonesian, Paulus came to realize his participation in MCC was more limited than that of his expatriate colleagues. He saw himself as displaced from MCC in relation to expatriate staff.

A certain parallel between Frank and Paulus becomes apparent. Just as Frank was conceptualized as being a guest in his work in an Indonesian institution, so too was Paulus, as a local staff member in MCC, conceptualized as a guest. The ideology of guesthood situates MCC's work in Indonesia as "away from home." Certain forms of behavior and expectations ensue from this understanding. One key consequence is that this necessarily situates local staff as being away from home while they are within MCC structures. MCC is not an Indonesian organization, not *their* organization. Their ability to belong within this North American "peoplehood movement" is significantly constrained. As guests in MCC, local staff are welcomed and relied on but are ultimately denied full participation in the politics of the NGO. Therefore, while the stance of guest is taken up by expatriates as they begin their voluntary service in Indonesia, it is also ascribed to local staff in their work within MCC.

This differentiation was further highlighted in an office meeting in Central Java where the MCC Reps explained to their Indonesian staff that they had struggled in deciding whether to hire local staff to work for "a North American organization." As a general rule it was thought more appropriate to have Indonesian colleagues working within Indonesian organizations, because Indonesian staff "must put on a North American mindset" when working for

MCC. Furthermore, "you folks are in a difficult position to represent weird North American ways of thinking to partners." As a result of MCC being at heart North American, local staff are structurally displaced as guests within the organization. The expatriate–local split is a result of the different status of each group in terms of employment contracts, work contexts, and identity within MCC—all of which are structurally built into wider MCC policy and practices. Local staff were expected to have to adapt to the culture of MCC in the same sort of way that MCCers were expected to adapt to Indonesia. The guesthood ideology underlying this "peoplehood movement" enables therefore both the transcending of boundaries and the simultaneous reassertion of them.

Conclusion

Through the orientation rituals and biographical narratives described and analyzed in this chapter, I have traced MCC's distinctive ideology of guesthood and its effects on MCC practices in Indonesia. The ideology of guesthood enabled expatriate MCCers to imagine their work as livable and legitimate. Through performing a "good guest" identity, expatriate MCCers in Indonesia sought to negotiate the moral politics of development.

MCC's ideology of guesthood is distinctive because the NGO is intimately connected with the North American Mennonite peoplehood. Guesthood resonates deeply with the prominence of peacefulness and simplicity in Mennonite theology and ethics. Furthermore, as a consequence of this peoplehood and the national spaces of Canada and the United States being perceived as "home," MCC's work in Indonesia is necessarily understood as being "away." Guesthood emerges here in relation to the traditional conceptualization of Mennonites as *die Stillen im Lande* (the quiet in the land) in North America; guesthood guides ("quiet") behavior when in someone else's land. Because of MCC's intimate identification with the North American Mennonite peoplehood, expatriate MCCers were oriented to seeing themselves as foreign guests in Indonesia. As the two narratives highlighted, however, this leads to an awkward positioning within the organization for those who are not part of this peoplehood. Local staff were structurally displaced within MCC. For if MCC is a guest in Indonesia then Indonesians who work in MCC are likewise guests. This was an inevitable, if unintended, effect of MCC's guesthood ideology. MCC's ideology of guesthood therefore is paradoxical. Premised on noncoercion it affirms attempts at bonding and facilitates the transcending of cultural boundaries, yet it also reinscribes those same boundaries. The ideology of guesthood is both associative and disassociative. It is in the tension between the two that MCCers, both expatriates and locals, carry out their work and live their lives.

It is important to note that many MCCers in Indonesia were acutely aware of these tensions, and some took active steps to mitigate them. During the period of my field research, the very first orientation to MCC was held for local staff in Indonesia. This was the butt of frequent jokes by one Indonesian staff member who had already worked with the organization for almost a decade. Another initiative undertaken by the MCC Reps was to attempt to get all Indonesian staff to attend the two-week orientation in Akron, Pennsylvania, so as to parallel their experience to that of international volunteers. These orientations were attempts to minimize the differences between expatriate and local, and in so doing they illustrate an awareness of the tensions arising from the guesthood logic. They were not insignificant and demanded the allocation of time, funding, and energy. But neither were they structural adjustments to the MCC system. These were attempts to mitigate the tensions rather than resolve them. At least some expatriate MCCers left Indonesia for "home" haunted by these unresolved frictions. Such hauntings of course arise out of self-reflexivity and discomfort with privilege and therefore are also markers of the endeavor to be good guests even after the lived experience of guesthood has past.

Acknowledgments

Thanks to participants at an anthropology seminar at the Australian National University who provided feedback on an earlier draft of this chapter and also Gillian Dalgetty, Phil Enns, Patrick Guinness, Christine Helliwell, Dan Jantzi, Jeanne Jantzi, Vernon Jantzi, Kersty Hobson, Iris Lee, Elizabeth Phelps, Victor Sensenig, Anne-Meike Fechter, and Heather Hindman for valuable comments and suggestions. Remaining errors are entirely my own. Warm gratitude also to all MCCers who participated in my research. The fieldwork was made possible through grants from the Australian National University and the Religious Research Association's Constant H. Jacquet Award.

Notes

1. I undertook ethnographic fieldwork for 19 months in Indonesia, primarily in Central Java. A further 3 months of fieldwork was carried out in various locations in the United States and Canada.

2. I take "ideology" to be similar to Keane's (2007, 31) notion of "animating ideas" through which practices and actions are made "inhabitable and practicable."

3. Although it was considered possible for MCC's local Indonesian staff to hold senior leadership positions in another country, there is a long-standing hesitancy in MCC to appoint local staff to leadership of MCC programs within their home country.

4. There were a few rare exceptions to this focus on education secondments in MCC Indonesia.

5. For introductions to the Summer Institute of Linguistics, see Hartch (2006) and Svelmoe (2007).

6. In keeping with common anthropological practice, pseudonyms and composites are used in both narratives. These sketches are drawn from numerous interviews and discussions that took place over the duration of my fieldwork.

References

Bornstein, Erica. 2001. Child sponsorship, evangelism, and belonging in the work of World Vision Zimbabwe. *American Ethnologist* 28 (3): 595–622.

———. 2003. *The spirit of development: Protestant NGOs, morality, and economics in Zimbabwe.* New York: Routledge.

Brewster, E. Thomas, and Elizabeth S. Brewster. 1980. *Bonding, and the missionary task: Establishing a sense of belonging.* Dallas, TX: Summer Institute of Linguistics.

Bush, Perry. 1998. *Two kingdoms, two loyalties: Mennonite pacifism in modern America.* Baltimore and London: Johns Hopkins University Press.

Clarke, Gerard, and Michael Jennings, eds. 2008. *Development, civil society and faith-based organizations: Bridging the sacred and the secular.* Hampshire, UK: Palgrave Macmillan.

Cooke, Bill, and Uma Kothari, eds. 2001. *Participation: The new tyranny?* London: Zed Books.

Cornwall, Andrea, and Karen Brock. 2005. What do buzzwords do for development policy? A critical look at "participation," "empowerment" and "poverty reduction." *Third World Quarterly* 26 (7): 1043–60.

Crewe, Emma, and Elizabeth Harrison. 1998. *Whose development? An ethnography of aid.* London and New York: Zed Books.

Dicklitch, Susan, and Heather Rice. 2004. The Mennonite Central Committee (MCC) and faith-based NGO aid to Africa. *Development in Practice* 14 (5): 660–72.

Erb, Maribeth. 2000. Understanding tourists: Interpretations from Indonesia. *Annals of Tourism Research* 27 (3): 709–36.

Fechter, Anne-Meike. 2007. *Transnational lives: Expatriates in Indonesia.* London: Ashgate.

Fisher, William F. 1997. Doing good? The politics and antipolitics of NGO politics. *Annual Review of Anthropology* 26:439–64.

Fox, Diana Joyce. 1998. *An ethnography of four non-governmental organizations: Oxfam America, Grassroots International, ACCION International, and Cultural Survival Inc.* New York: Edward Mellen.

Graber Miller, Keith. 1996. *Wise as serpents, innocent as doves: American Mennonites engage Washington.* Knoxville: University of Tennessee Press.

Hartch, Todd. 2006. *Missionaries of the state: The Summer Institute of Linguistics, state formation, and indigenous Mexico, 1935–1985.* Tuscaloosa: University of Alabama Press.

Hilhorst, Dorothea. 2003. *The real world of NGOs: Discourses, diversity and development.* London and New York: Zed Books.

Keane, Webb. 2007. *Christian moderns: Freedom and fetish in the mission encounter.* Berkeley and Los Angeles: University of California Press.

Kilby, Patrick. 2006. Accountability for empowerment: Dilemmas facing non-governmental organizations. *World Development* 34 (6): 951–63.

Kreider, Robert S., and Rachel Waltner Goossen. 1988. *Hungry, thirsty, a stranger: The MCC experience.* Scottdale, PA: Herald Press.

Kreider, Robert S., and Ronald J.R. Mathies, eds. 1996. *Unity amidst diversity: Mennonite Central Committee at 75: MCC and the 20th century North American Mennonite experience.* Akron, PA: Mennonite Central Committee.

Lewis, David. 1998. Development NGOs and the challenge of partnership: Changing relations between north and south. *Social Policy and Administration* 32 (5): 501–12.

Loewen, Royden. 2008. The poetics of peoplehood: Ethnicity and religion among Canada's Mennonites. In *Christianity and ethnicity in Canada*, ed. Paul Bramadat and David Seljak, 330–64. Toronto: University of Toronto Press.

Marr, Lucille. 2003. *The transforming power of a century: MCC and its evolution in Ontario.* Kitchener, Ontario: Pandora Press.

McKnight, John. 1989. Why servanthood is bad. *The Other Side* 25 (1): 38–40.

McNaughton, Darlene. 2006. The "host" as uninvited "guest": Hospitality, violence and tourism. *Annals of Tourism Research* 33 (3): 645–65.

Mennonite Central Committee. 2007. *In the name of Christ: Mennonite Central Committee calendar 2008.* Akron, PA: Mennonite Central Committee.

———. 2009. Front matter. *A Common Place* 15 (3): 2.

———. n.d. *Considering MCC?* Akron, PA: Mennonite Central Committee.

Morse, Stephen, and Nora McNamara. 2006. Analysing institutional partnerships in development: A contract between equals or a loaded process? *Progress in Development Studies* 6 (4): 321–36.

Mosse, David. 2005. *Cultivating development: An ethnography of aid policy and practice.* London: Pluto Press.

Mosse, David, and David Lewis. 2006. Theoretical approaches to brokerage and translation in development. In *Development brokers and translators: The ethnography of aid and agencies*, ed. David Lewis and David Mosse, 1–26. Bloomfield, CT: Kumarian Press.

Nolt, Steve. 1999. A two-kingdom people in a world of multiple identities: Religion, ethnicity and American Mennonites. *The Mennonite Quarterly Review* 73 (3): 485–502.

Quarles van Ufford, Philip, and Matthew Schoffeleers, eds. 1988. *Religion and development: Towards an integrated approach.* Amsterdam, the Netherlands: Free University Press.

Selwyn, T. 2000. An anthropology of hospitality. In *In search of hospitality: Theoretical perspectives and debates*, ed. Conrad Lashley and Alison Morrison, 18–36. Oxford and Woburn, MA: Butterworth Heinemann.

Smith, Valene L., ed. 1989. *Hosts and guests: The anthropology of tourism.* 2nd ed. Philadelphia: University of Pennsylvania Press.

Svelmoe, William. 2007. William Cameron Townsend and missionary linguistics. In *Anthropology's Debt to Missionaries*, 62–85. Ethnology Monographs. Pittsburgh, PA: University of Pittsburgh.

Ter Haar, Gerrie, and Stephen Ellis. 2006. The role of religion in development: Towards a new relationship between the European Union and Africa. *The European Journal of Development Research* 18 (3): 351–67.

Tsing, Anna Lowenhaupt. 2005. *Friction: An ethnography of global connection*. Princeton, NJ: Princeton University Press.

Turner, Victor Witter. 1979. Betwixt and between: The liminal period in rites de passage. In *Reader in comparative religion: An anthropological approach*, ed. William Armand Lessa and Evon Zartman Vogt, 234–43. New York: Harper and Row.

Unruh, John D. 1952. *In the name of Christ: A history of the Mennonite Central Committee*. Scottdale, PA: Herald Press.

Urry, James. 2006. *Mennonites, politics, and peoplehood: Europe—Russia—Canada: 1925 to 1980*. Winnipeg: University of Manitoba Press.

Wierzbicka, Anna. 1997. *Understanding cultures through their key words: English, Russian, Polish, German, and Japanese*. Oxford Studies in Anthropological Linguistics 8. New York: Oxford University Press.

Winland, Daphne Naomi. 1993. The quest for Mennonite peoplehood: Ethno-religious identity and the dilemma of definitions. *Canadian Review of Sociology and Anthropology* 30 (1): 110–38.

Yoder, Richard A., Calvin W. Redekop, and Vernon E. Jantzi. 2004. *Development to a different drummer: Anabaptist/Mennonite experiences and perspectives*. Intercourse, PA: Good Books.

Zehr, Howard. 1996. *Doing life*. Akron, PA: Mennonite Central Committee.

6

Everywhere and Everthrough
Rethinking Aidland

Keith Brown ·

Introduction

This chapter traces the birth, implementation, and afterlife of one USAID-funded civil society program that ran from 1995 to 2004. It adopts Raymond Apthorpe's definition of Aidland as "the *trail* (to use a word that usefully is both verb and noun, and about both process and place) of where foreign aid comes from, where it goes, and what then" (Apthorpe 2005, cited in Denskus 2007, 3) and the methods of "following the thing" or "studying through" advocated by a number of anthropologists of policy (Marcus 1995; Wedel 1998; Shore and Wright 1997, 11). It seeks in particular to explore what Apthorpe described as the virtuality of Aidland, whereby it constitutes "not a nowhere exactly but inexactly a somewhere, with the characteristics of a nowhere. An idea of a somewhere but about which more is desired" (Apthorpe 2003). Whereas others have picked up on the illusory qualities that Apthorpe described—referring, for example, to the way in which the development industry conjures a "'lala-land' . . . where standard inputs can be turned into predicted and desirable outcomes in a causally linked and apparently unproblematic way" (Wallace, Bornstein, and Chapman 2006, 172)—I seek here to pursue the more substantive, though often attenuated, connections between the virtual and the actual dimensions of Aidland.

Specifically, I suggest that the socioeconomic properties of Aidland—whereby aid professionals act at a distance, maintain relations with both home offices and field sites, and through their labor create the sector from which they draw their livelihood—can be illuminated by comparison with recent studies of alternative, online worlds. In particular, Tom Boellstorff, in his recent work on Second Life, called for anthropologists to move beyond the apparent dualism of "virtual" and "real" and to pay attention to the relation between them. For Boellstorff, "'virtual' connotes approaching the actual *without arriving there*. This gap between virtual and actual is critical: were it to be filled in, there would be no virtual worlds, and in a sense no actual world either" (Boellstorff 2008, 19, emphasis in original). Read back into Aidland, Boellstorff's observation offers an ontological reading of the coproductive distance between idea and impact in almost all international assistance programs. It is not failure of design, lack of goodwill, cultural insensitivity or local incapacity, ingratitude, or corruption that derails good intentions: the goodness of intentions is in fact preserved by their persistent virtual and virtuous intentionality.

Apthorpe captured this quality elsewhere in his work, where he wrote that modernist rural development projects operate not "in" or even "on" but rather "over" any particular country (Apthorpe 2003). Although it is commonplace to perceive this gap between the virtual and the actual simply as a disconnect, I argue here that it is a relation that constitutes the two objects that it interconnects. And, as Apthorpe's invocation of the vertical plane signals, resonating with Escobar's (1995, 214) point that development colonizes reality rather more so than the other way around, it does so asymmetrically. While seeking to avoid the seduction of locality, in which voices and analyses "from below" are privileged as more real than their "top-down" interlocutors, this chapter argues that the constitutive relations of Aidland are traceable at almost every point of the trail, as different formulations of the actual and the virtual brush against each other.

For throughout Aidland, as elsewhere, as Doreen Massey (1993, 67, cited in Li 2007) put it in her reflection on her native Kilburn, "locality is constructed out of particular interactions and mutual articulations of social relations, social processes, experiences and understandings, in a situation of co-presence, but where a large proportion of those relations, experiences and understandings are actually constructed in a far larger scale than what we happen to define as that place." The virtual quality ascribed to Aidland, I suggest, is a product of the apparent attenuation of the relations by which it is constituted. Geographers such as Massey remind us that ideas have social, cultural, and/or material impacts throughout their careers, however far they travel and whether they do so along newly blazed trails or well-established channels. Whatever we may conclude about the theoretical and practical impossibility that policymakers and implementers realize what they first virtualize in their plans and schemes, the actual outputs are traceable and can throw into relief the power geometry of the interventionist imagination that is this chapter's overarching concern.

The Empirical Context: USAID in the Republic of Macedonia, 1995–2004

So far, so theoretical. The empirical data on which I base this reading of Aidland are drawn from a case study of one of its constituent parts, a USAID-funded initiative in Eastern Europe launched in the 1990s. The Democracy Network Program (henceforth DemNet) was first conceived in 1994 to support the development of civil society and was implemented in 11 countries starting in 1995 by a variety of US-based NGOs.[1] A number of scholars have written about the program's place in portfolios of democracy assistance to different countries, in most of which it ended after an initial three-year grant period (Regulska 1998; Carothers 1999; Petrescu 2000). This chapter focuses on its longer history in the Republic of Macedonia, where after the first three-year phase, the program was extended three more times, finally ending in 2004.

This period marked the republic's progressive incorporation into Aidland, as international assistance escalated dramatically first after the Kosovo crisis in 1999 and then again after armed conflict within Macedonia in 2001. US bilateral assistance topped $60 million in each of the years 1999, 2002, and 2003, and European donors also made substantial investments over this period. DemNet, with a total budget of just over $8 million over its decade of operation, was just one component in a mix of foreign-funded initiatives that at different points included media training, legal reform, business development, and confidence building. Its relations with those other programs, though important and interesting, are not explored in this chapter.

I offer instead a calculatedly simple narrative frame. Taking at face value USAID's slogan "From the American People," I set out in 2007 to document and describe the "aid chain" that delivered assistance from American taxpayers to particular individuals, communities, and organizations in Macedonia through this program and to see what traces it had left behind for those involved. In this enterprise I collaborated with a former country director for the program in Macedonia, Paul Nuti, whom I had first met in Skopje, the capital of Macedonia, in 2001 and who had subsequently reflected on his own experiences and understandings as a practitioner of democracy promotion (Nuti 2006). In 2008 we tracked down and interviewed his Skopje-based Macedonian colleagues from Phase III of DemNet, which ran from 2000 to 2002, and then worked up and down, back and forth, in and out from that spatial and temporal start point in the chain. So moving up or back or in, we interviewed Institute for Sustainable Communities (ISC) personnel in Vermont and US-AID personnel in both Washington DC and Macedonia. Moving down or forth or out, we interviewed community leaders in towns and villages outside Skopje. In the course of the project, we conducted open-ended interviews and slightly more formal focus groups of between one and two hours with over 50 individuals connected to the DemNet program in Macedonia—as designers, implementers, advisors, employees, trainees, grantees, beneficiaries, and evaluators.[2] Obviously, this chapter cannot do justice to the richness of their reflections or the diversity of their perspectives. What I offer here is a set of accounts of the program in which all were involved to different degrees, which I hope illustrates the utility of a reflexive and ethnographic emphasis on the interplay of the virtual and the actual to better discern the larger scale relations that give shape and substance to Aidland.

Design at a Distance: Envisioning a Virtuous Network

DemNet was first conjured on the public record by President Bill Clinton. In a news conference in Prague on January 12, 1994, following a meeting with Visegrad country leaders, he reported,

> We're supporting the development of a thriving civil society. And in our meeting I announced the creation of the democracy network, an initiative to bring new resources to grassroots and independent groups throughout the region. I stressed our interest in fostering regional cooperation.[3]

Clinton's visit to the region and these remarks were entangled with Washington politics. With the end of the Cold War, and powerful pressures to reduce perceived government waste, USAID's very reason for existence was called into question (Brown 2009). Among the initiatives the agency took was to develop a new democracy promotion portfolio, and among the personnel charged with its development was Dr. Gerald Hyman, who joined USAID in 1990.[4] Originally situated in the Asia/Near East bureau, Hyman anticipated drawing on his legal training and anthropological background (having done fieldwork in Krian in Indonesia and completed a PhD supervised by Clifford Geertz) in programming for that region of the world. The US government, however, also sought ways to intervene in the political transformations in Eastern Europe and the Soviet Union, and when Congress approved new funding for that purpose, through the FREEDOM and SEED acts, USAID was tasked with work there.[5] And in the absence of regional specialists or a dedicated European bureau at that time, the Asia/Near East bureau and Gerald Hyman found themselves taking the lead. Speaking in 2008, Hyman recalled this sequence of events in somewhat self-deprecating terms, stating, "They chose the wrong person and put him in the wrong place." He recalled his early visits to the region vividly and his skepticism about what US assistance could bring, almost two decades later:

> There was a lot of fear in these countries about organizing, about associating, who was listening, who would report whom. They had come out of a pretty dark period. And perhaps more than others I was affected by that because I was often the first person from AID that went into any of these countries. Not in Poland and Hungary, but in the Balkans. . . . I remember both in Bulgaria and Romania, you know, the security forces, they penetrated everything. In Romania, your typewriters had to be registered. People talked to each other and turned themselves in, everything was bugged, people thought you couldn't have a conversation with anybody, when I went there first, it was dark. There was no electricity to speak of, there were few lamps, there were no restaurants. Your choice was between, you know, fried chicken and fried pork. . . . And people were not like they are now. So, people were afraid, people had been turned in, people had spent years in camps and jail. So, to come after that and say, "OK, great, now we're going to have this effervescence of NGOs and they're going to come out, and they're going to be so Tocquevillian, and people are going to cooperate with each other, and not only are they going to do common projects but then they're going to advocate and stuff." I mean, I had no belief that that was going to happen without a lot of help, without a lot of nurturing.

This account demonstrates clearly the gulf that Hyman, from his own visits to the region, saw existing between the ideal of associational life as expressed in Robert Putnam's work on social capital—popular in Clintonian circles—and the realities of social relations in the Balkans (Putnam 1993). Charged with putting procedural flesh on the conceptual bones tossed out by President Clinton—or, in the idiom of this chapter, adding actuality to a virtual program—he clearly rejected as unrealistic any simple bilateral model of the United States teaching (or preaching) its democratic template among the benighted. Instead, he conceived of a democratic space that was composed of relations among NGOs in neighboring countries and a program that would facilitate those relations. In his words, again,

> DemNet was an attempt to do several things at once, but one of them was to try to create some sense of regionalism. . . . In the very early period after the wall came down, you could not get anybody in any part of the region to talk about any other part of the region. No matter where you went, they wanted to go their own way . . . they had been through the Warsaw Pact arrangements . . . [and] they wanted nothing of regionalism. We thought that there was a really unsatisfactory . . . solipsism almost, of each one of these countries . . . each wanting to build their own country but not knowing what was going on in their neighbors'. . . . And so we thought DemNet would be a regional bridge, so to speak.

Hyman here articulates a vision in which nonstate actors in different Eastern and Southeastern European countries would interact, learn, and ultimately create genuinely reciprocal relations. The original Request for Proposals that he then authored envisages Aidland as a multi-country space in which activists would regularly meet to share experiences. USAID's role would be minimal and largely managerial, facilitating such meetings. As such, Hyman did not see any strong need for a permanent in-country presence for US personnel. The program would be administered by USAID in Washington, but the work of bringing the virtual into alignment with the actual would be carried out by stakeholders in the region—it would be their engagement with one another that would turn the largely hollow language of the network into a literal resource for its members.

Mission Maneuvers and Beltway Bandits: The Actualities of Implementation

As the brief description of DemNet in Macedonia made clear, Hyman's original design was never realized. A key factor was bureaucratic turf battles among and within US government agencies. In USAID in particular, since the 1970s, the main career track has been managerial rather than technical. The currency of professional advancement is the successful administration of ever-larger program budgets and, as in the State Department, jockeying to move up through missions overseas with the goal of ending as country director in a location of major significance for US foreign interests. The "opening" of Eastern Europe and the passage by the US Congress of the SEED and FREEDOM support acts, which allocated spending in the region, potentially created a host of entry-level opportunities for young diplomats and aid professionals eager to manage the disbursement of these funds. So even as Hyman designed DemNet to foster multilateral relations among Eastern European nonstate actors, with funding coming directly from Washington, others were advocating for embassies and start-up USAID missions in the region to have a major say in the allocation of funds. Their arguments constructed Aidland differently, as constituted of individual nation-states rather than intraregional relations, each tied to the United States primarily through embassy-based US personnel. Whereas for Hyman the actual action of DemNet was to take place across national boundaries within the region, in reality those relations were rendered virtual.

Hyman did not entirely lose this battle: the media and legal reform components of DemNet were administered at the regional rather than the national level. But the civil society component, which commanded the largest single slice of the overall budget, was sliced up and divided along national lines, with US Foreign Service officers in each country making the final decision on how the program would be implemented, in combination with other vehicles of US assistance. In terms of the distribution of decision-making power within USAID, this had a decentralizing effect, in keeping with the overall rhetoric of reform within the agency at this time, spearheaded by Brian Atwood, to bring government within the reach of "the people" (and away from Washington).

For the people of Eastern and Southeastern Europe, especially those seeking to think beyond the borders of the nation-state, the actual effects were less clearly virtuous. In the first case, because of the physical location of US embassies, this so-called decentralization in fact reinscribed the importance of national capitals and relations with governmental agencies. Less obviously, but perhaps more significantly, it lengthened the trail of the DemNet program substantially. For in keeping with the Clinton administration's pledge to make government more efficient and nimble, the actual implementation of DemNet was outsourced to NGOs or private voluntary organizations (PVOs) based in the United States. In Hyman's original design, a small group of organizations would have been involved, building close working relationships over the course of the program through regular meetings in Washington DC, and travel to and between the countries of the region. But in DemNet as implemented, seven different US-based NGOs were contracted by US officials in the 11 countries (see Table 6.1). In place of the straightforward, direct path

Table 6.1
DemNet Nongovernmental Implementors, by Country

Implementing Organization	Country
Academy for Educational Development	Poland
Foundation for Civil Society	Slovakia, Czech Republic
United Way International	Hungary
World Learning	Romania
US-Baltic Foundation	Latvia, Lithuania, Estonia
Institute for Sustainable Communities	Bulgaria, Macedonia
Organization for Educational Resources and Technological Training	Albania

of assistance described by President Clinton and designed by Gerald Hyman, which would leave a singular transatlantic trail, DemNet's resources traveled within USAID from Washington to its country missions, then back to the home offices of US-based NGOs, then back again to the in-country offices that each established. Information and authority flowed back and forth along these multiple trails, and also along channels of oversight created inside each country. The intensity and turbulence of all these flows connecting up the territorial United States and its extrusions on foreign soil was largely self-contained: by contrast, in place of the lively intra-regional exchanges that Hyman had envisaged, each country's civil society sector was treated as an island unto itself, to be enriched by North American expertise and idealism.

The range of US-based organizations that implemented the civil society portion of the DemNet program reveals the wide scope covered by the shorthand categories of NGO and PVO. Formally alike, they were and remain a diverse group, with backgrounds in education and humanitarian relief as well as civil society promotion, annual operating budgets that in the years 2007 and 2008 that ranged from around $3 million (Foundation for Civil Society [FCS]) to over $400 million (Academy for Educational Development [AED]), and histories that date back only to the end of the Cold War (FCS, US-Baltic Foundation, ISC) or to the late nineteenth century (Organization for Educational Resources and Technological Training [ORT], United Way). Whereas younger organizations such as FCS and the US-Baltic Foundation defined themselves by their interest and expertise in particular parts of the region, others such as AED or World Learning had operated across the globe, often as contractors for US government–funded programs. What most shared was the derogatory label of "Beltway bandits," with their operations headquartered close to Washington DC.

Intercontinental Activists: Community Participation in Theory and Practice

In this regard, the ISC was a literal outlier. It was founded in 1990 by Vermont governor Madeleine Kunin after she and her policy advisor, George Hamilton, monitored democratic elections in Bulgaria that year. Based in Vermont, the organization focused in its early years on environmental issues in the United States and in Eastern Europe, drawing in a variety of practitioners with experience of nonprofit work and community activism in the United States, which linked environmentalism with an expanded vision of citizenship. ISC's successful application to implement DemNet in both Bulgaria and Macedonia prompted further expansion, and today the organization has an annual operating budget of around $10 million, mostly through USAID cooperative agreements.

At time of writing, George Hamilton remains as the executive director. When we spoke in January 2009, in ISC's offices in an environmentally efficient building in Montpelier, he was still able to recall the sense of excitement that he and Governor Kunin felt in Bulgaria in 1990, when they witnessed the vibrancy and energy of the environmental organization Ekoglasnost.[6] He also stressed the strong connection that ISC has persistently recognized between the living tradition of participatory democracy (still manifest in Vermont's annual town hall meetings every March to approve budgets) and environmental awareness (Bryan 2004). This, he recalled, shaped ISC's initial approach to its work in Bulgaria and Macedonia.

> The environment was our initial entry point, because that's what people wanted to focus on, but it's a useful one, from a sustainable community development standpoint, because the environmental problems affect everyone in a community equally. So unlike economic development programs, which tend to have winners and losers, in an environment, everyone benefits from having clean air, clean water, clean land, healthy food. So that's a good way of trying to get everybody involved. That's a great way to mobilize people to come together and to work together on solutions, and once they work

together on solutions and accomplish things together, they're more likely to take other challenges on.

Whereas Hyman envisaged supranational regional cooperation as a corrective to unproductive thought and action within state borders, Hamilton argued that the key to unlocking the human potential of Eastern and Southeastern Europe was for intervention at the level of "face-to-face" community. This demonstrated a fundamental faith in civic virtue in the same vein that John Dewey (a Vermonter himself) articulated in the 1920s and certainly traceable to the Tocquevillean tradition of direct democracy. Hyman, visiting the region in the early 1990s, had perceived widespread fear and distrust: Hamilton's specific encounter with Ekoglasnost also stayed with him, sustaining his confidence that the principles of small-town community activism translate across oceans and continents, whatever diplomats and bureaucrats might believe to the contrary. Both built their designs out of their interpretations of on-the-ground experience.

Hamilton recruited staff who shared this vision. Among them was Steve Nicholas, had worked in local government in Seattle during the 1980s and had also established an NGO committed to greening the city. He initially consulted with ISC on environmentally oriented projects in Russia and Hungary and, when offered the opportunity of directing DemNet in Macedonia, took it eagerly. In early 2009 he recalled his initial arrival in Macedonia's capital city in 1995:

I literally flew into Skopje with nothing but an address for a temporary office, which I also slept at for a while until I found an apartment. I slept on the floor of what became ISC's office for I forget for how many weeks. And I had one or two contact people, Macedonians, and, of course, some money from the USAID contract, but [I was operating] almost from scratch, really. And that was quite a challenge, obviously. I didn't speak the language. And so I just went about the business of creating both ISC's office and presence in Macedonia. And so that was everything from establishing the office, you know, buying furniture, hiring a local staff, paying a lot of attention to hiring a staff that had an ethnic diversity that mirrored the country—we paid a lot of attention to that—getting registered, you know ... all of the things that go into establishing a brand-new field office. And it was especially challenging because our office in Macedonia and Bulgaria, those were the first two field offices that ISC had ever created, so myself and a guy named Aaron Bornstein, who was the country director in Bulgaria, we were very much the guinea pigs for the organization in terms of how to do that. It's much more systematic and formalized now.

This self-deprecating narrative highlights the on-the-ground practicalities involved when Aidland extended onto, into, or over Macedonia. Nicholas went on to describe how he threw himself into establishing the kind of authentic human partnerships at the heart of the ISC approach. He worked particularly closely with environmental activists and existing organizations, including the Macedonian staff of the Regional Environmental Center (a Budapest-based organization that had been funded, in part, by the Environmental Protection Agency) and a number of robust ecological movements. A significant number of younger activists in these circles were attracted to the dynamic participatory networking meetings that Nicholas organized. Beyond hiring a small skeleton office staff, Nicholas did not hire project personnel but rather identified what particular skills people felt they needed—action planning, grant writing, database management, and the like—and set up trainings to teach them, thereby creating ties among already-active and motivated individuals and enhancing their professional profiles. Over a decade later, in interviews with Macedonian citizens who had been involved in DemNet, the sense of excitement and volunteerism that marked the first phase was still a salient memory.

Nicholas's Aidland, then, in keeping with ISC's philosophy, was a landscape of possibility and promise and a journey of adventure and collaboration. Strikingly, what many Macedonians remember most vividly is his commitment to learning and speaking their language—in which ISC was the *Institut za Trajni Zaednici*.[7] As his account of sleeping in the office indicates, he was committed to establishing an intimate relationship with the country: he also cultivated ties with a variety of local counterparts, which served to blur easy distinctions between "expatriate" and "local." He recalled, for example, relying on the judgment and guidance of Josif Tanevski, the energetic and principled leader of an ecological umbrella organization, DEM, who was already active in global forums.[8] At the same time as he acknowledged this level of professionalism, he also remembered fondly his own adaptation to Balkan modes of sociality. A friend would call him, and they would go out and sit over coffee for two hours even though, as Nicholas put it, he had a program to run. What he and his Macedonian colleagues shared, in fact, was something of a pioneer spirit in which they worked together, on an equal footing, to address a set of issues and in which they could see in their own life-changes the evidence that actual progressive change and learning was possible.

Committed Colleagues or Hired Hands? The Effects of Actuality

ISC's initial experiences in Macedonia, then, and its translational transformation into Institut za Trajni Zaednici, appeared to transcend the concerns that Hyman had expressed about the blinkeredness of citizens of the region and also US personnel in local embassies and AID missions. Nicholas had identified a network of activists already in dialogue with counterparts elsewhere in Eastern Europe and beyond, and it turned out that the techniques and philosophies he had developed as a professional and an activist in Seattle were both of interest and did translate. He also operated with greater freedom than DemNet implementers elsewhere, whose grant giving was in some cases subjected to close scrutiny by embassy-appointed "democracy commissions" (Petrescu 2000, 225–26; Carothers 1999, 272).

With each subsequent phase, though, this picture shifted. This was in part a product of the steady worsening of the political situation in the Republic of Macedonia. Although Nicholas made note of the sensitivity of ethnic relations, and also was a near witness to the dramatic assassination attempt on Macedonian president Kiro Gligorov in October 1995, security was not a major concern during his tenure as country director. In addition, his community-level focus was in synch with national-level initiatives, including, for example, a new law mandating that every municipality should create an environmental action plan that created a channel for citizen-activists to shape their communities' vision for the future.

By contrast, during Phase II (1998–2000) national politics became more polarized along ethnic and also party lines. Financial scandals were also widely reported, as it became clear that political and business elites had disproportionately benefited from the privatization process insisted on by the international community. This period, too, saw the US-led NATO intervention in Kosovo, in the course of which hundreds of thousands of ethnic Albanian refugees crossed into Macedonia, putting additional strain on the republic and prompting public suspicion of US motives (Brown and Theodossopoulos 2003). In a situation where a majority of citizens were worse off, and were also increasingly pessimistic about the country's future, the pool of energetic activists whose efforts Nicholas had sought to assist and compound was no longer so evident. At the point where it sought to expand its reach beyond the environmental sector to foster participation and advocacy in other domains, ISC found it-self now trying to promote views and practices that ran counter to increasing trends toward self-interest and individual survival. Conditions grew still more inhospitable during Phase III, in the course of which an armed insurgency broke out in the northwest of the country, where ethnic Albanian citizens of Macedonia constitute a local majority. By the summer of 2001, insurgents had taken control of a suburb of Skopje, prompting the US government to evacu-ate nonessential personnel to Bulgaria—including Paul Nuti, then director of the DemNet program.

By this time, ISC had expanded the scale of its operations. As noted earlier, USAID increased its level of funding to the republic after the Kosovo crisis of spring 1999, and this included a larger commitment to the DemNet program.[9] By 2000 the organization had over a dozen full-time paid employ-ees, including both Macedonians and Albanians, and was promoting citizen participation at the community level through support for a number of "pilot" local environmental action plans and also broader community action plans. Si-multaneously, other staff delivered training and grants to over 50 issue-specific NGOs across the country.

When Paul Nuti was evacuated, the Macedonian staff (including both ethnic Macedonians and ethnic Albanians) continued to work together. Besim Nebiu served as country director in Nuti's absence: in an interview in July 2008, he recalled the sense of cognitive dissonance they felt, feelings shared by the NGOs with whom they were working:

> It was a very difficult time, I think on a personal level it was very dif-ficult because it was, you know, basically a conflict happening around 15, 20 kilometers and you have to be present in order to understand how it is, and of course, we'd been close to other conflicts, but this was immediate, so there is a human reaction to that, which is I think sort of scary if you put it in the context. Though, it was also—it was a difficult time, for all of us, because it wasn't easy to live in the country when there is a conflict, and . . . friends and family and we are there. In terms of ISC doing its work, I think it was very difficult, not just because of security reasons, I think it was very difficult to be pursu-ing most of what we were doing at the time, because those things just didn't seem to be the priority, in the months, especially, of June, July, August of 2001. And when people were not preoccupied, because in times of conflict, I think priorities of people and organizations and groups of people switch, or change, dramatically, and, you know, they

involve things like making sure you have enough food supply, making sure that you're in a safe place, making sure that your family is in a safe place, and so on and so forth, so I think talking about environmental action plans, or community action plans, is very difficult, or bringing people to work on those subjects.

Other members of staff at that time recalled the practical and existential challenges of 2001. However committed the organization's staff were to their mission, and to each other, security realities interfered with what Escobar termed the "busy, repetitive reality" of democracy and development work (Escobar 1995, 214) and pushed programs back into the domain of virtuality. The pressures on the Macedonian staff were considerable: in a climate of interethnic suspicion, ISC's policy of diversity in hiring made its employees suspect to nationalists on both sides. A number of political parties also demonized the United States for its role and perceived bias in the conflict, which again created difficulties for those who, in the absence of international staff, were taken as associated with the United States. In interviews in 2008, one person expressed a sense of betrayal by ISC. So after Paul Nuti recalled how hard it was for him to be evacuated to Sofia, a female employee responded as follows:

It was quite frustrating for local staff too, because when you work with Americans and you see that they're evacuating, and from ISC Vermont they're sending these plans for evacuating, transferring all the data and documents, packing, and we're just left there, and we're trying to pretend that we're working—like, not to pretend—but it's really a psychotic thing, you are supposed to act normal and come to work and do all these preparations.

The apparent callousness that this signaled, that the organization attached more value to the preservation of its archival record than the security of its non-US employees, clearly rankled. It also served as a concrete reminder of the hierarchies of power—and, in particular, the increasing pressure that was applied on ISC Macedonia and ISC Vermont to comply with the requirements of USAID and with US government interests more generally. A further demonstration of this occurred soon after Paul Nuti's return from Sofia to resume work as country director. As noted previously, since 1999 the institute had been working with a larger network of Macedonian NGOs than before. In the aftermath of the conflict, the United States committed considerable resources to confidence-building initiatives intended to heal the wounds of armed conflict and avert its resurgence. As well as committing $16 million—more than twice ISC Macedonia's total budget to that point—to media and infrastructure projects across northwestern and northern Macedonia, USAID also pressured ISC to mobilize its NGO network to win public support for the unpopular Framework Agreement. Another ISC member from the period, Zoki Stojkoski, remembered the incident well:

> Somebody came from outside to be responsible for support of the framework agreement. And at that time we had a meeting with him, and USAID, when our position in DemNet in Macedonia was to be flexible but in a way to keep relations with everybody. In terms of our assessment of the situation, if we were asked to implement this campaign, we thought that would be in conflict with our general approach and would further influence our presence and our roles. We as a staff said that we were definitely not interested. And I know that there was a lot of pressure from that particular person . . . some PR guy that was working in similar situations. But it was pretty much top-down approach for us, so we decided, you know. He even said, "You'll see, I'll stop you, your program, you must agree with us" and we said [incredulously], "Come on."

This reaction speaks to the level of engagement and partnership that ISC staff had enjoyed in programming up to this point and also their sense of the challenges of the work and their own standards with regard to fairness, respect, and priorities. The year 2001 presented them with a difficult dilemma, as they acknowledged the right of the communities and organizations that they served to their own opinions and action around the situation in the country, even as they were financially and programmatically entangled with a US donor organization that, whatever its own values, was in turn beholden to the US government.

In this principled stand, ISC's Macedonian staff had the support of key allies within USAID Macedonia as well as ISC Vermont (Nuti 2006). But the incident was indicative of an ongoing shift in the salient understandings and social relations that enmeshed Macedonia with Aidland. It was all too easy for critics to see the outbreak of violence in 2001 as indictment of ISC's patient, community-based approach to building civil society over the prior six years. The appointment of a new USAID administrator by the incoming Republican administration, and an intensified regime of financial audits and reporting requirements, also generated pressure for ISC Vermont to conduct a major strategic review of its operating practices. In the United States, the outcome was an overhaul of ISC's brand, including moving to its new premises in Montpelier, opening an office in Washington DC, and deploying a new professionally designed logo. In Macedonia, Paul Nuti was succeeded by Paul Parks, who had worked for USAID in the past and who replaced ISC's program of broad-spectrum, holistic NGO and community support with a focus on supporting organizations working in priority areas identified by USAID. Parks in turn stayed only one year in post and was succeeded by DemNet's sixth country director, Stephanie Rust, who closed out DemNet IV. Speaking in 2008, she gave this overview of the program's evolution:

> I would say it's gone from "Throw the seeds and the fertilizer wide and let a thousand little flowers bloom"—the George Hamilton– Johnny Appleseed approach—to now, you know, "Let's focus on the plants that survived and flourishing and starting up their own little seedlings" and that kind of thing. But it's been a lot of kinks and I think [apart from] the brief foray—brief, I mean it was kind of big—into CAPS and LEAPS,[10] I would say the general trajectory has been along the lines of USAID, which has been more professional organizations, more policy advocacy type of things . . . that model of NGOs, like you know professional staff, formal organization, working on advocacy issues.

The foci for ISC in this final phase included HIV/AIDS, human trafficking, and work with Roma, Macedonia's most marginalized and stigmatized community in terms of levels of literacy, employment, and living standard. In addition, a number of core staff decided, with the blessing and support of ISC, to set up a "legacy" organization named the Center for Institutional Development and known by its Macedonian acronym CIRa.[11] CIRa was established as a citizen association in early 2004: of its 15 original charter members, 9 had been employees of ISC Macedonia for four years or longer, testimony to the stability of the organization. CIRa inherited ISC Macedonia's office space and equipment, client list, training materials, and the expertise that its staff had accumulated over the course of a total of over 50 years' experience with ISC. From one point of view, this was the "Macedonianization" of assistance, by which a particular set of resources previously distributed throughout an attenuated network was concentrated locally and in the hands of a group of new professionals versed in and committed to community planning and association building. The establishment of CIRa can thus be seen as in itself a (virtuous) fulfillment of the interventionist imagination articulated by President Clinton over a decade earlier, actualized through the intermediating efforts of USAID and ISC.

Discerning Beneficiaries: Where the Asphalt Ends

This conclusion reflects the viewpoint of a variety of mobile professionals located along the aid chain that connects Washington DC, Montpelier, and Skopje, who worked to turn idea into impact. Beyond that, though, the trail of DemNet leads out to a variety of communities and NGOs across Macedonia, where different perspectives on the persistence of virtuality can be glimpsed. In July 2008 Paul Nuti, a member of CIRa, a documentary crew, and I drove from Skopje to the town of Prilep, in western Macedonia, to meet with two grant recipient organizations. The first, the Center for Civic Initiatives (CCI), is a well-established, professionalized NGO. Our questions prompted a narrative that began from the organization's pioneering role in setting up citizen-information centers to increase the transparency and accountability of local government and concluded with a brief account of their now-enlarged portfolio of projects, all implemented with assistance from a range of international donors. One particular result of their growing reputation and reach, they told us, was that they were in a position to help organizations with more limited capacities in grant writing, fund-raising, and strategic planning to find their way. The conversation took place in an air-conditioned conference room surrounded by the trappings of institutional stability and longevity—binder folders of training materials, certificates of participation in multiple trainings, and accreditation from national and international authorities. We spoke mostly in English: the tone was relaxed, the register for the most part quite technical, and the overall feel very much like that in meetings in Skopje and Vermont. It was tempting to conclude that the organization had gone native in Aidland.

After two hours we left to visit the neighborhood of Trizla, home to Prilep's substantial Roma community, where a more recently established Roma NGO that ISC, CIRa, and CCI had all reportedly helped establish was based. Even though Trizla is within the city limits, the sense of distance was palpable; for all the active collaboration between the three organizations, CCI and CIRa staff still have a hard time finding their way through the unpaved streets of the Roma community. In the end, after extended cell phone conversations failed to clarify matters, the NGO leader had to walk down to meet us where the asphalt ended, and we bumped up the narrow dirt road to our destination. Inside, he had assembled a group of citizens, including other NGO leaders

(Roma and non-Roma) as well as representatives of a Roma political party, who had been waiting for us for some time. Several neighborhood children were using the four or five desktop computers in the hot, crowded room and continued to do so throughout our meeting.

Our conversation here was conducted in Macedonian and was much more closely concerned with the stuff of community activism. Our primary host, together with the other NGO representatives, talked about the need for multiconstituency collaboration, involving governmental and nongovernmental actors. He used as his primary example the main output from the community's DemNet grant: a community action plan produced by Trizla's citizens in 2003. He pressed the case for local government—including the political representatives present—to implement the plan and thereby show that citizens' voices counted.

The party spokesmen, though, disagreed. They made clear their frustration with the NGO talk, suggesting that talk of "multiethnic collaboration" was an unproductive distraction from their Roma constituents' real needs—jobs. So in place of democracy promotion, they said, foreigners should invest in new factories, which would generate reliable employment for less-educated citizens: only the provision of basic financial security to families, they said, would create the conditions for the next generation to stay in school and thereby at least move toward genuine opportunity and inclusion.

It was a contentious, compelling meeting, in which the range of challenges still facing Macedonia's Roma community and the range of tactics that different leaders espouse were made abundantly clear. It concluded, though, with an abrupt change of topic. After 90 minutes of passionate advocacy for the importance of DemNet for his community's future, the NGO director turned to the CIRa member (who had been guiding the conversation) and posed a seemingly simple question: Who created ISC, and who created CIRa? After the CIRa member provided an answer laying out a similar timeline to the one provided previously, the NGO director offered a clarification of his interest:

> Do you know why I asked this question? Because you forced me to create and give you a project in three days, so that you could give me some equipment. That is why I asked why ISC founded CIRa or, again, why CIRa asks its partners to help out, quickly. At a particular moment, CIRa turns to its own people [that is, its partners] so that it can provide some assistance to them, at the end of the year. I am grateful. That was the question directly to you.

What this comment revealed was that behind the seemingly easy question lay an acute awareness of the codependent relations that constitute Aidland. The Roma director understood clearly where his organization stood in the hierarchical order—and he also, clearly, felt warmth and gratitude toward members of CIRa as well as to Paul Nuti, whom he remembered from a visit back before 2002. But he also recognized that CIRa and ISC were enmeshed in a larger set of expectations set from further up the aid chain, which centered around meeting spending targets by the end of a funding cycle. This might seem distant from the activity of NGOs like his. But the different domains were in fact entangled together by the equipment that his organization receives and the line item that, together with administrative overheads, makes expenditure match projection for the US government auditors of NGOs' books. ISC, he was suggesting, as well as CIRa and also (though he did not name it) CCI, depended for their ongoing existence and purpose on one another: what drove the economy of which they were all a part, though, was the activity of NGOs like his. Their air-conditioned offices, vehicles, and technical discussions were all built on, or perhaps "over," his labor. From where he stood, they operated at one or more remove from the messy realities with which he had to contend.

Conclusion: Virtual Places, Actual Trails?

This seemingly offhand comment, the last piece of material I offer from interviews, came almost as an afterthought at the end of a 90-minute session, at the close of a full day's travel and discussion, in the course of an intense two-week period of back-to-back interviews and focus groups, which was part of a research project stretching over a year or more. But that, of course, is what ethnography, even in the punctate, multisited form represented here, can provide. Prague, Washington DC, Montpelier, Skopje, Prilep, and Trizla—or, at least, briefing rooms, conference rooms, and offices in those places—are just some of the sites along the attenuated trail of DemNet.

I conclude with this observation from an old man in the economically depressed quarter of a provincial town in a tiny young country, because it so succinctly captures the radically contingent status of these two NGOs—one Macedonian, one North American. An important subtext—never explicitly raised—was the widely known friction that had arisen between CIRa and ISC since CIRa's formation in 2004. Stephanie Rust did not come to Skopje simply to complete Paul Parks's term and close out the program: she successfully applied for a USAID continuation program in Macedonia, the Civil Society Strengthening Project. ISC partnered with CIRa in the application; in early

2008, though, ISC Skopje severed its organizational relationship with CIRa, which had been operating the corporate philanthropy promotion component of the award. Instead, ISC supported a new NGO to perform this same role, which was set up by a CIRa member who had been working on philanthropy before leaving CIRa in early summer 2008.

ISC's continuing presence in Macedonia, after ISC apparently handed off its portfolio to CIRa, confused many Macedonians, and the course described previously—which in the name of strengthening civil society undermined CIRa—added to that sense of bewilderment. Yet in this event, I suggest, the Roma NGO director correctly saw a larger pattern of relations at work. In particular, the virtual and actual dimensions of Aidland are not as easily untangled as we might suggest. As Apthorpe aptly noted, Aidland must be envisaged as constituted by paths of movement, as much as by places of work, residence, or leisure of particular, determinate types: it is everthrough as much as it is everywhere. Each of the localities visited in this chapter is made out of its relations with others and constituted by the virtuality and actuality of those relations: the same can be said of the voices represented here. The quality of these relations is also dynamic and susceptible to modification in ways that affect the entire system. When, for example, in 2001 ISC Vermont followed the terms of its agreement with USAID and secured the financial records of its activities in Macedonia, the action impacted the way in which Macedonian employees perceived their own relationship with the organization: the actualization of an obligation up the chain simultaneously virtualized what had been built as a horizontal and reciprocal bond between ISC and its local staff. In similar fashion, the decentralization of funding decisions over DemNet to embassies actualized a national frame of locality and virtualized the regional dimensions. And in the opposite direction, program staff and grantees during and after the program recognized the ways in which actual conditions on the ground were continuously shaped by less tangible priorities being set and followed elsewhere.

Living in, traveling through, or acquiring citizenship in Aidland, then, is not quite like doing so in either Kilburn or Second Life. In the former case, Massey alerts us to the central role of British imperialist history in constituting an apparently localized tapestry of ethnic and economic diversity. In the latter, Boellstorff takes note of the ways in which personal boundaries and social expectations seemingly anchored in actual physically proximate interaction get reinscribed via keyboard, mouse, and avatar. What these innovative theorists share is an acute awareness of how the play of actual and virtual relations shapes these contexts of human place making. Here I have explored only one fragment of one of Aidland's trails, stretching between President Clinton's Prague remarks in 1994 and the Roma NGO director's query in 2008. But I hope to have demonstrated the ways in which theoretically informed ethnography can enrich our understanding of the consequential effects of seemingly attenuated connections.

Notes

1. The abbreviation DemNet is used throughout this chapter, though some authors use the acronym DNP (Democracy Network Program).

2. The Center for Institutional Development (CIRa) provided considerable support to our research. Our research was funded by a grant from IREX—an organization that, we learned late in our research, competed for USAID contracts with ISC elsewhere in the Balkans. For a discussion of some of the issues around co-optation facing ethnographers studying NGOs, see Markowitz (2001).

3. See "The President's News Conference With Visegrad Leaders in Prague" at http://www.presidency.ucsb.edu/ws/index.php?pid=49832&st=democracy&st1. Accessed March 29, 2010.

4. While many anthropologists continue to use pseudonyms in their research, in this chapter I use the actual names of all organizations and individuals. We were transparent about our plans to publish our research, and we obtained signed permissions from all interviewees.

5. The Support for East European Democracy (hence SEED) act was signed into law in 1989, and the Freedom for Russia and Emerging Eurasian Democracies and Open Markets (hence FREEDOM) Support Act in 1992, both by President George W. Bush.

6. For a short history of Ekoglasnost's formation and early activities, see Baumgartl (1993).

7. The choice of *trajni*—long lasting—to translate *sustainable* is considered by many staff as a suboptimal translation. Some suggest *izdržlivni*, or enduring or persisting, would have more faithfully captured the nuances of the term.

8. DEM was an acronym for the *Dviženje na ekologistite na Makedonija*, or Movement of Ecologists (more accurately, ecologically minded citizens) in Macedonia, established at least two years before the invention of DemNet.

9. This increase was overseen by USAID program officer Kathy Stermer, who had previously served as chief of the Democracy and Governance Division in Slovakia and shaped the DemNet program in that country.

10. CAPs are community action programs, and LEAPS are local environmental action programs. On their conceptualization, see Markowitz (2000); on their implementation, see Cook and Popovski (2002) and Wilhelm (2002). For a critique of their implication with neoliberalism, see Buzarovski (2001, 2004).

11. Centar za Institucionalen Razvoj.

References

Apthorpe, Raymond. 2003. Virtual reality: An allegory of international aidland and its people. Paper presented to a conference on Order and Disjuncture: The Organisation of Aid and Development, London, School of Asian and Oriental Studies.

———. 2005. Postcards from Aidland. Paper presented at the Institute of Development Studies, Brighton, United Kingdom.

Baumgartl, Bernd. 1993. Environmental protest as a vehicle for transition: The case of Ekoglasnost in Bulgaria. In *Environment and democratic transition: Policy and politics in Central and Eastern Europe*, ed. Anna Vari and Pal Tamas, 157–75. Dordrecht, the Netherlands: Kluwer Academic.

Boellstorff, Tom. 2008. *Coming of age in Second Life: An anthropologist explores the virtually human*. Princeton, NJ: Princeton University Press.

Brown, Keith. 2009. Do we know how yet? Insider perspectives on international democracy promotion in the western Balkans. *Southeastern Europe* 33 (July): 1–25.

Brown, K., and D. Theodossopoulos. 2003. Rearranging solidarity: Conspiracy and world order in Greek and Macedonian commentaries of Kosovo. *Journal of Southern Europe and the Balkans* 5 (3): 315–35.

Bryan, F.M. 2004. *Real democracy: The New England town meeting and how it works*. Chicago: University of Chicago Press.

Buzarovski, Stefan. 2001. Local environmental action plans and the "glocalisation" of postsocialist governance: The Macedonian experience. *GeoJournal* 55:555–68.

———. 2004. The growing role of civil society in neo-liberalizing state: Environmental education in the Republic of Macedonia. *International Research in Geographical and Environmental Education* 13 (1): 79–89.

Carothers, Thomas. 1999. *Aiding democracy abroad: The learning curve*. Washington, DC: Carnegie Endowment for International Peace.

Cook, Thomas J., and Mihajlo Popovski. 2002. *Evaluation of the Macedonia DemNet program, task order no. 805*, 1–59. Washington DC: USAID.

Denskus, Tobias. 2007. What are all these people doing in their offices all day? The challenges of writing-up stories from "post-conflict" Kathmandu. *Journal of Peace, Conflict and Development* 11 (November). http://www.peacestudiesjournal.org.uk.

Escobar, Arturo. 1995. Imagining a post-development era. In *The power of development*, ed. Jonathan Crush, 211–28. London: Routledge.

Li, Tania. 2007. *The will to improve: Governmentality, development and the practice of politics*. Durham, NC: Duke University Press.

Marcus, George. 1995. Ethnography in/of the world system: The emergence of multi-sited ethnography. *Annual Review of Anthropology* 24:95–117.

Markowitz, Paul. 2000. *Guide to implementing local environmental action programs in Central and Eastern Europe*, 1–166. Szentendre, Hungary: Regional Environmental Center for Central and Eastern Europe and Institute for Sustainable Communities. http://www.iscvt.org/who_we_are/publications/LEAP%20Guide.pdf.

Massey, Doreen. 1993. Power geometry and a progressive sense of place. In *Mapping the futures: Local cultures, global change*, ed. Jon Bird, Barry Curtis, Tim Putnam, George Robertson, and Lisa Tickner, 60–70. London: Routledge.

Nuti, Paul. 2006. Toward reflective practice: Understanding and negotiating democracy in Macedonia. In *Transacting transition: The micropolitics of democracy assistance in the former Yugoslavia*, ed. Keith Brown, 69–94. Bloomfield, CT: Kumarian Press.

Petrescu, Dan. 2000. Civil society in Romania: From donor supply to citizen demand. In *Funding virtue: Civil society aid and democracy promotion*, ed. Marina Ottaway and Thomas Carothers, 217–42. Washington, DC: Carnegie Endowment for International Peace.

Putnam, R., with R. Leonardi and R.Y. Nanetti. 1993. *Making democracy work: Civic traditions in modern Italy*. Princeton, NJ: Princeton University Press.

Regulska, Joanna. 1998. Building local democracy: The role of western assistance in Poland. *Voluntas: International Journal of Voluntary and Nonprofit Organizations* 10 (1): 61–71.

Shore, Cris, and Sue Wright. 1997. Policy: A new field of anthropology. In *Anthropology of policy: Critical perspectives on governance and power*, ed. Cris Shore and Sue Wright, 3–33. London: Routledge.

Wallace, Tina, Lisa Bornstein, and Jennifer Chapman. 2006. *The aid chain: Coercion and commitment in development NGOs*. Warwickshire UK: ITDG.

Wedel, Janine. 1998. *Collision and collusion: The strange case of western aid to Eastern Europe, 1989–1998*. New York: St. Martin's Press.

Wilhelm, Doug. 2002. *Shaping peaceful change: A field report on building civil society in Macedonia*, 1–18. Skopje, Macedonia, and Montpelier, VT: Institute for Sustainable Communities.

7

Anybody at Home?
The Inhabitants of Aidland

Anne-Meike Fechter

Over the past few years, the term "Aidland" has slowly but steadily made its way into academic accounts of the world of aid and development (Apthorpe 2005, in press; Eyben 2007; Denskus 2007). It seems to have a resonance with academics and practitioners alike—hence also its inclusion in the title of this collection. Apthorpe (this volume), who can be credited with bringing the term into wider circulation within discourses of development, readily points out that "Aidland" was coined as a metaphor, a rhetorical device that suggests particular traits and characteristics of the development sector and that conceptualizes, in a shorthand, the world of aid as a complex, almost self-contained web of institutions, people, and activities, with sets of attitudes, discourses, and practices all of its own.

As such, "Aidland" links to terms such as the "Aidbuck" (Shutt 2008) and to broader concepts such as "Aidnography" (Gould 2004). A risk contained in using metaphors, however, as Lakoff and Johnson (1980) argued, is not only that they possess agentive powers of their own and shape people's behavior in accordance with the metaphor but that they may reify and render simple what are more intricate realities. Thinking of a uniform sphere of Aidland, inhabited by a clearly defined type of aid worker, would not be appropriate, as becomes evident in Apthorpe's own observations (this volume). I suggest, though, that the idea of Aidland with aid people has heuristic potential and may generate key questions about who aid people are.

As argued in the introduction to this volume, the bulk of ethnographic work on Aidland has so far been focused on its institutions and its policy production and practices (Mosse 2005; Mosse and Lewis 2006; Mosse in press (a), in press (b)) but less so on the individuals who inhabit it: the "citizens of Aidland," as they could be called (though see Hilhorst [2003] on NGOs, as well as Stirrat [2000, 2008] and Rajak and Stirrat [in press] on development workers). In the wake of efforts to document the inner workings of Aidland institutions, the roles and agency of individuals associated with them—especially those of implementers of aid—have been somewhat neglected. This has occurred in spite of the emphasis given in recent decades to "participatory approaches" in development practice and of the recognition of the importance of individual actors, both local and international, for development processes. The present chapter thus aims to address these issues—that is, the risk of reifying Aidland and its constituent parts, as well as the relative invisibility of people in discussions of Aidland so far. In the first instance, the chapter therefore attempts to populate Aidland through identifying the people who might be considered its inhabitants, however transient they may be. Through this, it aims to inspect more closely the uniform category of the aid community or the aid workers, who are at the center of this collection. This chapter is intended as a companion piece to Apthorpe's chapter (this volume), which discursively traverses Aidland, highlighting some of its poignancies and contradictions. The issues identified in these two pieces and in the introduction thus contribute to an agenda for future ethnographic work on aid workers. This chapter's purpose is thus to show that in-depth studies of "people in aid" may produce innovative lines of inquiry and emergent themes in aid work that have not been systematically pursued so far and thus contribute to a more comprehensive understanding of development processes.

Thinking about what kinds of aid workers there are also means probing the validity of the term "aid worker" as an analytical category. If these people turn out to be so diverse, how meaningful is the term "aid worker" to describe them, whose only commonality may be that they are involved with development activities? Although I cannot attempt to answer this question here, I hope to contribute to the discussion through both the case profiles to follow and the shared issues arising from them. With regard to self-ascription, there is evidence that the term "aid worker" has some currency among practitioners themselves, as visible, for example, in the name of the Internet-based support group Aid Workers Network (www.aidworkers.net); in a similar vein, an organization for those working in humanitarian human resources is called People in Aid (www.peopleinaid.org). To what extent the label "aid worker" is used by individuals to self-identify varies. Some of my interlocutors found the term inappropriate for their role and preferred to describe themselves as "managers" or "administrators," especially if their work was based in the country office rather than mostly in the field. Also, many were keen to distinguish themselves from humanitarian relief workers, who are typically concerned with short-term emergency response operations. Many of those working for NGOs or international aid agencies, however, seemed at ease with describing themselves as "working in aid" or "working in development." One might take this as an indication that the term "aid worker" is a meaningful one—at the very least for practitioners themselves.

As part of an ethnographic approach, the basis for the discussion here is research conducted in one particular country—Cambodia—to allow for in-depth familiarity with a small set of aid workers but also to share aid workers' experience of a particular place and participate as far as possible in their lives there. This is useful, I suggest, to enable comparisons between them, as they share their current country of work and residence, even if they differ in many or most other aspects of their lives. Cambodia itself constitutes a good case study, since it ranks among the poorest and most aid-dependent countries in Southeast Asia and has been receiving substantial foreign assistance since the arrival of the United Nations Transitional Authority (UNTAC) in 1992. Consequently, there is a continuing strong presence of national and international NGOs and bi- and multilateral aid agencies and their personnel there. According to latest estimates, the number of NGOs registered in Cambodia is near 1,800 (Samnang 2010, 2), and the substantial presence of international aid workers is especially visible in the capital, Phnom Penh, but also, to a lesser extent, in the provinces.

Cambodia, and the nationally and professionally diverse aid community it houses, therefore lends itself to studying aid workers. These particular circumstances though also mean that manifestations of Aidland can be observed in especially pronounced forms there. While insights gained in Cambodia may thus not be representative of other countries, I argue that they nevertheless hold relevance for, and resonate with, situations found in other parts of the developing world.

The data that I draw on for this chapter were gathered as part of a broader research project on international aid workers in Cambodia, considering them as migrants or mobile professionals.[1] Fieldwork for this project was conducted in Cambodia, the United Kingdom, and Germany. Data collection took place during a series of fieldtrips in 2007, 2009, and 2010; a total of 48 informants have been interviewed in depth so far. The focus of the study was not development organizations but individuals, who were accessed initially through personal contacts and then through widening social networks. The main methods used were participant observation, such as accompanying aid workers on trips to the provinces or meetings and workshops in the capital, as well as semistructured interviews, informal conversations, and material such as aid workers' blogs and memoirs. The names and some of the personal details of informants presented here have been changed to preserve their anonymity and confidentiality.

Who Are "People Working in Aid"?

During my fieldwork in Phnom Penh, an informant once commented that the aid community there resembled a zoo—referring to the sheer diversity of the people who were in some form associated with aid or development work. Identifying subgroups among them could be likened to the efforts described by the writer Jose Luis Borges, from an essay titled "The Analytical Language of John Wilkins" (1964, 101–03):

> These ambiguities, redundancies, and deficiencies recall those attributed by Dr. Franz Kuhn to a certain Chinese encyclopaedia called the *Heavenly Emporium of Benevolent Knowledge*. In its distant pages it is written that animals are divided into (a) those that belong to the emperor; (b) embalmed ones; (c) those that are trained; (d) suckling pigs; (e) mermaids; (f) fabulous ones; (g) stray dogs; (h) those that are included in this classification; (i) those that tremble as if they were mad; (j) innumerable ones; (k) those drawn with a very fine camel's-hair brush; (l) etcetera; (m) those that have just broken the flower vase; (n) those that at a distance resemble flies.

As Borges mockingly suggested, the lines along which scholars subdivide groups sometimes appear ridiculous or at least questionable. Parallels might be drawn here between difficulties in classifying animals and aid workers. Applying the spirit of Borges's list to the world of aid, one might ask what the equivalent would be to distinguishing animals according to whether they are embalmed, mermaids, or have just broken the flower vase. Such an exercise might loosen preconceived ideas about who aid workers are and counteract essentializing tendencies in thinking about Aidland's population. A list of attributes to distinguish one subgroup of aid workers from another might divide them into those who (a) live in a traditional wooden house on stilts; (b) see themselves as managers; (c) have just left high school; (d) want to pursue a comfortable lifestyle; (e) have taken Cambodian citizenship; (f) are feminists; (g) think rescuing a single soul is enough; (h) are corrupt, incompetent, or greedy; (i) use local sex workers; (j) adopt a Cambodian child; (k) could not get a job at home; (l) fly business class; (m) belong to a religious organization; or (n) are divorced.

I suggest that rather than abolishing classificatory efforts in the face of difficulties in determining who are aid workers, one could instead identify possible lines of division and exploit their heuristic potential.

To populate the category of "aid worker" with individuals and highlight commonalities as well as fundamental differences between them, I present a cast of six characters who were among the aid workers I encountered during my fieldwork in Cambodia. Having sketched their personal and professional situations, I discuss shared lines of inquiry that might emerge from these.

Russell, the Independent Volunteer

We meet Russell in a small hamlet, some kilometers outside of a provincial town, accessed by a dirt road. Wearing a faded T-shirt, flip-flops, and shorts, he is wiping the sweat off his face and talks enthusiastically. He is standing in front of a simple house with a wooden frame, a raised platform on stilts, the walls and roof made of woven bamboo leaves. Russell, an Australian, is in his mid-20s and has recently started a project that works with poor villagers to help them set up, repair, and complete their own houses, within a scheme that requires families first to acquire and prepare rudimentary building materials, with Russell's program then matching their efforts, supplying the rest of the building materials. Together with international volunteers, the family members themselves, and local people, complete building their house.

He says, "We help them to have a secure home, shelter, which is a basis for them being able to look for work, and generally to plan their lives and livelihoods on this basis." Russell is a trained car mechanic who had been working in Australia for several years before coming to Cambodia on a holiday. "When I saw the place, I really liked it, and I also thought I can do something here." Enabled partly by private donations that he collected on his return to Australia, he came to Cambodia some time later and set up a scheme that invites international volunteers who are often passing through to help build houses; he works with Cambodians living in the area to identify families who are most in need of secure housing. "These are mostly seasonal laborers working, and since it's dry season, they don't have any income at the moment," he explains and gestures toward small groups of villagers who are sitting on wooden platforms underneath their houses, many of which are in a state of disrepair. "We think that having a proper, simple house is the launching pad for all kinds of things. Our scheme links the house-building to the kids getting to school regularly, and it generally gives them a feeling that they can manage their livelihoods better."

Russell is aware, however, that his own savings, which he has partly used to establish this project, will run out, and he will have to look to sustainable sources of funding, but he is hopeful. His girlfriend has joined him in Cambodia, and they are thinking of setting up a small business as a basis of supporting their own presence here.

Martha, the Human Rights Activist

Martha is an American in her early 30s, whom I meet on a Saturday morning, as she is cycling to her office at a local NGO. She is a human rights activist and has been working in Cambodia, for several different organizations, for the past five years. She came as a traveler to Cambodia in the late 1990s, before completing a postgraduate degree in the United States, and then was offered a job with a local NGO in a northeastern province working on rural health issues. After two years working there, she relocated to Phnom Penh to take up a job with another local NGO, with an emphasis on human rights issues. Martha speaks Khmer fluently and is living with her Cambodian partner. She shakes her head as she tells me about the human rights situation in the country, which she thinks has been declining over the past few years:

> There is just so much to do. It's crazy. I have to constantly do firefighting. I'm responsible for linking several organizations working in this area, and I constantly get phone calls about what's been happening, there are Cambodian activists, colleagues, who are being threatened or shot or just disappear. Something happens all the time. Then we have to put out statements, coordinate campaigns, work on policy documents. I am constantly behind and can't support every organization that needs it.

Martha is usually in the office by 7:00 a.m. and rarely leaves it before 6:00 or 7:00 p.m. This work pressure also means that she is on the way to work on a Saturday. "There won't be everybody in the office, of course, but some," she explains. She is being paid a considerably higher wage than her Cambodian colleagues, but she points out, "I also have a lot more responsibility, I have to work harder, and that is what I'm being paid for." For the time being, her foreseeable future lies in Cambodia. "We have a nice, cheap apartment that we rent in the center of Phnom Penh, we have lots of Cambodian friends, and here is where my work is, where I want to be."

About two years after our initial meeting, Martha experiences a bad period at work, followed by disagreements with her new boss, and decides, after having spent six years in Cambodia, to return to the United States. There she takes up a post with an international human rights NGO, with an emphasis on Southeast Asia, utilizing her specialist regional expertise. She is happy with her new job and feels that this was the right move to make at this point in her life.

Robert, the Civil Servant

Robert, a Canadian, is in his early 30s and works for a bilateral aid agency. After studying for a postgraduate degree in international relations in Canada and doing a stint as a volunteer in Bolivia, he applied for a government trainee scheme and has since worked in two African countries for several years and has been in Cambodia for about a year. Robert enjoys living in Phnom Penh: "There are great leisure facilities, I can do all kinds of sports, squash, golf, football, you name it. I've got good friends, both here in the city and across the region. I wouldn't want to stay here forever, but it's good for now." Robert mainly works with the Cambodian government on national initiatives. "We don't do projects," he explains. "We advise them in implementing long-term programs, such as their decentralization program, and good governance." He is wearing a smart shirt, pin-striped trousers, and leather shoes, and his plastic ID card is dangling from his neck.

Although he finds his work interesting and rewarding to some extent, he is slightly wistful about the time spent in African countries. "I had more in-depth knowledge of the history of the place, politics, and so on. I spoke the language to a decent level. . . . I knew more how to do things. It was a very different feel." He speaks some Khmer but only enough to get around in everyday life; his actual work, he says, is conducted in English. His girlfriend, whom he met at university, is an independent development consultant and joins him in Cambodia in between her stints working in other overseas countries. They aim to coordinate their career plans as much as possible and have talked about returning to Canada to start a family before moving on to new overseas posts.

Christina, the Technical Expert

Christina, a Scandinavian woman in her mid-40s, works for a multilateral aid agency; she considers herself a technical expert and has worked in a succession of countries on the same broad issues, matching her specialist expertise. She has been married for over 10 years, and she and her husband adopted two children from one of the countries she worked in. She and her husband both have professional expertise that predestines them to work abroad, and this has been a shared goal since the time they met at university. In the course of events, however, her husband has agreed to take the role of accompanying spouse, looking after the children and household, while she has taken on the role of main breadwinner. She appreciates her husband's work but also relishes the power and responsibility she has both professionally and privately. So far, she has not spent more than about three years in each of the countries she has worked in; she finds this refreshing rather than tiresome and finds that she becomes jaded if she stays in one place any longer than that: "I like to have a fresh challenge and bring new perspectives to the situations I'm brought into." She also appreciates the ease with which friendly relations are established between international aid workers, though she concedes that it can become wearing to reestablish them time after time and finds that the depth of engagement with others can be limited. She enjoys her lifestyle, her job, and what being part of the international community affords her, such as the availability of good international schools for her children; she attends dance classes and barbecues and goes on weekend trips within Cambodia or occasionally to other countries in the region. While in Cambodia, she is mindful of where she would like to work next and is keen to maintain relations with people in headquarters and in other regions, to pave the way for her to take up a job in the region she has set her sights on.

Helene, the Lifelong Aid Worker

Helene is in her late 50s and has worked overseas, with some intermittent periods in the Netherlands, since her early 20s. She is a trained nurse and has worked for different international organizations across a number of countries over the years, living between two and five years in each. Her stations have included, among others, Rwanda, Ethiopia, Pakistan, Afghanistan, and India, and now she is halfway through a four-year posting in Cambodia. She is based in a provincial town, working at the state-run hospital, and is involved in training nurses. Helene is constantly in motion, with short white hair and a scarf made of local fabric, and is wearing comfortable clothes and sandals. She talks fondly of her recent return trip to the Netherlands on holiday, where she had been traveling around, visiting friends, and spending time with her aging mother. "We had some good conversations," she says contentedly. Helene finds that her work in the hospital, after initial difficulties, is slowly showing results. She has a good relationship with her counterpart, a middle-aged Cambodian trained nurse, who is currently having domestic difficulties and is trying to divorce her estranged husband. Helene says, "We are talking about that a lot. I think I am one of the few people she can really confide in." Helene plans to stay in Cambodia for a few more years: "Who knows, when I am done here, I might stay on, because there are still so many places I want to go to!" Her next planned holiday trip is to Myanmar, which she will undertake together with an American friend, in her 60s, who is working as a volunteer for an international NGO. Helene is on friendly terms with many of the other aid workers in town, who informally socialize in only one or two bars. Some of them she knows through her work in the hospital, and when they get together in the evenings, their chat often turns to work. "It's sometimes hard to switch off," she admits, "but I like this life."

Pierre, the Cambodian Resident

Pierre lives in a pleasant house that he built himself overlooking a river. A French national and medical doctor by training, he first came in contact with Cambodians when he worked as a doctor in the refugee camps on the Thai border in 1979, where he treated, among others, malnourished children who had fled from Cambodia after the end of the Khmer Rouge regime and Vietnamese troops entered Cambodia. He then stayed on and has lived in Cambodia, for the most part, for the past 30 years. He was given official recognition by the government and has taken on Cambodian citizenship. He has been working in different capacities and in different provinces over the years and is running a charitable foundation, which works to provide poor and academically bright children with an education, enabling them to finish high school, and supports their further training or university until they are able to sustain themselves. He is not married and lives on a large plot of land he bought, where he built a house. A bunch of elderly roaming dogs, motorbikes, and a pick-up truck surround his property. The sounds of geese squeaking drift over. His veranda, furnished with faded rattan and wooden chairs, is facing a river. He explains,

> In order to support the children, I rely on private donations that I'm raising all the time. I have a few people who have been very good over the years, they sponsor individual children, or sometimes many. But the last two years have been hard; my sponsors are getting older. The financial crisis is a problem, people don't have that much to spare, they don't know what they are doing for their retirement either.

The children need help, he says, as some of them are missing a parent or are orphans, and although state schools are meant to be free, teachers often require children to pay for lessons, since teachers' salaries are very low—sometimes about $40 a month, which is not enough to sustain them. He explains, "We go through the villages and identify who is very poor and academically very bright, and those get our help. I need 2,000 riel [about 50 US cents] to pay for one student's lessons for one day at secondary school." He talks about a celebration he held recently in his garden, where all the children whom he had supported over the years gathered: "Everybody was there, it was like a family."

These brief vignettes, the cast of six characters from Aidland, are in the first instance a reminder that an ideal type of aid worker does not exist. As mentioned in the introduction to this volume, in the public imagination, aid workers are often perceived as people who are toiling away in selfless endeavor for years in a remote part of a tropical countryside, living simply on a meager allowance, and working to establish a local basket-weaving cooperative. At the same time, the other stereotype looming large is that established by critical texts such as Hancock's book *Lords of Poverty* (1989): they are the "aid bureaucrats" or "development managers," who are based in the capital in air-conditioned offices and whose working days are filled with meetings with government officials and international agency staff and who rarely ever leave the city and the comfortable lifestyles it offers. Considering the previous small selection of aid workers' lives, it becomes clear that both extreme types of aid worker exist—as well as many in between. As indicated at the beginning, I will take the vignettes as a starting point to explore commonalities and differences between these people by discussing a series of issues that pertain to all of their lives, albeit in different forms and with different consequences. Thus the lines that divide aid workers also tell us more about who they are. In particular, I will be discussing in turn their motivations, mobility and the life course, their relations to place, and the futures of Aidland.

Mixed Motivations

As de Jong (this volume) pointed out in her chapter, a related set of assumptions among the general public in addition to those mentioned previously is that aid workers have come to developing countries to help. If we consider the six individuals just sketched, however, it becomes apparent that in many cases, their motivations for entering the world of development were mixed. This is not to say that the desire to help was not important or not existent. Russell, for example, after having traveled in Cambodia, thought that he might be able "to do something" there and returned with the explicit aim to improve poor people's housing. He also explained to me that this opportunity had come up at a time after he had already been working for several years as a car mechanic and that it was, he said, "time for a change," a desire for new challenges, which setting up a project in Cambodia would fulfill.

Similarly, Pierre first worked in his capacity as a medical doctor in the refugee camps on the Cambodian–Thai border; it emerged gradually over a number of years that the life he was able to establish in Cambodia suited him in many ways. Expounding the virtues of living in a tropical climate, he recounts, for example, "I have not spent a single winter in Europe since 1982. . . . I was one of the world's first climate refugees, hehe," followed by a hearty cackle. The fact that Pierre might thoroughly enjoy himself in this respect does not diminish the benefits he is able to provide to the poor students sponsored by his foundation. In the case of Christina, in comparison, the main drivers for her life abroad are associated with her profession: she relishes the challenges of implementing democratization programs and the problems this poses in different country contexts; she is not concerned about her limited involvement with each country in turn and is explicit that furthering her career and her reputation as an expert in this area is of central importance for her.

While Helene shares with Christina the relatively high mobility, having worked in more than six countries in Africa and Asia as an advisor, she was lured from the beginning, as she says, by a sense of adventure and the desire to escape the social limitations of her close family and small hometown, which she experienced as particularly oppressive as she grew up in the 1950s. Despite the hardships and personal risks she faced, for example, working in Afghanistan as a single woman in the 1970s, her aid worker's life abroad also brought her a considerable freedom from the restrictions of life in her home country at the time.

It should be clear that detailing such mixed motivations or the financial, professional, or personal benefits derived by aid workers through their work abroad is not meant to diminish their altruistic intentions and efforts. Rather I suggest that the diversity of people's motivations visible in this small selection belies a general, often implicit assumption that aid workers' motivations are, or should be, purely altruistic. I suggest that recognizing the intricate array of people's passions, attitudes, and perceived rewards is useful for raising questions on the moral economies of aid work and aid workers, both in their own minds and in the Western popular imagination.

Mobility, Uncertainty and the Life Course

Apart from people's motivations, a further dimension that is central to understanding aid workers' lives is their mobility—and, as its flipside, their relations to particular places and regions, which I turn to next. As the case examples suggest, the aid workers' length of stay in one country varies considerably and often depends on circumstance: funding for projects may be extended or cut short, people may leave at short notice, and vacancies and new opportunities may arise unexpectedly. Helene, for example, has spent most of her life on different postings abroad, but while she always harbored the wish to work overseas, at several points she returned to the Netherlands, and it was not clear at each turn whether she would be able to reembark on an overseas career. As far as her future is concerned, she wants to retire in the Netherlands, but when exactly that will be remains uncertain. A similar open-endedness character-izes Christina's situation: as she now has a so-called overseas CV, her skills set is most suitable for work in developing countries rather than in her Western home country. While a series of further posts abroad are thus most likely in store for her, the when and where is to be determined. For people like her and Robert, job mobility and therefore a limited stay in Cambodia are a given and intrinsic to the nature of their careers and employers.

In the case of Martha and Russell, the length of their time in Cambodia, for example, is to some extent in their own hands. Russell will see how things develop with his project, and he is comfortable with not knowing exactly how long his Cambodian venture will last. At the time when I first met Martha, she broadly expected to settle in Cambodia and perhaps to even start a family there. When I interviewed her two years later, however, she had left Cambodia and was living and working in Washington.

As such unpredictability is relatively typical, many aid workers frequently have to consider the next stage of their career, job, or project and which orga-nizations they will be working with and where. Neither their professional nor their geographical trajectories are mapped out long in advance. In contrast, though, the question of mobility does not arise for Pierre in this form; as far as he is concerned, he plans to stay in Cambodia. The only issue arising might be being cared for in old age, since he would have to organize his own support network, in absence of provision by the Cambodian state.

Working in the development sector thus by definition involves working outside of one's home country, and for many, moving from one developing country to another is an intrinsic feature of their professional lives. One issue arising is how this regular change is experienced. For some, like Christina, who consider themselves "technical experts," this is something they thrive on. As she says, "Every country is a new challenge for me. I love getting into new situ-ations, having to figure out my way around. I wouldn't want to stay in a one place for too long. I think I would get jaded and complacent." Even among those people who envisaged staying in Cambodia for the foreseeable future, like Russell and Martha, many valued being in a position to determine how long to stay or when to leave. At the same time, for those who are employed on fixed-term contracts or for a particular project, this uncertainty can be also wearing. For example, in conversations between Helene and her friends, it was frequently debated whether to extend one's stay for another six months or a year or not at all; possible future destinations, which jobs were on offer in the region or with the same organizations, and the advantages and disadvantages of one's current workplace were weighed up against other interests such as being curious about other countries and preferences for certain employers. Some individuals expressed anxiety about regularly having to consider the prospect of identifying new job opportunities or projects to work on and how to avoid possibly stressful periods of unemployment. Such concerns might overshadow their lives months before their current contract is going to come to an end.

Relations to Place, and Local Knowledge

Mobility is thus an intrinsic feature of aid workers' lives, whether this consists of residing long-term outside of their country of origin or moving every two to three years from one developing country to another. A pertinent question, then, is how aid workers relate to place, including their countries of origin, places where they have worked before, and where they currently reside. Future destinations also matter, that is, countries where aid workers would like to move to next or favored places to spend their retirement. It is useful, again, to look at the far ends of the spectrum to grasp the divergence between people's engagements with a place. Pierre, for instance, has witnessed firsthand the political and social developments in Cambodia over the past 30 years; he speaks Khmer fluently; he is well-known in his local community and beyond; he regularly visits villages to identify what he calls "very poor and very bright" children to see if they might qualify for the support of his foundation; he is used to negotiating with schools, state institutions, and government officials; and children who have graduated from his program have now settled all over the country. He is therefore one among a relatively small group of foreigners, casually referred to as "old-timers," who often know each other and who share an intimate knowledge of the country. In comparison, people like Martha, who lived in Cambodia for about five years, often speak Khmer to a level where they can conduct business. As an activist, Martha has a good understanding of, and close relationships with, those Cambodians who, like her, are engaged with human rights issues. While being based in Phnom Penh, she personally knows and works with colleagues across the country and has access to inside information on current political developments, even though she may lack the long-term perspective gained by people like Pierre, which is accumulated partly by virtue of their decades-long stay in the country.

On the other side of the spectrum are those who work in Cambodia on relatively short, fixed-term contracts between one and three years, and rarely longer.

This group includes civil servants like Robert or technical experts like Christina, who have come to work on particular tasks within a given time frame. They often have a basic knowledge of Khmer, which allows them to deal with everyday life, but their main language at work is English; when necessary, they resort to working with an interpreter. Such kinds of aid workers are usually based in the capital, and most of their social interactions are typically with other members of the international community, their close work colleagues, or their national compatriots. While they might not have specifically aimed to live in Cambodia, they are often content being there for a limited time period, especially since Phnom Penh offers a range of Western-style amenities and services, including international schools, supermarkets, restaurants, and sports facilities. As they do not necessarily receive much country-specific preparation before they arrive, their knowledge of the country's political history and social and cultural characteristics depends on their own efforts to find out more, which can be considerable in some cases and rather limited in others. Given the near-sedentary lifestyle of some aid workers and the ultra-high mobility of others, a key question is how they respectively relate to place or, more precisely, the society and country in which they are living more or less temporarily. What kinds of attachments or engagements do they form? What are their expectations and experiences in this respect? And, perhaps most important, how do these affect their work? This matters, as a prominent theme in development debates has been the relevance of local or "indigenous knowledge" (Pottier, Bicker, and Sillitoe 2003; Sillitoe 2010); by extension, I would argue, the familiarity of aid workers with this local knowledge is relevant, too. This is contrasted by the perceived influence of "travelling rationalities" (Mosse in press (a), in press (b)), which are seen as originating from Western aid agencies and are being implemented by Western experts. The extent to which aid workers are familiar with such local knowledge thus not only influences their individual experience of a country but also provides concrete insights into how local knowledge variously matters, or is thought to matter, in development processes. While this topic merits a separate discussion, it is worth noting just a few basic issues here. First of all, there appears to be an underlying distinction between "knowledge possessed by the locals," which may refer, for example, to indigenous natural resource management strategies or traditional midwifery practices, and "knowledge of the local," which is often presented by nonindigenous authors regarding the social and cultural characteristics of a country and its language, history, and political development. Examples of the latter can be found, in their most basic form, in guidebooks such as *Culture Shock! Cambodia* (North 2005) or, more subtly, in publications aimed specifically at development practitioners such as *Learning for Transformation* (O'Leary and Nee 2001) or Leng and Pearson's (2006) study on expatriates and Cambodians working together. It is interesting to note—based on anecdotal evidence—that there seems to be an inverse relation between job responsibility and country-specific training given. Thus aid workers who are in many respect on the lowest rungs of the professional and income ladder, such as volunteers, often receive comparatively extensive predeparture and in-country training, whereas technical experts in high-profile positions are given relatively little, if any. There is a range of reasons for this, which cannot be fully explored here, but there is a sense that some aid workers (those in the field) need more local knowledge(s) to operate successfully than do others, such as technical experts or development managers, whose expertise in particular areas is seen as not country specific and as applicable, with few modifications, almost anywhere. With respect to the broader agenda of studying aid workers, the questions would not only be how much local knowledge (of all kinds) people have, how they acquire it, or in what ways it influences their work. Perhaps as important, how aid workers rate local knowledge might be an indicator of where they position themselves on the social and political spectrum of Aidland—whether in the ethos of, for example, religious groups focused on "serving Cambodia" or as part of a more managerialist, globally operating "development elite."

Futures of Aidland

Finally, of key interest to policymakers, beneficiaries, and development scholars are the futures of Aidland, as flagged in the subtitle of this collection. This refers to the shapes and forms development assistance might take in the future, as well as their associated problems and challenges. I suggest that studying aid workers, as individuals, provides highly relevant material for identifying such issues. For example, a trend that has been discussed recently by development scholars is the increasing "professionalization," as well as "managerialization," of aid work, and the career profiles of Robert, the civil servant, and Christina, the technical expert, seem to be good examples of this. I would also argue, however, that these developments are paralleled by an increasing diversification of participants and practices in the aid sector.

While the people I described work mostly in topical areas that are prominent in the popular imagination, such as health (Helene), education (Pierre), housing (Russell), and, more recently, good governance or democratization (Christina), others I encountered during my fieldwork included, for example, journalists employed by an aid agency to provide media training at a local radio station, and European psychologists involved in setting up new degree programs at a local university. There were also those foreigners with a fine arts background working in the Cambodian art scene, organizing exhibitions and workshops and generally fostering exchange between foreign and Cambodian artists. Furthermore, because of Cambodia's particular recent history, a small but significant proportion of the international community in Phnom Penh works with the Extraordinary Chambers in the Courts of Cambodia, which is holding a tribunal on the crimes of the Khmer Rouge regime. These include lawyers, prosecutors, a substantial number of international legal interns, and those working within NGOs on peace building, transitional justice, and care of trauma victims. I am not suggesting that all those identify themselves as aid workers. In a wider sense, however, they are involved in attempts to restore justice and enhance democracy, processes that are seen as vital to ensure the long-term political and social stability of the country and as such arguably occupy the margins of what has traditionally been considered development work.

With regard to the broader agenda, all of these examples suggest that when thinking about aid workers, it is useful to maintain a broad scope in terms of who counts as an aid worker, as it is likely that activity at the margins is pointing to changing understandings and practices of what constitutes aid. This also involves recognizing the entanglement of private funds as well as those channeled through large government organizations or NGOs; it involves taking people into account who are employed by such organizations, as well as the myriad individuals who arrive and operate in Cambodia independently of them, as exemplified in some of the case studies. A further issue to bear in mind here concerns the less than clear-cut division between aid workers and beneficiaries. As Crewe and Harrison (1998) pointed out, some of the main beneficiaries of foreign assistance to developing countries may be Western consultants and expert advisors themselves, as some of them are financially highly rewarded for their efforts. In a different vein, it has been observed that for national employees, a job at a local or international NGO can be a key opportunity that allows them to build their professional capacities and opens career possibilities and overseas travel opportunities that might otherwise not have been available to them. In this sense, they are also beneficiaries of overseas aid, even though they do not represent the impoverished, rural population at which much aid is targeted. They, like the international experts, could thus be described as being aid workers and beneficiaries at the same time. Such blurring of boundaries characterizes distinctions not just between aid worker and recipient but also between volunteers and professionals, public and private sector workers, and those in traditional versus emerging forms of development assistance, all of which contribute to the shifting contours of Aidland.

Conclusion

At the beginning of this chapter, the question was raised about who might be considered the inhabitants of Aidland—thus tracing a thread that runs through all chapters gathered here and is discussed most explicitly in Apthorpe's contribution. One of the aims of this chapter was to populate the paradigm of Aidland while avoiding the reifying tendencies of Aidland as a metaphor and of aid workers as a category. The case examples presented highlighted, in the first instance, the diversity of individuals who work in aid. I suggested that sets of differences between aid workers can be valuable for establishing future research agendas. More particularly, I argued that each of the themes identified bears significance for quite fundamental questions on aid work that lie at the heart of the development paradigm. First, the issue of aid workers' mixed motivations speaks directly to debates about their presumed altruism—or indeed selfishness, as portrayed by polemical accounts such as Hancock's (1989) *Lords of Poverty*. Studying the biographies and motivations of individual aid workers would provide a much more grounded and nuanced debate than has been held so far. Second, a growing area in development studies concerns the linkages between migration and development—usually conceived of as poor people trying to escape poverty. Turning this on its head, one can argue that migration is in fact intrinsic to the lives of international developers too—as by definition, they are working outside their home countries and are furthermore mobile throughout their careers. Recognizing this, and establishing how this affects their work, is one key question for future research on aid workers. Third, studying aid workers allows for revisiting the debate on indigenous knowledge from a different point of view, asking how local knowledges are valued and used among those who implement aid projects. In the broadest sense, it also raises the issue about whether it is beneficial or detrimental if aid workers become very familiar with the place they are working in—up to the possibility of "going native." Finally, paying attention to the multitude of current and emerging kinds of aid workers—and thus forms of aid work—means not to take development for granted but to be alive to the future directions it may be taking.

Note

1. The research was carried out as part of a research project on "aid workers as mobile professionals," supported by a grant from the Economic and Social Research Council (RES000 22 3481), whose assistance is gratefully acknowledged.

References

Apthorpe, Raymond. 2005. Postcards from Aidland. Paper presented at the Institute of Development Studies, Brighton, United Kingdom.

Apthorpe, Raymond. In press. With Alice in Aidland. In *Adventures in Aidland: The anthropology of professionals in international development*, ed. David Mosse. Oxford: Berghahn.

Borges, Jose Luis. 1964. The analytical language of John Wilkins. In *Other inquisitions 1937–1952*, trans. Ruth L.C. Simms, 101–05. Austin: University of Texas Press.

Crewe, Emma, and Elizabeth Harrison. 1998. *Whose development? An ethnography of aid*. London: Zed Books.

Denskus, Tobias. 2007. Peacebuilding does not build peace. *Development in Practice* 17 (4–5): 656–62.

Eyben, Rosalind. 2007. Becoming a feminist in Aidland. In *Gender and family among transnational professionals*, ed. Anne Coles and Anne-Meike Fechter, 149–69. London: Routledge.

Gould, Jeremy. 2004. Introducing aidnography. In *Ethnographies of aid: Exploring development texts and encounters*, ed. Jeremy Gould and Henrik Secher Marcussen, 1–13. Occasional Paper 24. Roskilde, Denmark: International Development Studies.

Hancock, Graham. 1989. *Lords of poverty: The power, prestige, and corruption of the international aid business*. London: Atlantic Monthly Press.

Hilhorst, Dorothea. 2003. *The real world of NGOs: Discourses, diversity and development*. London: Zed Books.

Lakoff, Georg, and Mark Johnson. 1980. *Metaphors we live by*. Chicago: Chicago University Press.

Leng, Chhay, and Jenny Pearson. 2006. *Working in Cambodia: Perspectives on the complexities of Cambodians and expatriates working together*. Phnom Penh, Cambodia: VBNK.

Mosse, David. 2005. *Cultivating development: An ethnography of aid policy and practice*. London and Ann Arbor, MI: Pluto Press.

———. In press (a). Introduction: The anthropology of expertise and professionals in international development. In *Adventures in Aidland: The anthropology of professionals in international development*, ed. David Mosse. Oxford: Berghahn.

———. In press (b). Social analysis as corporate product: Non-economists/anthropologists at work in the World Bank in Washington DC. In *Adventures in Aidland: The anthropology of professionals in international development*, ed. David Mosse. Oxford: Berghahn.

Mosse, David, and David Lewis, eds. 2006. *Development brokers and translators: The ethnography of aid and agencies*. Bloomfield, CT: Kumarian Press.

North, Peter. 2005. *Culture shock! Cambodia: A survival guide to customs and etiquette.* Portland, OR: Graphic Arts Center.

O'Leary, Moira, and Meas Nee. 2001. *Learning for transformation: A study of the relationship between culture, values, experience and development practice in Cambodia.* Battambang, Cambodia: Krom Akphiwat Phum.

Pottier, Johan, Alan Bicker, and Paul Sillitoe, eds. 2003. *Negotiating local knowledge: Power and identity in development.* London: Pluto Press.

Rajak, Dinah, and Roderick L. Stirrat. In press. Parochial cosmopolitanism and the power of nostalgia. In *Adventures in Aidland: The anthropology of professionals in international development,* ed. David Mosse. Oxford: Berghahn.

Samnang, Chum. 2010. NGO coordination and the changing aid environment in Cambodia: Challenges and opportunities. MA thesis, University of Wellington, Victoria.

Shutt, Cathy. 2008. Power and aid relations: A study of Cambodian NGOs and their international funders. PhD diss., Institute of Development Studies, Brighton, United Kingdom.

Sillitoe, Paul. 2010. Trust in development: Some implications of knowing in indigenous knowledge. *Journal of the Royal Anthropological Institute* 16 (1): 12–30.

Stirrat, Roderick L. 2000. Cultures of consultancy. *Critique of Anthropology* 20 (1): 31–46.

———. 2008. Missionaries, mercenaries, misfits: Representations of development personnel. *Critique of Anthropology* 28 (4): 406–25.

8

Dealing With Danger

Risk and Security in the Everyday Lives of Aid Workers

Silke Roth

Aid work has become "dangerous business" (Thomas 2005, 123). The international media regularly report about aid workers who have been kidnapped or killed while conducting their assignments.[1] A new genre of "aid worker memoir" has emerged in which authors present vivid accounts of dangers encountered in the field, ranging from vehicle accidents and tropical diseases to outright attacks (see, e.g., Burnett 2005; Cain, Postlewaite, and Thomson 2004; Olson 1999). This chapter is based on semistructured biographical interviews with aid workers and addresses how respondents perceived and dealt with danger and insecurity in their everyday lives. To provide a context for the narratives of the aid workers, I briefly summarize changes in overseas aid since the 1990s that have contributed to the increased vulnerability of aid workers. I then discuss what role danger plays in the narratives of aid workers, what they identify as dangerous situations, how they describe themselves in such circumstances, and what strategies of dealing with danger are presented in the interviews. Three main approaches will be identified: applying security procedures, relying on the support of the community, and seeking solace in religious beliefs. I argue that risk is overall downplayed in the interviews and that respondents emphasized that they were responsible and in control of their security and the security of their colleagues and clients. I interpret these narratives of control and risk-distancing as efforts to assume positions of "professionalization," which, as I argue, interacts with the current securitization of aid.

Risky Business

Although attacks on aid workers are not new (Hammond 2008), since the 1990s and in particular since September 11, 2001, the number of attacks on aid workers, including killings, kidnappings, and armed attacks, has steadily increased (Stoddard, Harmer, and DiDomenico 2008). Between the second half of the 1990s and 2005, the number of major incidents per year more than doubled. The increased number of victims, however, needs to be related to the growing number of aid personnel.[2] Furthermore, more than three times as many national compared to international aid workers were among the victims. Thus the security situation of international staff has actually improved, whereas the risk of national aid workers who represent the majority of victims has increased. This reflects the strategy of "localization," that is, that in situations of increased insecurity, the management of aid programs is transferred from international to local staff (Stoddard, Harmer, and Haver 2006, 1f).

The attacks on aid workers are related to the fact that since the 1990s and in particular since the beginning of the "global war on terror" (GWAT), humanitarian aid has been increasingly militarized and politicized (Torrente 2004). Howell and Lind (2009, 4; see also Duffield 2007) analyzed how the GWAT has deepened and intensified relations between development and security actors, which they described as "securitization," that is, the "absorption of global and national security interests into the framing, structuring and implementation of development of aid." This development led to a reallocation of aid to frontline states in the GWAT (Afghanistan, Pakistan, Iraq), a nexus of aid policy and national and global security objectives, and a closer interaction between ministries of defense, foreign policy, development, and domestic affairs (cf. Howell and Lind 2009). Parallel to securitization, humanitarian aid is also undergoing a process of professionalization that is reflected in the introduction of codes of conduct, a proliferation of university- and NGO-based humanitarian training, and the establishment of a professional organization, the International Humanitarian Studies Association (2009) (cf. Walker and Russ 2010; see also Walker and Maxwell 2009, 129–35). These professionalization processes are closely related to the need for skilled staff (Richardson 2006) and to minimize staff turnover (Loquercio, Hammersley, and Emmens 2006).

The increasing involvement of humanitarians in complex emergencies and military humanitarian interventions caused reflections regarding security management of aid organizations already in the 1990s (Duffield 1997; Van Brabant 1998). The attacks on the UN and the International Committee of the Red Cross in Bagdad in 2003, however, represent a turning point and have resulted in an increased interest of aid organizations in security and the creation of new structures. In December 2004 the UN General Assembly approved the establishment of the Department of Safety and Security while international aid organizations started to develop security systems and to employ security advisors (Bruderlein and Gassmann 2006, 76–77). Nevertheless, while it has become increasingly common for aid organizations to contract certain security functions to external professionals, the hiring of armed protection remains the exception (Stoddard, Harmer, and DiDomenico 2008). Instead, organizations tend to employ international security advisors who provide training, risk assessment, and security management consulting; in addition some organizations also hire unarmed local guards.

Humanitarian aid or emergency relief that focuses on lifesaving activities providing food, medical assistance, and shelter can be distinguished from long-term development cooperation that focuses on capacity building and support for infrastructure. The boundaries between humanitarian aid and development cooperation, however, cannot always be neatly drawn. In particular in the processes of peace building and humanitarian relief in the conflict and postconflict settings of the so-called New Wars of the 1990s (Kosovo, Sierra Leone, and Bosnia), "development and security actors also started to interact in new and overlapping ways" (Howell and Lind 2009, 8). Multimandated organizations are involved in providing emergency relief as well as development cooperation and peace efforts (Bruderlein and Gassmann 2006, 69), and confusion over what constitutes humanitarian work and what constitutes development work has been noted (Riddell 2007, 330). Some organizations involved in development cooperation have started to become involved in humanitarian assistance without being familiar with security issues (Martin 2003). Furthermore, the Department for International Development in the United Kingdom expanded its support to insecure countries and in particular provides support for development projects, which now outweigh humanitarian expenditures in insecure environments (National Audit Office 2008, 5).

While it is well justified to think about humanitarian aid and development cooperation as a continuum, given the fact that poverty and need are closely related to conflict and disaster, the blurring boundaries between these two types of aid have significant consequences for the safety and security of aid workers. Whereas humanitarianism is defined by neutrality and impartiality (Anderson 2004),[3] development cooperation is taking sides in that it stabilizes local governments and is implemented with their approval. Nearly a decade ago, Bakhet and Diamond (2002) observed that although development workers such as United Nations Development Program staff were not necessarily viewed as relief workers, they were often responsible for UN security matters, whether or not they were prepared for the lack of security and hardship they could expect. Briefing, support, and debriefing structures for development workers in postconflict regions were often missing (Bakhet and Diamond 2002). While my respondents still identified a lack of briefing and debriefing structures, they were overall quite satisfied with the security procedures of their organizations.

Data and Methods

This chapter is part of a study that explores the transnational lifestyle and experience of mobility of aid workers. I asked respondents to tell me how their life developed before and since they became involved in international aid work, what they found satisfying and frustrating about this work, what impact this involvement had on their relationships and sense of self, and what their future plans were.

Between 2004 and 2006, I conducted 44 biographical interviews with aid workers working in development cooperation and emergency relief with smaller and larger NGOs and various UN agencies. These organizations differ not only with respect to their programs but also regarding salaries and benefits, training, and career opportunities. The respondents were born between 1937 and 1980 and included 23 women and 21 men. Fourteen (32%) were younger than 35, 18 (41%) were between 35 and 39, and 12 (27%) were over 40. Seventeen of the respondents came from Western Europe, 8 came from North America, 3 came from Central and Eastern Europe, 8 came from Asia and the Middle East, 4 came from Africa, and 4 came from South America. Respondents differed with respect to marital status and work area (e.g., education, medical support, logistics, refugees, human rights).[4]

Most of the respondents came from a middle-class background, had attended university, and had been volunteers during school, university, or work. A few had been politically active before they became aid workers. Some had parents who had been working abroad, and others came from an immigrant background, had been refugees, or started in development NGOs in their own countries before they became international aid workers. University studies or other training, voluntary activism, and paid employment alternated over the life course of the respondents. On the basis of the biographical interviews, I distinguish three different patterns of getting involved in aid work. Those in the first group stated that they were interested since their childhood in helping those living in poverty. The second group is characterized by gradual involvement. A turning point or epiphany that led respondents to their work overseas is typical for those in the third group.

Some interviews were conducted in a European city with a snowball sample of respondents who were in between jobs or working at organization headquarters. The majority of interviews were conducted while interviewees participated in a humanitarian studies course at a North American university.[5] Thus my research is based on the narratives and perceptions of aid workers themselves who spoke about their experiences outside the risk context.

Danger in Aid Work

Danger rarely was a major theme in the interviews, even though some respondents mentioned acquaintances, coworkers, or friends who had been injured or killed in accidents or attacks. In a few interviews, dangerous situations, in particular fights that were going on in the streets, encounters with rebels, or the overall security situation in the country where the respondents had been based, were mentioned when they described their living and working conditions. If the respondents spoke about dangerous situations at all, they mentioned them casually rather than emotionally. A few respondents, however, addressed situations in which they felt vulnerable, for example, if they received warnings about suicide bombs or other attacks in public places or encountered child soldiers. But in most cases I prompted respondents to tell me whether they had encountered risks and how they dealt with them.

In particular respondents who were involved in human rights and relief work emphasized that taking risks was part of their work and that they knew what one could expect "on the job" and how to handle it. This means not that they were seeking risk but that they accepted that the involvement in humanitarian assistance and human rights work involves dangerous situations. Not only did the decision to get involved in aid work require a decision about the acceptance of danger, carrying out this work on a day-to-day basis also required constant choices. A single childless woman who has worked in a South American country for several NGOs providing psychosocial support for victims of violence explained that she accepted the risk, for example, the frequent encounters with guerrilla

> because it is part of my job. It is nothing that I can do about it, in order to do my job. . . . So then I feel that for me is like an issue of commitment, and know that there are some high spots in my job and

also low spots, but these low spots that I find are less significant than the high spots that I found there.

In this quote she highlights her commitment to human rights work and emphasizes that the satisfaction that she gains from this kind of work outweighs the danger she has to accept as part of the job. One married respondent and father of two children pointed out that if one would accept only safe assignments, nobody would do this kind of work, because humanitarian situations tend to involve risks. He admitted, however, that when he had the choice, he chose assignments in more secure environments. Organizations experience difficulties recruiting highly qualified and experienced staff to high-risk environments (National Audit Office 2008). Another female respondent who is married without children and has worked for various UN missions in South Asia, the Middle East, Eastern Europe, and Africa stated,

> I think that when you do this sort of work, you have to accept the "wrong time, wrong place" scenario that you could end up in the wrong place at the wrong time and then be dead. . . . It is something that you have to accept, and if you can't accept it, you shouldn't do this work. And I have no sympathy with people who think that they are going to, these places are not safe, you are going to a postconflict scenario; it is not safe. And anybody who wants to be somewhere safe should stay at home.

Accepting danger as part of the job, however, does not mean that respondents did not carefully assess the situation and made a conscious decision whether to take an assignment. Respondents emphasized that they were very conscious and careful about the risks they were taking. They furthermore stressed that it was their decision whether they went on a mission. A female respondent working for an NGO providing medical relief, who as a logistician was responsible for security procedures in the field, emphasized that she felt in control of the situation:

> I am convinced that what I am doing is worth it. And that is what I am trying to balance is the things that could happen to me . . . I told my mom . . . "I made sure that before I went there, I was in control of what needed to be known, what is not controllable, is not controllable." And I am happy with my life and with the risk I am taking, and I don't take stupid risks. I really don't take stupid risks, I mean,

although I am working in a tough context, I am very, very conscious. So in the end, anything, things can happen anywhere.

Normalization of Danger

In their accounts of how they experienced and dealt with danger, respondents employed three comparisons and were thus putting risk into context. First, they juxtaposed the risks they encountered in the field (e.g., land mines, child soldiers, organized crime) with risks typical for their home countries such as property thefts, muggings, and car accidents. They pointed out that while they were aware of dangerous situations—and took every precaution to avoid them—risk taking was part of everyday life everywhere. The risks simply varied according to the circumstances. Second, they pointed out they were getting used to security threats, which were seen as normal in the field, while they seemed scary at home. A single childless woman who has worked as a human rights activist for NGOs as well as intergovernmental organizations in Eastern Europe and the Middle East recalled that the fact that "someone had just been killed" before she went on an assignment "didn't really bother" her. She explained,

> When you are in the field, you rationalize the most peculiar things. So obviously if it was happening here [in Western Europe], you would be scared. There when everybody else is doing it and they are all going about their business, it is a herd mentality; if everyone else is still carrying on working, it must be OK, even if a bomb has just dropped into that particular city or there has been a threat against Western women and there are really only five in the town. If everyone else is still going to work, you think it is OK.

Thus just as the majority of the Western population travels by car regardless of deadly car accidents (and the impact on the environment) without considering this as risk, the risks encountered in the field are normalized. Third, respondents pointed out that even if they put their lives at risk, the situation was much worse for local staff and beneficiaries,[6] who in contrast to international aid workers were not evacuated and could not take a break from the dangerous and stressful situation in which they lived and worked. In particular internationals who were evacuated felt guilty about leaving local staff and beneficiaries behind.[7] A female respondent who worked in several human rights

NGOs in South America recalled a situation in which she was responsible for a group of schoolchildren:

> So I had the guerrilla on this side and the paramilitary on that side, and they were like fight, but what really, really, really was hard for me was when I went back to the classroom, I was worried about how to gather the little kids and put them into a safe spot. When I came back, everything worked like automatically, the kids had their back-packs, they were going to the classroom, face the floor. They knew how to do it, they already had, they knew how to work that out, that really shocked me, because like the little ones, like 3 years, 4 years, up to the ones who where 12, they all knew what they had to do.

The fact that even very young children were so familiar with violence and knew how to deal with it was harder for her than the dangerous situation itself. Another respondent who has worked for several NGOs in Eastern Europe, the Middle East, and Africa pointed out that as an international staff member, he would travel in armed vehicles and thus had less security problems than the local population whose safety he was assigned to guarantee.

Respondents emphasized that it was important to create security rules and guidelines that were followed by everyone and to pay close attention to the surroundings. Having lived in a country where violence was considered an aspect of everyday life was perceived as a good preparation for aid work. A male respondent from South America, who was married to another aid worker without having children and had been on a number of missions in various African countries for an NGO providing medical aid, explained,

> And being [national] or having lived in [South America], it helped a lot, because I tried to be aware who moved behind me, what is happening there, what noise. And we have discovered that some of my colleagues, they don't know anything of what is going on next to them, they could be robbed. . . . It is part of this job; we cannot avoid it being in places with risk, when you really want to reach the population.

Another single childless male respondent, who had been working with NGOs in the Middle East and Southeast Asia, stated that he had moments in which he had fears, felt uncomfortable, and was afraid. He was convinced that it was better to be cautious rather than go ahead with the mission:

I think 10 times before I move in those difficult situations, I don't think, just to prove to the people that you are brave, you should take a risk. Sometimes, I mean there is an element of risk in everything you know, going downtown or wherever in a taxi it can be very risky, there is an element in there. But you know, you make sure that, you know, at least you are prepared for bad moments.

While taking risks appears to have become an integral part of not only humanitarian assistance but also development cooperation in postconflict and conflict situations, necessary to provide aid and engage in peace building and human rights work, respondents mentioned that they decided to accept a position in a dangerous place because of the "challenge" or for the "sake of the career." In addition to such pragmatic reasons, danger might also be "attractive." A single childless female respondent engaged in human rights work in Eastern Europe and Southeast Asia observed among her male colleagues that

there was this machismo, "I have been close to danger," you know, and it's a fascination with danger and excitement that is part of the human psyche. But if you have actually seen it and gone over the edge, you don't want to talk about it and share your experiences. So there is a spectrum there of people, constantly fascinated with that edge, cliff edge, and those who have actually gone over it don't want to talk about it. . . . But that sort of, we would always sit around analyzing each other: Why are we here? Because it is a big part, you find yourself in some hellholes. What is it about me?

This respondent highlighted the attraction and fascinating aspects of risky situations. It is important to note that in this study, male respondents rather than female respondents stated that they would avoid assignments that appeared too dangerous for them and reported feelings of vulnerability. It also needs to be emphasized that this sample is small and not representative. Furthermore, this quote also addresses the fact that it was particularly difficult for aid workers to convey their experiences with those who have not been in similar situations. While they found it difficult to share with friends and family back home what they had lived through, they considered dangerous situations that they experienced together with their colleagues as a "bonding experience" and referred to the exchange of such experiences as "war stories."

As the quotes indicate, the respondents emphasized that they were responsible in assessing and taking risks. I interpret this as an effort of aid workers to highlight their professionalism and to distance themselves from those who were inexperienced and naive or irresponsible risk seekers. Respondents emphasized that it was ultimately their decision which jobs they took and how they dealt with the security situation in the field and were thus emphasizing the individual self. They also highlighted communal aspects, however, when they described how they trusted their colleagues in risky situations and their organizations concerning the adherence to security procedures.

Security Procedures of Organizations

Respondents' risk assessment included not only the situation in the country but also the security measures provided by the organization. Because the interviews were carried out between 2004 and 2006, that is, after the Baghdad bombings of the UN and International Committee of the Red Cross in 2003 and the subsequent increase in security measures of international humanitarian organizations, it appears that the international aid workers I interviewed were satisfied with the attention their organizations paid to security matters. In 2004 one respondent referred to security as the new buzzword of NGOs. A female respondent, also interviewed in 2004, who had been on missions in various regions of the world including the Middle East, stated,

> Several heads rolled as a result of the Canal hotel bombing [August 2003]. People lost their jobs and were severely criticized, and nobody else wants to lose their jobs. So in order to avoid losing your job, you make sure that nobody goes into danger. It is not that they are concerned about the safety of individuals; it is their concern about their own jobs. And of course concern—quite rightly—that if something happens to any UN staff, it would be a major problem for the future. They can't afford it. So it's, I'm being cynical by saying, "It's just people looking after their own backsides," it's not just that.

Field staff sometimes disagreed about the evaluation of the security situation and the adequate response. In the view of field staff, the head office might view a country as a monolithic entity disregarding the fact that the level of threat might vary widely within the country. Security measures that were mentioned in the interviews included daily security updates, security advisors, joint accommodation in secure neighborhoods, curfew, guards and full-time security officers, training of drivers, use of armed vehicles, radio contact during travel from accommodation to field office, security provided by national military or international peacekeepers, and evacuation. To ensure the safety of their (international) staff, organizations thus might withdraw their operation or restrict the movement of their staff or protect them with armed or unarmed guards, military escorts or peacekeepers. A female respondent involved in human rights work recalled,

> I was very strictly controlled. Like for instance, I [would] go for a run each morning, I would have a military personnel running with me. I had to radio every single movement. When I got into the car, I had to radio when I was leaving, radio at the halfway point, and radio on arrival. And everything, going to bed at night and ring the military as I was going to bed at night, in the morning, if I wanted to go down for a swim, I needed to take a military person with me down to the beach.

This quote not only illustrates the concern of organizations to ensure the safety of their international staff but also shows the privileges international aid workers enjoyed in specific locations.

In contrast to the security procedures of international NGOs and UN agencies, in particular regarding their international staff, national NGOs tend to lack the resources to provide security and psychosocial support for their staff. A female respondent who has worked for NGOs in her South American home country reported that when she tried to raise the security issue, she was told,

> "You are not as committed as we are, you have to go to the field, you have to be with the people. So if that means you have to lose your life, you have to lose it." So it is very, very hard, very hard, because nobody cares about it, nobody is paying attention to what you are going through.... They say upfront, "If you are taken hostage, we are not paying for that."

Her experience reflects the fact that smaller NGOs tend to lack the resources to provide insurance for their staff and volunteers (Bruderlein and Gassmann 2006, 91). In addition to the lack of security, she also experienced a lack of psychosocial support and felt that there was no space for "being sad . . . for being affected or being depressed." It is, however, important that organizations address not only the security of their personnel but also the psychological consequences of traumatic experiences (Thomas 2005).

So why do they do it? Several respondents mentioned that friends and family thought that they were "crazy" to do this kind of work or that they often ask themselves why they are doing it. They presented three aspects that make aid work rewarding: it is meaningful work and "makes a difference" in the lives of beneficiaries, it is complex and challenging work that requires skills and the ability to adapt to changing environments, and respondents greatly appreciated traveling to and living in foreign places and meeting foreigners, such as international and local colleagues, beneficiaries, and the local population in general.

Community Support

In particular NGOs and their staff sought the acceptance (Van Brabant 2000) from the local community. For aid workers this means, on the one hand, being protected by the local community and, on the other hand, not being attacked from within their midst. A female respondent who was married, had adult children, and had been based in the Middle East explains that being attacked by "the people that you think you are helping" was one of the most difficult experiences to overcome and made her doubt continuing relief work: "I remember, I thought I could never go back, to tell the truth." This quote very clearly indicates that aid work is rarely neutral but is supporting different sides of a conflict—or seen to do so locally. In some cases, respondents described that they were both attacked and defended by different factions of the local community. This becomes clear in the following account in which a single female respondent recalled how those in the family with whom she lived while she was doing human rights work in Southeast Asia endangered their own lives by defending her against local men:

> I had maybe six or seven [local] men outside my house with machetes, and they are saying to my family, "Give us the [foreign] woman with the black heart," because they knew that I was defending militia, they knew the job I was doing, and I had a black heart, as far as they were concerned. And [foreign] is any woman, any international, not [local]. So the young boy probably had said, "No, no, she is not there." And they were hiding me under the, no, in the shadows, down in the corner, they were putting their own selves at risk.

The support of the local community is not only important in providing security for aid workers but also vital for other reasons. One male respondent working for an NGO in Africa recalled a situation in which he and his colleagues were threatened by young men who intended to loot the warehouse in which the aid organization stored food:

> So what the community did, they lined up along the road, then we drove through. And I always take that as an example. Once you build the best relationship with the community, then you can be sure that nothing will happen. Well, it can still happen, but at least you have minimized the risk.

Speaking the local language or even sharing the same cultural background or political background can make it easier to gain the trust of the local community (cf. Cordier 2009). One of the interviewees, who worked for an NGO, described the suspicion of the local community toward the international NGO and how sharing language and cultural background helped him to gain trust:

> You know, we weren't hassled actually, but I knew that there was always somebody there, watching us, see what we are doing. I didn't have a problem with that. . . . You know, I spoke the language, even though it was a different dialect, but it was easier for me to learn. And I come from a similar background, culture, and political background. . . . I am not a very good Muslim, but I know how it is to live in a Muslim community. . . . I know what is allowed, what is not allowed.

Furthermore, learning the local language and making friends with the locals enables international aid workers to go out even under curfew.

As noted earlier, getting immersed in the local culture and developing relationships with locals was described as one of the pleasures of aid work. It not only contributes to work satisfaction and is one reason to do this kind of work but also contributes to the safety of aid workers. Respondents had to follow security regulations that did not permit them to move freely and make contact with locals, which they described as unsatisfying. Some avoided taking on assignments if security regulations would have restricted them to staying in guarded compounds and traveling in armed vehicles.

Family and Faith

Respondents addressed their relationship not only to the local population but also to friends and family back home. Overall, single childless respondents stated that they would take more risks as long as they did not have a partner or children. Some single respondents, however, anticipated the effect on their friends and family before they made a decision to take an assignment in a high-risk setting. One single childless woman who has worked on numerous missions for an NGO providing medical relief in various African countries explained,

> I relate security more to my parents than to me. . . . Really, if I am dead, I am dead and that's it. It will affect my parents. If I am taken hostage, I guess I have to deal with the fact that I am taken, but I am more worried how my parents would perceive it and if it happens to me, I will have to deal with it.

Furthermore, aid workers might not take assignments in their own countries if that would put family members at risk as one married childless male respondent from a South American country explained.

The fact that younger, childless, and single relief workers stated that they were willing to take risks supports McAdam's (1986) notion of biographical availability based on his study of college students volunteering for the Freedom summer campaign of the American civil rights movement in 1964. Nepstad and Smith (1999), however, found that activists in the Nicaraguan solidarity movement took on risks in midlife, despite the fact that they had families and careers. Echoing Nepstad and Smith's findings, not all relief workers are single. Respondents who were married and had children tended to live separately from their families, as it would be too dangerous and not allowed by the organization to bring them to the field. Married relief workers thus had to cope not only with stressful situations in the field but also with frequent and long-term separations from their families.

Several respondents emphasized that friends, partners, and family members sustained their involvement in humanitarian aid. They described their families as being proud of them and encouraging them to continue their work. One female respondent reported that although her mother was worried about her, she was also full of pride of the human rights work her daughter was engaged in and that she prayed for her daughter. Some Christian respondents reported that they started to pray in situations when they were under attack and could neither leave their location nor expect any support at that moment. Furthermore, as another single female respondent who had been on missions in Western and South Asia stated, faith was important not only in a situation of clear and present danger but also to cope with the stress of conducting aid work in a dangerous environment.

[Starting a mission] we landed, it was getting dark . . . and I thought there is nothing there, it is just desolate. And I think this is really where I have to say that it is my faith that has kept me sane and emotionally secure, and coming from a very tight family has kept me together mentally. Because it's, I am able to talk about it in a very nonchalant way, but it was quite a difficult situation to be in.

This quote illustrates the "emotion work" (Hochschild 1979) that is performed by aid workers who emphasize their professionalism. Two Muslim women, who both worked as national staff in international organizations, described themselves as good believers and provided accounts of how they convinced their relatives that it was the right decision to undertake humanitarian work in conflict situations. As this single female respondent who was from and worked in an East African country recalls,

I said, "Father, I want to remind you that when your day comes for death, you only have one day, you die, this one day is written, and it is known by the Almighty Lord. Where am I going to die? How am I going to die is something on his hand. So being away from you or being in insecure situations will not stop me, it is not a cause of death for me. No. If Allah, our Lord, wants me to die this way, it is written, OK, its faith and dignity, we have to believe in this." So they supported me.

Faith did not replace the security procedures or the support of the local community. It provided an additional resource for some of the respondents, however. In addition to the "wrong time, wrong place" assessment, the belief that their fate was predetermined allowed some respondents to trust that risking their lives was well justified.

Conclusions

This study indicates that aid workers accepted the dangerous situations they were facing but stressed that they were not taking them lightly. The respondents emphasized that they took necessary precautions and avoided unnecessary risks. Dangerous situations were put into context and compared to risks that were encountered at home such as car accidents, robbery, or mugging. It was accepted that risk was part of the challenges faced by humanitarian aid work that many of the respondents took on because they found their previous work unsatisfying. Accepting risk while at the same time taking every possible precaution, they accepted a "wrong place, wrong time" scenario. Religious respondents coped with risk through their belief that their destiny was determined, and it was therefore unnecessary as well as useless to avoid insecure contexts.

The interviews reflect two interacting processes that characterize recent changes in humanitarian aid and development cooperation: securitization and professionalization. Securitization has paradox effects: on the one hand it led to an increase of danger for aid workers, because of the increasing shift of humanitarian and development aid to conflict and postconflict situations; on the other hand it has resulted in the adoption of security procedures in aid organizations. Professionalization seeks to improve the performance of aid organizations and their staff through the introduction of codes of conduct, standards, and—often university-based—training. Respondents emphasized their professionalism by presenting themselves as risk accepting and cautious.

Acknowledgments

This research was funded by the University of Pennsylvania and the University of Southampton, which also provided support through a research leave. I am deeply grateful to the respondents who took the time to share their experiences with me as well as to those who helped me to identify respondents. I thank Heidi Armbruster, the anonymous reviewer, and the editors for their helpful comments.

Notes

1. In a narrow sense, the term "aid worker" refers to field staff in emergency relief. As I point out in the description of my sample, I interviewed staff and volunteers of a broad range of organizations including NGOs and UN organizations working as field staff, in country offices or regional offices, or in headquarters in a wide range of different fields. Although field staff who are based in insecure environments are most at risk, staff of country or regional offices or headquarters make field trips and can also be victims of attacks (e.g., attack on UN headquarters in Baghdad in 2003) or disasters (e.g., Haiti earthquake; see obituaries in the *Guardian*, January 18, 2010).

2. Stoddard, Harmer, and Haver (2006, 16) estimated that the number of humanitarian field workers increased from 136,204 to 241,654 (77%) between 1997 and 2005. The increase was higher for the NGOs (91%) than for the UN (54%). As Walker and Russ (2010, 14) pointed out, the number of aid workers is not known because in general aid agencies do not keep complete and accurate data.

3. Because of securitization, however, even humanitarian aid is not neutral if, as in Afghanistan, aid agencies are "funded by the invading powers" (Lindisfarne 2010, 34).

4. The biographical interviews were supplemented with interviews with two human resources officers (one working for an NGO, one for a UN agency), a trainer who works with NGOs and UN agencies, two lecturers in a humanitarian studies course, and a staff member of an organization supporting HR management of humanitarian organization officers as well as with some people who were considering becoming aid workers or who as refugees had been clients of aid organizations but had not (yet) become aid workers. I also draw on biographical interviews with respondents who were involved in HR management.

5. To ensure confidentiality and anonymity of interviewees, I removed identifying information such as country of origin, organization, and country of assignment when I'm quoting from the interviews.

6. In the context of development cooperation and humanitarian aid, the term "beneficiaries" refers to the individuals and communities who are the recipients of aid and shall be empowered through development cooperation. The term implies an unequal relationship between donors and recipients of aid as well as passivity and paternalism (or maternalism). For a critical discussion of changing power and relationships in international aid, see Groves and Hinton (2005).

7. When organizations decide to evacuate, staff members have to leave—unless they decide to leave the organization.

References

Anderson, Kenneth. 2004. Humanitarian inviolability in crisis: The meaning of impartiality and neutrality for U.N. and NGO agencies following the 2003–2004 Afghanistan and Iraq conflicts. *Harvard Human Rights Journal* 17:41–74.

Bakhet, Omar, and Marie Diamond. 2002. Supporting staff during crisis and on the path to development. In *Sharing the front line and the back hills*, ed. Yael Danieli, 95–100. New York: Baywood.

Bruderlein, Claude, and Pierre Gassmann. 2006. Managing security risks in hazardous missions: The challenge of securing United Nations access to vulnerable groups. *Harvard Journal of Human Rights* 19:63–93.

Burnett, John S. 2005. *Where soldiers fear to tread: A relief worker's tale of survival.* New York: Bantam Books.

Cain, Kenneth, Heidi Postlewaite, and Andrew Thomson. 2004. *Emergency sex and other desperate measures: A true story from hell on earth.* New York: Miramax Books.

Cordier, Bruno De. 2009. Faith-based aid, globalisation and the humanitarian front-line: An analysis of Western-based Muslim aid organisations. *Disasters* 33:608–28.

Duffield, Mark. 1997. NGO relief in war zones: Towards an analysis of the new aid paradigm. *Third World Quarterly* 18:527–42.

———. 2007. *Development, security and the unending war: Governing the world of peoples.* London: Zed Books.

Groves, Leslie, and Rachel Hinton, eds. 2005. *Inclusive aid: Changing power and relationships in international development.* London: Earthscan.

Hammond, Laura. 2008. The power of holding humanitarianism hostage and the myth of protective principles. In *Humanitarianism in question: Power, politics and ethics*, ed. Michael Barnett and Thomas G. Weiss, 172–95. Cornell, NY: Cornell University Press.

Hochschild, Arlie. 1979. Emotion work, feeling rules and social structure. *American Journal of Sociology* 85 (3): 551–73.

Howell, Jude, and Jeremy Lind. 2009. *Counter-terrorism, aid and civil society: Before and after the war on terror.* Basingstoke, UK: Palgrave McMillan.

Lindisfarne, Nancy. 2010. Starting from below: Fieldwork, gender and imperialism now. In *Taking sides: Ethics, politics and fieldwork in anthropology,* ed. Heidi Armbruster and Anna Laerke, 23–44. New York: Berghahn Books.

Loquercio, David, Mark Hammersley, and Ben Emmens. 2006. Understanding and addressing staff turnover in humanitarian agencies. *Network Paper* 55. Humanitarian Practice Network. http://www.odihpn.org/report.asp?id=2806.

Martin, Randolph. 2003. An introduction to NGO field security. In *Emergency relief operations,* ed. Kevin M. Cahill, 225–63. New York: Fordham University Press.

McAdam, Doug. 1986. Recruitment to high-risk activism. *American Journal of Sociology* 92:64–90.

National Audit Office. 2008. *Department for International Development: Operating in insecure environments.* Report by the Comptroller and Auditor General. HC1048 Session 2007–2008/16 October 2008. London: The Stationary Office.

Nepstad, Sharon Erikson, and Christian S. Smith. 1999. Rethinking recruitment to high-risk activism: The case of Nicaragua exchange. *Mobilization* 4:40–51.

Olson, Leanne. 1999. *A cruel paradise: Journals of an international relief worker.* Toronto: Insomniac Press.

Richardson, Frances. 2006. Meeting the demand for skilled and experienced humanitarian workers. *Development in Practice* 16 (3): 334–41.

Riddell, Roger C. 2007. *Does foreign aid really work?* Oxford: Oxford University Press.

Stoddard, Abby, Adele Harmer, and Victoria DiDomenico. 2008. *HPG report: The use of private security providers and services in humanitarian operations.* New York: Center on International Cooperation, New York University.

Stoddard, Abby, Adele Harmer, and Katherine Haver. 2006. *HPG report: Providing aid in insecure environments: Trends in policy and operations.* New York: Center on International Cooperation, New York University.

Thomas, Ros. 2005. Caring for those who care—Aid worker safety and security as a source of stress and distress: A case for psychological support? In *Workplace violence: Issues, trends and strategies,* ed. Vaughan Bowie, Bonnie S. Fisher, and Cary L. Cooper, 121–40. Oxfordshire, UK: Willan Publishing.

Torrente, Nicolas de. 2004. Humanitarian action under attack: Reflections on the Iraq War. *Harvard Human Rights Journal* 17:1–29.

Van Brabant, Koenraad. 1998. Cool ground for aid providers: Towards better security management in aid agencies. *Disasters* 22:109–25.

———. 2000. Operational security management in violent environments: A field manual for aid agencies. In *Good practice review* (No. 8). London: Overseas Development Institute, Humanitarian Practice Network.

Walker, Peter, and Daniel G. Maxwell. 2009. *Shaping the humanitarian world.* New York: Routledge.

Walker, Peter, and Catherine Russ. 2010. *Professionalising the humanitarian sector.* London: Enhancing Learning and Research for Humanitarian Assistance. Retrieved from http://www.elrha.org/uploads/Professionalising_the_humanitarian_sector.pdf

9

The Hollowing Out of Aidland

Subcontracting and the New Development Family in Nepal

Heather Hindman

Introduction: The Hollow Men

Outsourcing, offshoring, and subcontracting are central aspects of contemporary practices of what is often called "neoliberalism" and associated with a growing rationalization of all forms of life, including of employment policies. The pursuit of corporate integration has been rejected in favor of complex networks of specialized service providers—companies have been hollowed out and transformed into supply chains. Organizations in the global North seek to "streamline" production in large part by eliminating tangible and human aspects of their operations, transferring the actual creation of goods and associated workforce to offshore entities that can be quickly dismissed in accord with changing fashion. These extreme forms of vertical disintegration have become synonymous with the "best practices" of multinational business and are designed to maximize "efficiency" while minimizing economic risk (LiPuma and Lee 2004) and corporate responsibility. While this rationalizing approach (Weber 1930/1992) has become banal to both its business adherents and its academic critics, many are surprised to observe the application of these same ideologies to seemingly sacrosanct domains such as academic labor (Strathern 2000) and development (Elyachar 2003, 2006). This chapter looks at how the employment practices of aid agencies in Nepal—through the increased use of short-term, subcontracted foreign staff—have changed the character of the expatriate community in Kathmandu.

Yet this is more than a story of demographic shift. These newly emergent prescriptions for efficient development work have also had an effect on how "aid workers" think about their profession and their lives. Fewer and fewer of those doing aid work are willing to label themselves as aid workers, identifying instead with the technical services companies who loan them out to various aid projects. The invisibility of employment policy to aid policy has led to a further depoliticizing of aid itself (Ferguson 1994) as more key decisions in development are made by administrative logics and "best practices." The complex problems of hiring and maintaining an international workforce of aid professionals becomes a management problem governed by a distinct set of accepted rules for global employment, unconnected with the intended type of work (Hindman 2007). Through a sleight-of-hand made possible by specialized service providers, both aid work itself and the maintenance of workers are transformed for their employers from matters of concern to mere matters of fact (Latour 2004, 2005)—removing the issue of care for both development and developers. In Nepal, this transformation has produced several changes explored in this chapter, including increased costs of expatriate labor in the form of large per diems, the move from families attending movie night to families chatting online from different locations, and the reversal of some small gains in the presence of women and employees of color in the offices of aid agencies in Kathmandu. The result is a simultaneous alienation of aid workers from any larger mission of development and the further disassociation of their professional and private lives—a hollowing out of private homes and professional offices.

Aid workers often find themselves categorized alongside a wide range of people in the "helping professions"—benevolent individuals who often sacrifice a level of compensation for the satisfaction of doing work that contributes to a better world. The expectation of aid work as, in part, charity work is particularly high in Nepal, where the beauty of the landscape is contrasted with the poverty of the country. This dissonance attracts many foreigners to the country for both tourism and gestures toward offering some contribution to the nation.[1] While the external perception of development workers is often of virtuous toilers sacrificing for the poor, a new collection of those doing aid work in Nepal does not identify with this image, relating instead to their professional affiliation as structural engineers or defining themselves in connection to an employer that outsources their skills to aid agencies, governments, or businesses. In contemporary Nepal, it is frequently hydrologists and accountants who are doing the daily work labeled "development," and fewer of these workers are full-time employees of an individual aid agency. In Kathmandu, the line between NGOs, government employment, and for-profit business is blurred among expatriate workers (see also the introduction to this volume). The same individual might act as a marketing consultant for a business in one posting, work for a private aid agency to promote maternal wellness in a second, and be a part of a government project to encourage good financial practices in a third location—all utilizations of their skills as a health care consultant. From the viewpoint of many aid agencies, these new practices of employment are merely strategies of efficient management of experts, the same use of on-demand, flexible services available in the global city and widely seen as a part of contemporary business practice (Sassen 1991). Beyond all this talk of efficiency, these changes have implications for the everyday lives of expatriate aid workers and alter the relationship between those who do the work of development and the product of their labors. While seeing the successful outcome of aid work has always been difficult, this process of commodifying development expertise further alienates the worker from the potential successes of an irrigation or literacy project when it is reduced to a series of unconnected microprocesses (Marx 1867/1990). To see these implications requires stepping outside of the traditional framing of critical development scholarship to consider aid work as related to other forms of labor.

The antagonism between "development anthropologists" and "anthropologists of development" has been thoroughly examined and critiqued (Escobar 1991), including in the introduction to this volume, with conclusions about the historical precursors to this division (Ferguson 1997), its ability to obscure relations of power (Crewe and Harrison 1999), and the potential of a postdevelopment era (Rahnema 1997; Ziai 2007; Escobar 2007). Yet few of these debates have sought to treat the development worker as subject, focusing more on policy and rhetoric than on the life of development laborers.[2] One reason for this lies in the "anthropological gambit" (di Leonardo 1998, 61; see also Trouillot 2003), a term that captures the changes that occur in applying the methods of anthropology to a population presumed by the anthropologist to be familiar to reader and writer alike. It is a conceit seen in humorous depictions of how "we" are tribal, irrational, or otherwise exotic in Gary Larson cartoons or "Body Rituals Among the Nacerima" (Miner 1956; Larson 1981, cited in di Leonardo 1998, 143). This approach does a disservice to the complexity of the not-so-other—"we" think "we" already know what "they" are like—and dehistoricizes the familiar in the same way as was once done to "people without history" (Wolf 1982).[3] The inability to study development workers with sincerity appears to have excluded them from the ethnographic record and from historical change, in part because they seem too familiar or too similar to anthropologists. Given the frequent accusations of development deploying neocolonial understandings of progress and linearity, it seems incumbent on anthropologists of aid workers to acknowledge the role of change in this community as well. Development workers are often depicted as mere conduits for modernizing projects, but they are targets of processes of accountability and progress as well—the selfsame modernizing enterprises that have often been the charge of development to implement.

The invisibility of aid workers in development criticism may also have to do with the way in which the problem of development is framed. The concept of governmentality and examination of the discursive work of aid have provided powerful tools in the pursuit of a critical lens to view aid work (Ferguson 1994; Escobar 1995; Scott 1998; Mitchell 2002), but this perspective often focuses on a dialectical relationship between policy and application that excludes aid workers as agentive actors and neglects the everyday life of aid workers as a potential source of influence on project outcomes. In this piece I want to highlight aid workers as first and foremost workers. Thus this is in large part an analysis of changing labor conditions in an industry rarely examined within the scholarship on work and labor, the development industry, and the effect of new employment policies directed toward those doing aid work. The changing economic situation of professional development workers offers an underexamined framework through which one can seek to understand the ongoing difficulties of doing "good aid."

Housing the New Aid Worker

A billboard appeared on the main street in Lazimpath advertising the "Hacienda Apartment Hotel," and just a few weeks later, the facility made its debut to the expatriate diplomatic and development community by hosting the monthly newcomers' meeting of the United Nations Women's Organization of Nepal. The newly constructed building was in the center of an area popular with expatriates, with proximity to many of the embassy offices and a major Western-style supermarket, and offered enough distance from the tourist district to provide a respite from street vendors. The Hacienda offered furnished apartments for either single residents or couples, including kitchen facilities, Internet connections, and all the expected "mod-cons."[4] At the women's group meeting, the appearance of this new business, as well as the reflection on the paucity of new expatriate arrivals who were the ostensible reason for the meeting, induced a conversation about the changing population of expatriate aid workers in Nepal. One woman remarked on the lack of families arriving, noting that her husband's employer had cut the expatriate staff in Kathmandu by half, and observed that future departures would be replaced by consultants or subcontractors. "We can't find anyone to work at the library anymore," remarked another woman, noting that this prime volunteer job used to be a favorite among expatriate spouses. After an enumeration of different social events and institutions that had seen declining attendance, a woman about to depart Kathmandu to return home to Australia seemed to offer an explanation: "Yes, things are changing. They aren't replacing Steve with a Globus employee, they are hiring another company to oversee their maintenance."[5] Her husband's employer had a long history of basing several expatriate workers in Kathmandu as part of international transportation management coordination, but the company was turning to secondary labor providers to fulfill many of the tasks and cutting back on the number of direct employees in Kathmandu. While their tour of posting had generally been three or four years, the workers who would replace her husband would be resident for nine months or less. They would work in Globus offices in Kathmandu, but their paychecks would come from their primary employer, TBR, which provided consultants and technical professionals both in their home country and abroad.

This new form of employment could be seen across the gamut of expatriate employment in Nepal, with repercussions for the social and family life of workers. The USAID staff in Nepal was being dramatically reduced, even as their facilities and responsibilities were expanding. The Community Liaison Officer (CLO) for the US government was experiencing a problem that her predecessor had not seen: a lack of available families to fill the USAID houses. At the height of US aid work in Nepal, the country had taken out long-term leases—the closest equivalent to land purchase available to non-Nepali citizens—on a number of properties in the Kathmandu Valley. This enabled the US government to adapt the houses to fit the needs of the American families coming to live in Nepal for three or more years as part of their work with the US Mission. In the small but geographically dispersed community of USAID workers, the various AID houses had their own reputations, and as workers circulated in and out of Nepal, they remembered both who had been resident in the homes in the past and the various peccadilloes of each family and house. Over Christmas dinner, the spouse of a USAID worker discussed how, when she was in the Peace Corps in Kathmandu, she had eaten Christmas dinner at the very same house that was now her home—and that the roof had leaked then as well. In 1997 USAID rivaled the UN as the largest employer of expatriate development professionals in Kathmandu, but just 10 years later, conversations were focused on how to encourage the departure of direct AID employees and the benefit of a reduced labor force to the capacity of the agency to "adapt quickly to changing circumstances"—a language of flexibility found in many job advertisements for USAID positions and criticisms of AID projects that echoes that heard in the rhetoric of multinational companies. Those associated with USAID in various capacities reflected on the changing atmosphere in the offices. "It's empty up there," remarked one AID employee. "Everyone I worked with is gone." The USAID offices were scheduled to be relocated in the fall of 2007, and the signs of moving were already underway in May, but his comment was also about the lack of colleagues. This retiring career AID worker was concerned not only about the future of his project, which would now be run by subcontractors, but for his way of life as well.

The manager of the US recreation club in Kathmandu was one of the first to remark on the effects of new employment practices on expatriate social life. The club, known locally as Phora Durbar, had once maintained a fairly strict policy restricting membership to those directly employed by the US government. He noted, "Under those rules, no one is eligible anymore." Although the membership policy allowed expatriates from other nations to join, often at a higher cost, it was fairly strict about what jobs members must hold in Nepal, as the goal was to exclude the many tourists and long-term foreign residents.[6] But the changing nature of expatriate employment meant that by the late 1990s, many of those in Kathmandu for professional reasons were also being excluded, as they lacked the appropriate official affiliation or visa status, and thus the manager had to change the rules in an attempt to generate membership. Changes similar to those occurring at Phora were taking place in many other key institutions for expatriates in Nepal, including local international schools, English-language Christian churches, and various government commissaries.

Some of the most poignant comments on the changing character of the development community in Nepal came from a family who saw the changes from their front window, as they lived in a house within the USAID compound. Tom had worked for many years for USAID in postings in Africa and South Asia as an engineer. His two daughters had been raised in countries around the world, gaining an appreciation of both world travel and humanitarianism, and although they had planned to follow in their father's footsteps, they had recently decided to do so from the private sector. "My career with USAID isn't an option anymore," he remarked. Although proud that his children had developed a desire to help the less fortunate, he was unsure about the way they were going about pursuing that as a career. His younger daughter was still in school, studying culture and language but majoring in business, while his older daughter had begun her own consulting company. She was encouraged to pursue this route when she was hired as a subcontractor in Nepal on a small health project being done through a government aid agency in Kathmandu. "It is the future of aid work," Tom remarked, shaking his head about his daughter's pathway to a future in international health. Tom's wife, Sheila, also saw the changes in her world. She had worked at various international schools during their postings. At Lincoln School, an international school in Kathmandu many expatriate children attend, enrollment was changing. "No one can bring their families anymore," she observed. She speculated that this was in part a product of the difficult political situation in Kathmandu. The prominence of Maoist activists in the early and mid-2000s had made some employers (as well as some employees) reluctant to bring children to what was seen as a dangerous posting. Yet the shift was also a reflection of the changing nature of development contracts. Sheila told the story of a young father near tears hearing the news of his children at home, about his toddler learning to walk in his absence. This coworker of her husband had been brought to Nepal as a subcontractor on a three-month posting to Kathmandu, not long enough to merit family resettlement. The job took longer than was initially budgeted, and he was now into his eighth month in the country, growing tired of the separation as well as living out of suitcases in a hotel. Tom mourned the lack of collegiality the new USAID approach generated. Most of his coworkers were not USAID employees but subcontractors with career commitments to other organizations. The frequent turnover also meant that there was little institutional memory, a frequent problem in international development that was exacerbated by this new style of employment. With his impending departure from Nepal and likely retirement from AID, he mused about being the last of a dying breed. The AID offices were moving, and he would be the last employee to live in this house; furthermore, his position was not going to be filled after his departure.

"The aid community is in decline," remarked Mary, an AID subcontractor's spouse. Their family had worked on a USAID contract 15 years ago, when her children were young, and in 2005 they took up the opportunity to come to Nepal for a three-year term as subcontractors. "It's different this time . . . as a subcontractor . . . we don't have many privileges. I mean I can shop at the commissary and that's about it." For Mary this second experience of expatriate life contrasted with her pleasant memories of a posting in South America. It had been at her urging that her husband had accepted this late-in-life overseas posting, as for her it was a final adventure before their retirement, but the experience of being an expatriate development family had changed. They had struggled to find a home in Kathmandu, as her husband's position did not make them eligible for USAID housing. Instead they were given the name of a housing broker, whom she suspected, on the basis of reports of her household staff, was engaging in some unethical practices, and her husband spent the first several weeks of his assignment trying to learn a new job and search for houses by himself. "We had to do everything ourselves . . . and they gave us only 30 days' notice before we had to move." The social community that had sustained Mary when she was posted to South America seemed absent in Kathmandu. Part of her reason for assenting to an overseas posting was the close friends she had made the last time, but without the immediate networks brought by having young children in school and with most of her husband's coworkers being in Nepal alone and on short-term contracts, she said, "I've had a hard time making friends." The shift from close relationships among employees working with USAID to a more distant and complex model for development employment changed the experience of both life and work among aid professionals. One employee captured this new structure in referring to himself as a "sub-sub-subcontractor for USAID."

The loss of an encompassing institutional umbrella that had facilitated many aspects of life in Kathmandu was one remarked on by both USAID contractors and other expatriates engaged in development work in Nepal. Many of those now working as subcontractors for aid agencies had experienced an earlier period of direct employment to an NGO or government, and even as they criticized the way in which the former employment system was restrictive and highly regulated, most shared the perspective that "I could never imagine living [abroad] without the [employer's] structure, not that it is that much of an advantage, but . . ." For those who self-identified as aid workers, the community of development families, both within a posting and beyond any single location, was central to how they thought about their lives and careers. The familiar faces and routines made continual mobility tolerable, and many described the difficulties they felt when they were not abroad. Most of their friends were fellow expatriate aid workers, and they had habituated to overseas life, in both its hassles and its pleasures. In the new millennium, several aid workers complained that they had watched as subcontractors were getting paid much more to do the same work they had done. One long-term aid worker lamented the decline in a shared sentiment about the value of the work they were doing: "I used to feel we were all in this together," but now, he worried, "it's all about money—bonuses and per diems." Suddenly the compensatory aspects of "doing good" appeared irrelevant to the system, and many career development workers were either retiring or seeking to turn themselves into subcontractors to access the higher rates of pay their new colleagues were able to claim.

Managing Aid Workers Out of Existence

These expatriate families were all experiencing a shift in their community that was a product not of changing development policy but of changing management policy. While many of them found the projects aid organizations were currently undertaking similar to those that had existed in the past, what had changed was how workers were employed and how their jobs were defined. Many of those inside and outside development are constructively (and sometimes not so constructively) critical of the ideologies and practices of development work. Among practitioners, there is a nearly constant process of evaluation, both of their own practices and of the methods of the field as a whole. Yet it has largely escaped the critical research on and of development that the same audit cultures and accountability measures applied to development practices (Escobar 1995) are now also applied to the developers themselves. The end of the millennium saw a number of valuable criticisms of development discourse that revealed the degree to which postcolonial aid practices relied on transforming aid work into technical problems solvable by scientific means (Scott 1998, 4) and in which bureaucracy itself served to discipline the "objects" of development (Escobar 1995, 145). Through "depoliticizing" the operations of development (Ferguson 1994), its ideological agenda could be masked behind a veneer of science and technocracy. Yet in the past dozen years, this agenda of "rational" administration and pursuit of efficiency has found a new place in the development world such that "best practices" are not only applied *by* aid workers but applied *to* them as well. The Western economistic thinking that Arturo Escobar pinpointed as the unquestionable norm of development (Escobar 1995, 58–63) has shifted its target. Thus while prescriptions for "alternative modernities" and "culturally appropriate" forms of development have gained widespread acceptance, "universal" ideas of economics and management have reappeared in strategies of development employment. The valuable criticisms of development policy as reliant on a teleological view of modernity and a hyperrational pursuit of progress have not been applied to the way these same rationalities now impinge on the lives and cultures of aid workers themselves. Those within aid work often claim a radical disjuncture between development and business, noting that "management for development is fundamentally different," but often enough they then "go on and adopt ideas that come from the corporate sector" (Dichter 1989, 384). The hope is that solving problems such as hunger and maternal mortality should be exempt from the logics of business. A *cordon sanitaire* is expected to exist between the universalized and decontextualized measures of success demanded of development work in evaluatory frames and the allowances that are expected to be made for cultural and historical distinctiveness in the actions aid workers take in the field. Aid recipients are permitted to have culture and difference, while aid workers are supposed to be replaceable units of expertise.

To see this application of corporate logics to everyday life, one must step back from the level of discourse to examine the restructuring of the everyday life of aid workers based on metrics of efficiency and rationalization (Weber 1930/1992). The disjuncture between the lessons of critical development literature and the expectations of those generating development policy may not be merely a matter of disciplinary pride or stubborn devotion to past practices. What if the "problem" of development is not (or not just) issues of academic jargon or ignorance of the realities of on-the-ground aid work but instead a matter of bad employment policy? Why should aid workers be eager to promote cultural specificity in their work even as they are not granted the same considerations in their own lives?

Many global practices are challenged by similar disjunctures between the producers of cosmopolitan theory and policy versus those delegated to the realms of "local context" and implementation (Freeman 2001; Nightingale 2005). That aid workers have been invisible within scholarship can be explained, if not justified, by a variety of assumptions. Yet such an academic lacuna does not and cannot explain the physical absence of aid workers on the ground—the hollowing out of self-identified aid workers seen in Nepal. Here, there is a problem separate from a debate about ill-considered policy versus uninformed application—the category of aid worker itself is being evacuated to be replaced by hydrologists, obstetricians, and office managers. The technologization of aid that many have observed, and that found particular play in the creation of US aid policy in Nepal (Hindman 2002), has been transformed beyond the "Green Revolution" policies, cast-off machines, and "unsustainable" practices. Specialization is now embedded in people, and through new management practices development agencies are able to utilize the sort of "just-in-time" strategies seen in global manufacturing, now put in service of the production of a new kind of product called "aid." In other words, what have appeared as new universal models of efficiency and best practices for all businesses have been applied to the hiring of professional aid workers, and this reformulation of development labor has permitted the elimination of direct employees in development organizations and a related transformation of development itself. The redefinition of the expertise required to do aid work has altered those qualified to work on aid contracts such that in Nepal few employees actually identify themselves as aid workers.

One aspect of this is the rise of the professional NGO managerial expert. While some in the field of development scholarship point to a shift to professional (as opposed to "do-gooder") managers within many NGOs (e.g., Dichter 1999), public understanding of the work of most aid agencies is still of benevolent and self-sacrificing volunteers (de Jong this volume). Similar phenomena have also been observed among civil society, social movement, and advocacy network scholars (W. Fisher 1997; Skocpol 2003; D. Fisher 2006). For political activist movements, this increasing specialization is seen to negatively influence the mission of organizations by increasing distance between investors/donors and the outcome of their funds (D. Fisher 2006) as well as problematizing the relationship between "stakeholders" and those who manage a project (Dichter 1999).[7] David Lewis (2003a, 2003b, 2005; Lewis and Mosse 2006) has devoted significant attention to how the rise of professional management techniques has changed the operations of development, producing NGOs as an industry. Lewis has also explored changes in the relationship between NGOs and partners in government and business, but there is little scholarship on how these transformations are experienced by managers themselves or the effect that their new lives have on the work that they do. Yet there are high stakes for this new class of NGO consultants and experts as the move "toward professionalization, jobs, careers, status, and a whole mix of difficult to define personal stakes are now in play and give weight to the survival instinct" (Dichter 1999, 49; see also Kothari 2005).[8] The new professionals doing aid work must continually massage networks to get information about forthcoming bids and continue to maintain contact with a home office, which might deploy them next on a for-profit job outside of the development world. The technical expert doing work with aid agencies has little financial or social incentive to identify with the "helping professions." The engineer plotted within a world of paper-pushing NGO managers and young do-gooder volunteers is quick to identify not with these coworkers but with his fellow technical professionals. In the second part of this chapter, I want to explore this new world of professionals doing development work and the way in which the shifting demography of this population might say something about the changing nature of development work as labor and about the effect of the expanding application of best practices and managerial rationality.

Happy Hour at the Antigone Hotel

The social impacts of this new form of development employment are seen not only in the declining numbers of Western expatriate children at local international schools and the shifting regulation of membership at the American Club and commissary but also in the arrival of new social institutions that accommodate the demands of a changing expatriate population. Happy hour in the garden of the Antigone Hotel had once been a weekly gathering of a half dozen coworkers on Fridays, but for a period of time in 2007, it became an almost daily gathering, mainly centered on employees associated with one government-sponsored development contract and expanded to include other expatriates they met along the way. Most of those who attended were staying at hotels and guesthouses in the Lazimpath area, near many of the foreign embassies. For those in this group, their stay in Nepal was usually associated with a discrete project—a bridge, an energy-generation project, or a literacy program—and their projected stays varied from three months to a year, although many found their three-month contracts lasting for six months or more. One significant addition to this group was the visiting administrators who often came from the home offices of a subcontractor or supervisory consultants. These executives usually came for only a week or so to check up on the operations of their employees, as well as to research future contracting opportunities.[9]

Happy hour was often an all-evening event. Most workers traveled by taxi or company car directly from the job site to the bar, although arrival times varied widely depending on traffic and if there were protests on the streets. "What else do I have to do," remarked one early arrival who was attending happy hour despite having taken the day off work. Many of the men who formed this loose group had come together to find something to occupy their evenings.[10] Although they were all given substantial per diems to pay for lodging and food in Kathmandu, many chose to stay at midrange hotels and save as much money as possible for potential future gaps between contracts. Rather than staying at the Radisson, which was the basis for calculating per diems for several employers, they stayed at hotels such as the Antigone that were out of the price range of most backpacking tourists but not associated with any international chains. At these two- and three-star hotels, they had Internet access, English-speaking staff, and useful amenities such as a bar and gift shop but little in the way of recreation or entertainment. After several weeks of eating room service while watching the limited offerings on the hotel's television or watching DVDs on their computer, many ventured out to the Antigone happy hour to sociably pass the evening and perhaps share dinner.

Conversation consisted mainly of complaints about either superiors at the home office or subordinate Nepali workers and the boredom of life in Kathmandu. Weekends were not a welcome break, as the men could find little to occupy their time. Many took advantage of the opportunity to work at least part of the day on Sunday, as many in Nepal do, merely as a diversion. At least once a week, someone would propose a cultural outing to visit one of the many tourist sites in Kathmandu. Sometimes with enough enthusiasm and new participants, they could be motivated to go on a group outing to locations such as "the monkey temple" or "this big Buddhist thing outside of town." Equally often, someone in the group would discourage the activity: "I went there last month; it's not that big a deal, and it is really hot and dirty." It took most workers only a few months before they felt they had exhausted all the possibilities in the city. The casinos were interesting for a visit or two but contradicted the need to save money, and the predominance of Indian businessmen in designer suits made some feel out of place. The local tourist bars in Thamel were a favorite weekend outing, but within a month most found that the backpackers' enthusiasm for "exotic Nepal" and the predominance of local youth seeking foreign girls became a deterrent. The American Club continued to be an attraction for those able to gain entrance, but many complained about the family orientation. "It's all kid's movies," noted one Antigone regular, observing the frequency of Disney movies on the weekend schedule. Although the films were shown on a large screen, with Foster's beer and burgers just steps away, the movie choices could not overcome those assets, especially when bootleg versions of first-run movies were available for just a few dollars in Thamel.

Family and home meant something different to this cohort of expatriates than to the previous generation of expatriate development workers. Their home and family were elsewhere. Life in Kathmandu was at once a break from the day-to-day responsibilities for children left behind in another country and a practical choice to fulfill the economic needs of their family. Three core members of the Antigone group exemplified this new paradigm of global aid subcontracting but were at different moments in their personal lives. For Jason, short-term contracts abroad were a way to save money for a future he had not yet begun. "It's time to get out," he remarked, "I need to find a wife soon. With six months on and only one or two months off, it's hard to meet someone at home." After nearly 10 years in the military or on these short duration contracts, Jason had recently celebrated his 30th birthday. He worried that years of short-term relationships with "Asian girls" would make finding a wife at home difficult—he also worried that the weight he had gained over that time would make him an unappealing partner. "But I have a lot of money saved up—I want to build a house somewhere. . . . I suppose that I should just stop doing this and settle down." As soon as Jason left, one of his coworkers was quick to gloss his melancholy comments: "He had a girlfriend in Malaysia—four months—thought they might get married" but apparently resistance from both families, the end of the job contract, and considerations of where the couple might share a permanent home had finished the relationship. "Now he's worried he won't ever find someone." Jason's hope for a secure future made possible by lucrative contracts abroad resonated with Alan's frugal ways in Kathmandu. The dream of a financially secure family life was one Alan shared, but he was working to sustain it in the present. Alan has five children and a wife who works only part time, and his income from engineering consulting was necessary to support his household in suburban Virginia. While Jason hoped to end his peripatetic ways, Alan worried that he would never be able to afford to do so. "Those kids will want to go to college too," he noted after enumerating the many expenses that were incurred to support his family. Alan was in daily e-mail contact with his wife and children and eschewed many of the drinking activities and pursuit of local women that were a part of his colleagues' socializing. He confessed that he missed his family and worried that he was becoming just a source of money for his kids. Tim had been through a similar fear but was now at a different point in his life. "I'm in it to get new bikes." He somewhat flippantly noted that his motivation for pursuing overseas contracts was to go to the Sturgis motorcycle rally and attend as many Grateful Dead and "Jam band" shows as possible. "This 'three months on–nine months off' thing is perfect for me . . . and it keeps me away from my wife." Tim and his wife own a home in North Carolina and have three children—each of them has a grown child from previous marriages, and they have one teenager at home. He had spent very little time in the past few years at his house working on bikes and going to concerts, despite claims to being always in pursuit of recreation. Every time he returned to the United States, he found the draw to overseas contracts too great to resist: "The money is too good." Although many others who worked for his company tried to avoid overseas positions, Tim leapt at them and had managed to pay off some of his credit card debt with savings from his per diem.

Tim shared with Jason, and almost half of those at the Antigone, a period of military or foreign service experience. He was often the instigator for conversations about exploits at past postings. An enthusiastic storyteller, he often regaled those present with the near misses he and his fellow soldiers had experienced: "The sandbags are higher in Iraq than Mogadishu, if they hadn't been, he would have been blown up. . . . Baghdad is fun—Mogadishu is 100% worse." As we waited for dinner to arrive, such ruminations led to comparative horror stories about the food in various places—the terrible steak in Somalia, the attempts to produce a birthday cake in Seoul, nothing but MREs (Meal,

Ready-to-Eat) to eat in parts of Africa. When a group of contractors arrived to help in the construction of the new USAID offices, Tim found an eager audience of fellow ex-military personnel to listen to his stories. Many parts of the new AID and embassy facilities, including "the secret squirrel rooms," had to be constructed using personnel cleared by the US government. Given both the demands of security clearance and the long delays taking place at the time in getting clearance, the Turkish subcontractor in charge of construction had hired a number of ex-military personnel from the United States with the request clearance (Hindman forthcoming). Many of these men had retired from the military by their mid-30s and now roamed the globe on contracts procured through a network of contacts from their military days. Tim explained this to me like this: "I went to college—didn't finish—but most of these guys didn't. For us, it's kind of like what college was for you. We hang out—drink a lot—get scared shitless together—and avoid the responsibilities of real life . . . [short-term overseas contracts] are just the same; the work is bullshit, but it's easy." In Tim's estimation, most of the ex-military guys were like him, avoiding responsibilities and/or wives at home, making a good deal of money, and enjoying a prolonged youth.

At the Antigone, the electronics professionals on short-term contracts for the construction of the American embassy offices shared stories and beer with technical experts working on development projects and consultants from governments and corporations. They often described similar reasons for their time in Nepal: to make money, take care of their part of the job, and facilitate future subcontracted overseas employment. Although more than half of those who regularly attended the happy hour did "aid work," few considered themselves "aid workers." Some felt an attachment to a team, project, or contract—associating with the Irrigation Development Project and their coworkers on that endeavor—but a single project often included employees from as many as five different employers, and workers circulated in and out of a project as their technical skills were needed elsewhere. One employer pulled an Antigone regular from the development contract he had been working on in Kathmandu because his unique skills were needed in a more profitable job elsewhere, and the population of happy hour turned over regularly.

The affiliative networks being established at the Antigone were the product of changing employment ideologies imported into development work from the wider business community as much as the rise in US security concerns (see Bebbington and Kothari 2006). The economization of hunger and health are familiar critiques of how development is made quantifiable (Escobar 1995, 101), and discovering of rationalization of many aspects of everyday life may not be surprising (Callon 1998). The novelty was that those seeking to economize the activities of others (as is the case in much of development policy) were becoming subject to the same process of efficiency. The concerns of aid workers, and expatriates in general, were becoming subsidiary to a financial model that expected workers to be fully interchangeable and independent. It was not an interest in the diverse cultures of the world or a desire to overcome the great wealth disparity that marks the twenty-first-century world that brought together workers at the Antigone. For some, it was having an up-to-date TS/SSBI or knowing the same crazy gunny at Osan.[11] The cheap beer brought another group to happy hour to share stories about what bonuses and incentives their employers offered, how much money they were able to save while abroad, and what contracting opportunities they had heard about down the line. The poverty of Nepal or any of their other work sites rarely entered into the conversation; after all "a job's a job."

"It's Just Good Business!": Efficiency and the Family Abroad

The contemporary policies of aid employers are generating a demographic change in the population of expatriates in Kathmandu, but links between institutional support for transnational employees and the family lives of those who work overseas have a much longer history. Choosing men for their marital and class status was a key element of European colonial policy, and changing the profile of who was appropriate for a given position was part of the arsenal deployed to bring about shifts in governance, economics, and the everyday life of both colonial officials and the local populace. The regulation of salary, hiring, and sexual relations by colonial powers was "central to the development of particular kinds of colonial settlements and to the allocation of economic activity within them" (Stoler 2002, 47). At one moment, sexual relations and the establishment of families with local populations was sanctioned by the colonial government as a means to gather "local knowledge" and to reduce costs through sending only bachelor officers overseas and paying only a single (rather than a "family") wage. At other moments in the colonial project, these families would be condemned and prosecuted when they detracted from the economic mission of the British East India Company (Ballhatchet 1980). Scholars of colonial rule and family relations have observed that sexual morality and racism were sporadically marshaled to promote one form of domestic arrangement over another, but these ethical arguments were often public performances used to justify shifts in colonial politics and economics (e.g., Hutchins 1967).

In looking at the problem-space of European colonialism in relation to the contemporary practices of Aidland, I do not want to argue for a more general parallel between development and colonialism. Even if those are in evidence, my point is that both situations present employers with a concern about the relationship between the worker's family and the job at hand. The situation of overseas employment unavoidably disturbs any illusion of a tidy public–private or work–leisure divide and highlights the links between "human resources" policy and the tasks demanded of a worker. The choice of whom to send to conduct operations away from home forces employers to be aware of the employee as something more than an atomized individual. The British crown thought and rethought the economics and sociology, as well as the public relations impact, of various forms of hiring and related family postings of colonists to its outposts in India and elsewhere (McClintock 1995; Blunt 2005; Stark 1926/2007). Likewise, family policy is a concern that exercises contemporary overseas employers, whether in the international human resources literatures on the role of families in the failure of expatriate careers (Hindman 2007) or in shifting policies about same-sex families in the US Foreign Service.[12]

In placing changes in development employment policy alongside shifting discourse around colonial families, one can see the elisions that are a part of the tense relationship between "family values" and regimes of corporate accountability. Various agendas of the British crown generated metrics that resulted in different deployments of British workers overseas, which intentionally or unintentionally shifted the likely profile of their employees, the nature of the family unit abroad, and ultimately the work of the empire. Demographic shifts in employees can result from worker interest (Pratt 1992; Jayawardena 1995); domestic or overseas anxieties about race, class, and gender (Stoler 1989; Young 1995; McClintock 1995; Cooper and Stoler 1997); large-scale policy shifts (Hutchins 1967); historical accidents (Stark 1926/2007, 8); or particular needs of the employer at the time (Strobel 1991). The explicit discussions of race and class used as justifications by colonial administrations are contemporarily unspeakable; nonetheless shifts in the race, class, and gender makeup of those sought for expatriate development employment are taking place (cf. Salzinger 2003). What has occurred is framed not as a change in ideology but as an advance in administration. The same processes of outsourcing and specialization that are occurring in most industries appear in the new logics of development as well, as the aid industry continues to borrow from the corporate world even as it decries it. Agencies find that rather than retaining a permanent staff, they can subcontract with secondary employers to fit the moment-to-moment needs of a project, resulting, they hope, in the efficient, just-in-time delivery of aid functions. The logics that drive this new form of aid employment are no different from those of other industries—unsurprisingly, as both are now often administered by the same professional human resources specialists. These compensation experts and head-hunting agencies are given the charge to look for a hydrology engineer, and it matters little if the underlying contract is for a corporation or a development project. The empty offices of aid agencies in Nepal are a visible reminder of this shift in employment rubrics, and the few who remained employed under the old system mourned the loss of friends and devotion to the mission of care work (e.g., Pigg 1993; de Vries 2005; Gould 2008).[13] Laments about how the community was once united by a common desire to help people in Nepal were frequent, as people pointed to the new style of aid workers with the claim that "they're just in it for the money now."

Focusing on aid workers as also people with families and lives offers another framework for considering contemporary changes in how the labor of aid work gets done. With the transformation of tasks in the development industry into contract labor, those employed by aid agencies must devote new attention to the expansion of their own networks of professional contacts. For these new flexibilized laborers, professional affiliations align not with development agencies but with subcontracting agencies and colleagues employed by other companies (Welch and Welch 2008). Yet the shift in the demographic profile of aid workers from development professionals deployed abroad with their families to single technical specialists on short-term contracts is presented merely as a business decision. The changes in the profile of USAID workers in Nepal is explained as "best practices" and as such goes unquestioned by most in the aid industry. The manipulation by colonial officials of the class, racial, and gender makeup of overseas employees was initially presented as economic good sense but in retrospect appears to have also included a desire to manage the social behavior of colonizers and colonized alike as well as to generate or discourage particular types of domestic units. While I do not want to go so far as to suggest that contemporary aid agencies are seeking to reconfigure the family of the aid worker, their policies are having this effect. This can be seen in the rise of former military personnel in some arenas, a preference justified by security concerns, which results in a largely male population of employees. Anxiety over the effects of this demographic shift were felt particularly by a female aid worker in Nepal who had spent 15 years in various postings across the Middle East, Asia, and Africa. She saw herself as a pioneer in the profession, telling stories about how Asian colleagues, initially skeptical about a woman in a position of leadership, came to respect her and about how she found ways of manipulating travel restrictions on women in the Middle East. "Things had really been looking up in the 1990s—more and more women . . . now, that is all gone." She searched for a reason for why the next generation of female aid professionals she had believed she was cultivating had not appeared in Nepal by 2007, and we speculated for nearly an hour, raising a variety of possible explanations such as the changing attitudes toward raising children, the rise of Maoist violence in Kathmandu, and general cutbacks in the money devoted to aid projects. In the end, she seemed unsatisfied with any of our conclusions—she decided it was not discrimination, it was not fear, "it was only business."

Notes

1. It is worth noting that many who come to Nepal in search of volunteer opportunities are disappointed in the offerings. As discussed in the body of this chapter, few organizations are in need of the skills travelers can provide, and agencies complain that employing youth for the short stints that they offer is more trouble than value. Several organizations in Kathmandu seek to match eager tourist volunteers with opportunities, but managers I spoke with struggled to find openings. Often jobs were unappealing to foreigners, either because of the tasks required or the location or because many agencies and organizations were interested only in those with high levels of training or a willingness to commit a year or more. In addition, many agencies are finding they can fill their volunteer positions with paid visitors. Through these programs, organizations benefit from the income from the programs and the work of volunteers and also access a population that often goes on to earn high incomes in their home countries and potentially donate at high levels to the cause in the future. People with experience in other aid settings see a different set of changing labor practices, in which student or gap-year adventurers bring together youthful volunteerism with entrepreneurial and networking skills to produce a style of aid worker that is not seen in any numbers in Kathmandu. I thank participants in the spring 2009 anthropology seminar at Sussex University for this important perspective.

2. For exceptions to this rule, see the introduction to this volume.

3. Understanding how the shifting racial profile of the academic anthropologist and of the development worker might change this is an important interjection into this dilemma—as both "us"s change.

4. The Hacienda itself went out of business in 2007, but several similar "residence hotels" have emerged to serve this market. In addition, many tourist hotels have either adapted or added apartments to serve long-term residents.

5. Although I have preserved the names of many institutions and businesses, I have changed all personal names, some employers, and a few job details in an attempt to provide anonymity to people in this very small community. I hope I have done so successfully, as without the kindness and openness of Tom, Sheila, Mary, Tim, Alan, Jason, and many others like them, this research would not have been possible.

6. For more on the complex field of foreigners in Nepal and work exerted by each segment to create distinction, see Moran (2004) and Liechty (2005).

7. Dana Fisher's *Activism, Inc.* (2006) focuses mainly on how outsourcing the footwork of grassroots campaigning has resulted in a greater need for "command and control" functions (Sassen 2000) and how this lack of face-to-face engagement between activists and the public has destroyed the idealism of a generation of progressive activists in the United States. I thank Evalyn Tennant for bringing this argument to my attention.

8. It is worth echoing Dichter's own footnote to this claim, where he wrote that this is a statement based on his own experience with NGO workers. I bring attention to this comment because it shows the need for NGO scholars to shift their focus and pull in different types of experience to be able to view the aid worker as part of the story of aid work.

9. The visits of home office executives were usually dreaded, as it put the expatriate in the position of local host and also forced everyone to be on their best behavior. Yet it also often brought more luxurious dinners and perhaps a trip outside of the city on the company's dime.

10. I was one of only two women to attend these gatherings. The other was an employee with one of the supervisory agencies who was responsible for the practical arrangement for many of the visiting contractors. Several other women worked with these men on occasion, although none of them were in the same circuit of hiring. When I spoke with one of the coworkers of these men about the happy hour event, she noted she "wouldn't have anything to talk about," as she presumed, somewhat correctly, that much of the conversation revolved around literal and figurative war stories.

11. TS/SSBI is Top Secret security clearance having formerly passed a Single Scope Background Investigation. A gunny is a gunnery sergeant, and Osan is a US military base in South Korea. Yet having the knowledge of such acronyms and conversing in these codes is in large part the content of the communality, as much as the status itself.

12. This refers to the June 2009 decision by the US government to permit domestic partners of Foreign Service workers to receive many of the same benefits as those married to Foreign Service workers. For the details and limits of this shift, consult the US Department of State *Foreign Affairs Manual*, 3 FAM 1600 (www.state.gov/m/a/dir/regs/fam/03fam/3_1600/).

13. De Jong (this volume) and others have questioned the rhetoric of altruism in aid work, and the protests of loss of caring were likely the last gasp of vanishing practices that were never as strong as is claimed in their absence.

References

Ballhatchet, Kenneth. 1980. *Race, sex and class under the Raj*. London: Weidenfeld and Nicolson.

Bebbington, Anthony, and Uma Kothari. 2006. Transnational development networks. *Environment and Planning A* 38:849–66.

Blunt, Alison. 2005. *Domicile and diaspora: Anglo-Indian women and the spatial politics of home*. Malden, MA: Blackwell.

Callon, Michel. 1998. The embeddedness of economic markets in economics. In *The laws of the markets*, ed. Michel Callon, 1–57. Malden, MA: Blackwell.

Cooper, Frederick, and Randall Packard. 1997. Introduction. In *International development and the social sciences: Essays on the history and the politics of knowledge*, ed. Frederick Cooper and Randall Packard, 1–41. Berkeley: University of California Press.

Crewe, Emma, and E. Harrison. 1999. *Whose development? An ethnography of aid*. London: Zed Books.

de Vries, Pieter. 2005. Critiquing governmentality: The social construction of participation and accountability in the Atlantic zone of Costa Rica. *Focaal—European Journal of Anthropology* 45:94–111.

Dichter, Thomas. 1989. Development management: Plain or fancy? Sorting out some muddles. *Public Administration and Development* 9:381–93.

———. 1999. Globalization and its effects on NGOs: Efflorescence or a blurring of roles and relevance? *Nonprofit and Voluntary Sector Quarterly* 28 (4): 38–58.

di Leonardo, Micaela. 1998. *Exotics at home: Anthropologies, others, American modernity*. Chicago: University of Chicago Press.

Elyachar, Julia. 2003. Mappings of power: The state, NGOs, and international organizations in the informal economy of Cairo. *Comparative Studies of Society and History* 45:571–605.

———. 2006. Best practices: Research, finance, and NGOs in Cairo. *American Ethnologist* 33 (3): 413–26.

Escobar, Arturo. 1991. Anthropology and the development encounter: The making and marketing of development anthropology. *American Ethnologist* 18 (4): 658–82.

———. 1995. *Encountering development: The making and unmaking of the third world*. Princeton, NJ: Princeton University Press.

———. 2007. "Post-development" as concept and social practice. In *Exploring post-development: Theory and practice, problems and perspectives*, ed. Aram Ziai, 18–31. New York: Routledge.

Ferguson, James. 1994. *The anti-politics machine: "Development," depoliticization, and bureaucratic power in Lesotho*. Minneapolis: University of Minnesota Press.

———. 1997. Anthropology and its evil twin: "Development" in the constitutions of a discipline. In *International development and the social sciences: Essays on the history and politics of knowledge*, ed. Frederick Cooper and Randall Packard, 150–75. Berkeley: University of California Press.

Fisher, Dana. 2006. *Activism, Inc.: How the outsourcing of grassroots campaigns is strangling progressive politics in America*. Stanford, CA: Stanford University Press.

Fisher, William. 1997. Doing good? The politics and antipolitics of NGO practices. *Annual Review of Anthropology* 26:439–64.

Freeman, Carla. 2001. Is local:global as feminine:masculine? Rethinking the gender of globalization. *Signs* 26 (4): 1007–37.

Gould, Jeremy. 2008. *Thinking outside development: Epistemological explorations 1994–2008*. Ebook. Accessed 9 April. http://www.valt.helsinki.fi/staff/gould/pubs/thinking%20outside%2096%20dpi%2017v08.pdf.

Harper, Richard. 2000. The social organization of the IMF's mission work: An examination of international auditing. In *Audit cultures: Anthropological studies in ethics and the academy*, ed. Marilyn Strathern, 19–53. New York: Routledge.

Hindman, Heather. 2002. The everyday life of American development in Nepal. *Studies in Nepali History and Society* 7 (1): 99–136.

———. 2007. Outsourcing difference: Expatriate training and the disciplining of culture. In *Deciphering the global*, ed. Saskia Sassen, 155–77. New York: Routledge.

———. Forthcoming. Performing security in Nepal's Little America: Bureaucracy and its malcontents. *Bodhi* 4(1).

Hutchins, Francis G. 1967. *The illusion of permanence: British imperialism in India.* Princeton, NJ: Princeton University Press.

Jayawardena, Kumari. 1995. *The white woman's other burden: Western women and South Asia during British rule.* New York: Routledge.

Kothari, Uma. 2005. Authority and expertise: The professionalization of international development and the ordering of dissent. *Antipode* 37:425–46.

Latour, Bruno. 2004. Why has critique run out of steam? From matters of fact to matters of concern. *Critical Inquiry* 30:225–48.

———. 2005. *Reassembling the social: An introduction to actor-network-theory.* New York: Oxford University Press.

Lewis, David. 2003a. Development organizations: Towards a composite approach. *Public Management Review* 5 (3): 325–44.

———. 2003b. NGOs, organizational culture, and institutional sustainability. *Annals of the American Academy of Political and Social Science* 590:212–26.

———. 2005. *Anthropology and development: The uneasy relationship.* London: LSE Research Online. http://eprints.lse.ac.uk/archive/00000253.

Lewis, David, and David Mosse. 2006. Encountering order and disjuncture: Contemporary anthropological perspectives on the organization of development. *Oxford Development Studies* 34 (1): 1–13.

Liechty, Mark. 2005. Building the road to Kathmandu: Notes on the history of tourism in Nepal. *Himalaya* 25 (1–2): 19–28.

LiPuma, Edward, and Benjamin Lee. 2004. *Financial derivatives and the globalization of risk.* Durham, NC: Duke University Press.

Marx, Karl. 1990 [1867]. *Capital Volume I.* New York: Penguin Classics.

McClintock, Anne. 1995. *Imperial leather: Race, gender and sexuality in the colonial context.* New York: Routledge.

Miner, Horace. 1956. Body rituals among the Nacirema. *American Anthropologist* 58:503–7.

Mitchell, Timothy. 2002. *Rule of experts: Egypt, techno-politics, modernity.* Berkeley: University of California Press.

Moran, Peter. 2004. *Buddhism observed: Travellers, exiles and Tibetan dharma in Kathmandu.* London: Routledge.

Nightingale, Andrea. 2005. "The experts taught us all we know": Professionalisation and knowledge in Nepalese community forestry. *Antipode* 37:582–603.

Pigg, Stacy Leigh. 1993. Unintended consequences: The ideological impact of development. *South Asia Bulletin* 13 (1–2): 45–58.

Pratt, Mary Louise. 1992. *Imperial eyes: Travel writing and transculturation.* New York: Routledge.

Rahnema, Majid (with Victoria Bawtree, eds.). 1997. *The post-development reader.* Atlantic Highlands, NJ: Zed Books.

Roberts, J. Timmons. 1995. Subcontracting and the omitted social dimensions of large development projects: Household survival at the Carajas mines in the Brazilian Amazon. *Economic Development and Cultural Change* 43 (4): 735–58.

Salzinger, Leslie. 2003. *Genders in production: Making workers in Mexico's global factories.* Berkeley: University of California Press.

Sassen, Saskia. 2000. *The global city: New York, London, Tokyo.* Princeton, NJ: Princeton University Press.

Scott, James C. 1998. *Seeing like a state: How certain schemes to improve the human condition have failed*. New Haven, CT: Yale University Press.

Skocpol, Theda. 2003. *Diminished democracy: From membership to management in American civic life*. Norman: University of Oklahoma Press.

Stark, Herbert Alick. 2007 [1926]. *Hostages to India: Or the life story of the Anglo Indian Race*. United States: Simon Wallenberg Press.

Stoler, Ann Laura. 1989. Rethinking colonial categories: European communities and the boundaries of rule. *Comparative Studies in Society and History* 31 (1): 134–61.

———. 2002. *Carnal knowledge and imperial power: Race and the intimate in colonial rule*. Berkeley: University of California Press.

Strathern, Marilyn, ed. 2000. Introduction: New accountabilities. In *Audit cultures: Anthropological studies in ethics and the academy*, 1–18. New York: Routledge.

Strobel, Margaret. 1991. *European women and the second British Empire*. Bloomington: Indiana University Press.

Trouillot, Michel-Rolph. 2003. *Global transformations*. New York: Palgrave Macmillan.

Weber, Max. 1992 [1930]. *The Protestant ethic and the spirit of Capitalism*. New York: Routledge.

Welch, Catherine, and Denice Welch. 2008. *The strength of strong ties: Career neworks [sic] in international development projects*. http://www.impgroup.org/paper_view_window.php?viewPaper=6784.

Wolf, Eric R. 1982. *Europe and the people without history*. Berkeley: University of California Press.

Young, Robert. 1995. *Colonial desire: Hybridity in theory, culture and race*. New York: Routledge.

Ziai, Aram. 2007. Development discourse and its critics: An introduction to post development. In *Exploring post-development: Theory and practice, problems and perspectives*, ed. Aram Ziai, 3–17. New York: Routledge.

Who Is International Aid?

Some Personal Observations

Raymond Apthorpe

The following impressions of some people in aid I met on travels are imaginative but not imaginary. The events and encounters on which they are based happened. But no claim is made for any representativeness these remarks might have on good—or bad—days, and they are of art and artifice not weights and measures.

The Anonymity of Aid

International aid talks a lot about itself as apolitical, asocial, humanitarian, "just helping across borders." Is it that, or, rather, is it *only* that? People who in one way or another work in or for aid are, like everyone else, not without social and political class and other category affiliations, special interests, philosophical and perhaps spiritual concerns about inequalities in their own and other countries, theories about development, attitudes about emergency relief in man-made conflicts perhaps contrasted with aid for nature-sent disasters, and closer or more distant encounters with the "other cultures" and "other societies" they say they serve. On *what* aid is and *what* aid does or doesn't do there are mountains of dedicated inquiry. But sociologically and biographically, *who* international aid is and *who* "civil society" is, is, save for a few famous names and a handful of studies of particular organizations, almost unknown.[1] (With poverty studies it is the same: mountains of *what is* and *how much* writing only molehills on who is poor and *their* thinking about what is to be done.) Dedicated social research could reveal what in the international world of aid traces to aiders' personal backgrounds, biographies, nationalities, professional

training, career choices, and much more. Hence this book. The following remarks, however, draw only on some of this occasional aid worker's—now re-
ceding—personal experience. Unlike the book's main contributions, this one
is not social-research based. Most of its content has, however, at least been
presented and examined interactively in my international education classes on
aid over the years, then sometimes reimagined and restated as a result.[2]

Casts of 100s and 1,000s

"My wife and I own 17 NGOs," a retired civil servant in Bangladesh told me,
admittedly now some years ago, "so that we can help the foreign aid to our
country." Remaining for the moment with just that one country, it has also
of course the two huge NGOs, BRAC and Proshika, each with some links,
declining now though they may be, to foreign aid. BRAC, however, is "by
far the largest [foreign] NGO in Afghanistan" (Smillie 2009, 225). Not that
either the media or academia has noticed this. Thus depending on where it
meets with the national, the world of international aid is populated by not less
than 100s of 1,000s of *people*. That in itself must be one of the reasons why
little is known about them. With countless numbers of persons, where to start?
(Also to be considered is the very wide range of donor and other international
aid *organizations*, which tend to be highly competitive in what they actually
do. Other than in particular regards and circumstances, they seldom work in
anything like close cooperation [patronage and contract relations excluded].
Interagency relations within "the UN family" are no exception [much as Kofi
Annan used to lament when calling for UN reform to bring "harmonization"].
Normally neither NGOs nor donors allow joint evaluations of their offices and
operations.)

While it may be difficult for some specialized humanitarian and development aid agencies to accept, it is the case that militaries and mercenaries, mul-
tinationals (with or without corporate social responsibility) and missionaries
(and other religionists of many faiths), media and academia are also part of the
scenario, scene, plot, and action. Each considers it has its own legitimate role
to play with regard to the assistance and protection needed or not, and when,
and how. Moreover within each there is yet more diversity. In different ech-
elons of personnel, people think and do aid differently, however variously and
to different degrees in different organizations (lesser in my experience, say, in
projects of the European Commission's humanitarian office—ECHO—where
it appears exceptionally high centralization prevails; perhaps greater than in
the case of bilateral donors with globally far-flung and sectorally multiple pro-

grams). Where chiefs and section heads of agencies are individually charismatic, other dimensions of difference are likely to emerge, again depending somewhat on the specifics of the organization concerned including of course its history, economics, and politics.

Drivers. The convoy truck driver leader hired by the World Food Program risks absolutely all on the job in active war zones by actually delivering relief supplies under fire. One such driver, not yet 30 perhaps, I met in Liberia, a Sudanese. He was carrying the heaviest imaginable burdens of duty and responsibility, including those of negotiating, unarmed and with loaded trucks of food just waiting to be seized, with heavily armed rebels. (I confess back in Monrovia indulgently as an academic I asked him in a quiet moment whether at least he could draw on some sort of training for such greatest possible personal danger. "No, but neither have my college mates at home who are in a war too.")

Directors. In the head offices and boardrooms of major agencies, the top brass have signed up to what they have been convinced is essential for good aidship: codes of ethics. At other levels, such codes and whether they are needed may be seen in an entirely different light if, that is, they are known and seen at all. A woman working for a food relief agency in Pristina, when I asked her about such things, began by simply dismissing them as "Anglo-Saxon obsessions." (For a Frenchwoman from the land of *Code Napoleon*, that seemed, eventually to both of us, so over the top that finally we did have a good discussion.) Her view was that they were more executive playthings, "toys of boys," than anything else. Most chiefs, she said, were male, and what was opium for one gender and one class—top management—was seldom anyone else's.

Refugee camp managers. An assistant refugee camp manager in Macedonia told me when I asked him for his views on the pertinence of the international benchmarks of minimum emergency humanitarian provision known as the Sphere Standards that, *yes*, he had heard of them but, *no*, had never seen them. "Only the manager himself might have." So off I went to him. "Yes, I did see a copy somewhere but not here; anyway what might be acceptable for Rwanda would not be for the Balkans." (More recently, as, for example, in the Pacific region, the Sphere organization has stepped up its education campaigns to disseminate its standards and wisdom, perhaps in adapted form.)

Desk officers. In the Ukraine a donor agency's desk officer explained that much of her work in actually getting things done in the world of aid, whether there are codes of conduct or not, comes down to "ordinary practice," the likes of which might be familiar in business and trade but which are normally unassociated with aid work. "Someone with degrees from Oxford and LSE

[London School of Economics] and a Ph.D. in development studies from the University of Sussex arrived at BRAC expecting to find genius around every corner . . . what struck her instead was the ordinariness of everything . . . she discovered that the magic lies in . . . making ordinary things happen in the extraordinarily difficult situations and turning the whole into something quite amazing" (Smillie 2009, 258).

Volunteers with relief agencies. Some people you meet have considerable experience and/or training in technical matters in various sectors—medicine, nutrition, water and sanitation, and physical construction and reconstruction say. Perhaps also serious international experience and sensibility. Others, such as volunteers recruited short term to assist with emergency relief, have less, or even none, of either perhaps, as well as even orientation, let alone training. An Australian I met in Kosovo was in normal life back in Queensland in management PR, but, as she said, "I desperately wanted to do my bit and help." So she volunteered, was instantly hired by an international agency headquartered in Canberra to its emergency staff, and was flown immediately there from Brisbane. On the very next day, it was off to Skopje in Macedonia. Then after again just a one night stopover, she went next by road to Pristina—from where without any stopover at all, it was on to her work station hours away by road. To start work immediately without having been given by her new employer any significant orientation, let alone training, whatsoever: "There was no time."

Some of her duties turned out to be holding meetings of what in aid speak are called "beneficiaries," hearing their complaints, and then passing things on for whatever redress to her station chief. She told me she simply hated chairing those meetings. Having no knowledge whatsoever of how people in that part of the world lived, she had no idea as to whether it would be best or not to call both genders to the meetings. Normally there was nothing anyway, she said, that anyone could do by way of redress and accountability (Which, however, was not quite the case: as invited by her agency—which was hosting my visit—I helped set up some monitoring and evaluation provision. The World Food Program had received complaints about some of the distribution of its food and demanded that some inquiry be done there.)

Besides staffers and volunteers of all kinds, there are also of course the *committed individuals who take part on their own account*, as well as perhaps ad hoc interest groups at home. Here again there is much diversity. Think, for example, of the many "one-man-and-a-truck NGOs rolling into war-ravaged ex-Yugoslavia or Guatemala with loads of donated relief goods" (Sogge 2002, 69) a decade ago. Today *Viva Palestina* trucks and convoys bravely seek to break Israel's blockade of Gaza. Many such aid workers—like of course many others—work tirelessly if (to the media and also academia) largely invisibly, in all manner of practical ways. A few, however, stand defiantly—and highly visibly—in front of tanks and in other public demonstrations. Others boldly write their stands, perhaps taking on think tanks. Others stand independently in front of their classes. Across all such—and all the other—divides, what aiders *believe* about what they say or do in the name of aid varies a great deal, including as to what they consider to be properly aid and what is not aid. In Haiti, for example, after the earthquake in January 2010, whether foreigners allegedly attempting forcibly to evacuate children in need were aiding or child trafficking in what appear to be at best clumsy and at worst illegal and violent ways is a vexed issue again, as it was two or three years ago in Chad. Particularly, however, "my true belief" can fluctuate between extremes as wildly in aid as in other "I was a communist" walks of life and letters. Other examples might be "The formal sector has failed," but never fear, "The informal sector if duly assisted will succeed," and views such as "No, not top-down military-like management for aided irrigated agricultural development; better never anything but bottom-up."

Independent scholar-consultants such as this writer and academics from other disciplines on leave from their normal settings and scenes may be seen in the world of aid as nothing but nuisances if they respond to their formal terms of reference through plying a critical theory trade. While being, yet not belonging, in the world of aid, some do behave that way, most, as I believe, don't. There are after all many ways of taking a perspective and scarcely fewer as to why one is there, for how long, and with what degree of mental and other comfort or discomfort, or arrogance or empathy, or ignorance or knowledge. Also independence.

Minders, guides. On arriving at the field office of the organization into whose affairs you have come to pry as invited, you may kindly be provided with a minder or guide. What at times I have found, however, is how very nimbly such a guide can seize on the opportunity of perhaps getting out of the office for a day or two, with an evidently well-connected foreigner, to tell you as much as he or she can squeeze in about themselves and their personal plans "to move on" ("Can you possibly help me?"). In other ways too there can be some surprises when you arrive as to official narrative and the actual situation on the ground, not excluding at the extreme "You couldn't have come at a worse time; we requested you delayed your visit for a month or two."

From the different ways in which it is truly—or otherwise and perhaps less unstably—believed that aid should be done emerge other angles on belief as to what aid is and should be, including the case for "premature exit." Emergency relief aid bosses may decide to quit a scene before the job they came to do is done, on the calculation that staying might make either no significant difference or outcomes even worse. (The participants in my international classes each year formerly in Canberra and elsewhere, who included international practitioners, staffers of government disaster relief agencies, and the like, as well as regular graduate students, many of whom planned to seek careers in international aid, tended to take very different positions on such "principled aid" and exit. For one thing, participants from the "South" rarely ever agreed with those from the "North" as to whether that was just, that is, whether moral fervor—and political correctness—should bow in such cases to judgment, good or bad, about the practicalities of risk management and the politics of intervention and exit.)

On the whole, I find international—and other—aiders of all stripes mostly to agree with their interlocutors (perhaps after bringing up the matter themselves in the first place) that what they and their organizations nobly *say* about aiding and what they can or cannot *do* are very different. For such fracturation a variety of reasons is given. *Why* one works in aid may be important here, also for how long and whether in larger or smaller organizations or lower and higher positions. Certainly the complexities of being and doing, and of true belief and other forms of imagining and believing, which may be less unstable, and of not saying what you are doing besides not doing what you say, are as intricate in and around international aid as they are in other worlds. Perhaps more so, given the circumstances of the moralities and urgencies involved—as in the case, for example, of a consultancy team struggling against all odds: "At least two people in the mission are mad. They have made the mistake of confusing what they say they are doing with what they are doing" (Frank 1986, 237).

Aidlandery

Generalizing about a cultural formation at large is a high-wire act. Where 100s or 1,000s of people and organizations are involved, of course, no would-be totalizing single construct about scenes and scenarios could possibly be other than itself highly figurative and connotative, as well as being about sometimes only figurations and connotations. Similarly with Aidland (Apthorpe in press). No meta-high generalization on stilts could possibly be plainly denotative. Images aren't; they are not meant to be. Similarly as with feudalism, tribalism, imperialism, capitalism, and socialism (not that, so far as I know, Aidland has ever been ism'd). "None" is a descriptive term to which there corresponds a slice of life that can be . . . pointed out to bystanders as though it were a creature or an organism of some kind. . . . There have been thinkers who held that to every concept there properly corresponds an entity designated by some name, but *they never supposed that such entities walk about on two legs* [or] can be statistically weighed and measured. [While all connote] something real . . . there are no simple entities to which they refer. (Lichtheim 1971, 10–12, italics added)

What *does* "walk about on two legs" are not steep abstractions but real— and in such abstraction allegorical—people (when, that is, they are walking I suppose I should add for pedants—and sedants). Again thus this book. Different aiders, perhaps consonantly with their different aiding, live with different Aidlands, each with perhaps its own degrees of internal homogeneity and porosity, operational as well as virtual ways of linking (or not) with actual countries, as well as their own demographics and sociographics.

In opting in the previously mentioned seriously satirical "overview" of the world of international aid for the image Aid*land*, and not say Aid*space*, my intent was to take an anthropological approach to the intelligibility of international aid and aiders working across borders, and cultural and other "othering" wherever and in whatever forms it comes. In one year, Alice, the celebrity rhetorical device, joined my class and me "through the looking glass" from Wonderland. That only somewhat chance maneuver (I have long been a fan of Lewis Carroll the public logician) turned out so perfectly to serve a university course's week three "curious and curiouser" moments of high allegory and serious satire about the complexities of the *virtual* reality of a macroinstitutional culture that she stayed for the subsequent four years. "Land" and "country" metaphors tend to accentuate the essentialist, holistic, singular, and perennial in an institutionalized authority pattern. "Space" metaphors, such as Pierre Gourou's *l'espace sociale* (1973), also the aid world's own "humanitarian space," tend to accentuate the interpretivist, plural, and the dynamics of a pattern of organization and power.

Because mostly our social sciences disciplines lack rules of *cultural*—that is, *culturological* (cf. *sociological*)—methods to learn (and contest), a more or less laissez-faire regime reigns instead. "Any holistic ethnological image is distorted, since it necessarily preselects certain features of a cross-cultural encounter for extra emphasis" (Boon 1976, 71). Why Alice (and not, say, Snow White)? Why the sharpest focus on what aid people say rather than what they do? Why an extraterrestrial (or nonterrestrial) "global" construction that is not reflective of any particular region of the world, or type of agency, or gender, or religion, or for that matter one kind of conflict or disaster, or one kind of aid and aiding rather than another? When the social anthropologist Audrey Richards revisited in the 1950s the traditional Bembaland in what is now Zambia where originally she had worked in the 1930s, she let the shiny new Land Rover the mining company now had put at her disposal do the ruling. When, in mine (a much older model), I was driving Audrey back from Ndola to the Rhodes-Livingstone Institute in Lusaka, she said (and I believe later wrote somewhere) that "If only I'd had a Land Rover in those days, I'd have been able to travel around and would not have written so unqualifiedly about a centralized Bemba kingdom." Lacking in the 1930s such means of getting about outside the Paramount Chief's village, she had perforce been captured by, as it were, the accident of her point of entry into (mis-) representing "Bemba political culture" accordingly. Without, as one might say today, any triangulating to correct—or spread—the bias. While as more a projection of fears and desires, possibilities and impossibilities, than even a geographical, let alone a historical, expression, neither Aidland's past nor future is another country, there are nonetheless all the ordinary issues of representation and misrepresentation, and contingent everyday life, beyond the categorically positional and historic to contend with. To some of these I turn next.

Getting Real About Virtuals?

Going to an assignment country, whether as a seasoned hand on a new posting or mission or as a first-time "youth ambassador," is a more complex undertaking than on the surface of it may at first appear. For one thing it involves traveling to an outpost of one, as well perhaps to the heart of another, world. That is, *two*—as some would see them foreign—lands are involved, not one. "On top"—Aidland—is the one in which you are already inscribed. "Beneath" lies the actual country of your assignment—say Côte d'Ivoire—to which you'll need to be admitted by *its* framing and recognition procedures.

It is on the language and speak of the former that you will depend to survive and get around. The language (and customs) of the latter, very few foreign aiders ever practice, let alone learn: "It is not needed in the office." For expatriates living in whatever passes for the local version of a "green zone" (the in that case heavily militarily defended residential *canton* where the occupying expatriates sequestered themselves in Baghdad), a "kitchen kaffir" (a speak expatriates in east and south Africa use to communicate with their domestic servants) "is all that you'll need." For a normal aid career intending to reach the highest offices, it is absolutely essential not to get labeled as "gone native," which most likely is how your superiors would read any "camel corps" testimony (as Blair's Downing Street abruptly dismissed the Foreign Office expertise that advised against an Iraq invasion). There is simply no place for such "eccentricity" seen in international aid (unlike as in some colonial administrations, where at least it was contained, to prevent any contagion, through a "shunting off" process—say to a posting at an isolated station—where "no harm could come of it" and perhaps even some useful intelligence on "native customs" or "local land tenure" or such).

In the aid-recipient countries to which as foreign aiders we go, the ruler may in earlier life have been a rebel. Now his worries are more likely to be, one, that "too much" democracy would mean "too little" gross national product (as well as possibly regime change) but also, two, that "too little" would translate only into the same so far as aid is concerned: too little democracy would endanger foreign aid coming in. *Yes*, there is much to be said for the "foreign aid is a sideshow" view (Sogge 2002, 32), but, *no*, that does not mean that aid is no show at all. One of the principal reasons for one-party states, also strong centralization as against decentralization, has to do with control of access to foreign aid and influence: lose that control, and there is another risk that the center falls apart. Furthermore, in poor countries, there are precipitous and deep social, economic, and spatial divides and inequalities. Immediately after independence, openly displayed for anyone to see, for example, in charts on the walls of the project's offices (some of which were formerly settlers' ballrooms) in Kenya's formerly "White Highlands," then under resettlement in the name of poverty reduction and decolonization, were detailed facts and figures showing precisely the extent to which it was none other than to the national political elite that the biggest loans, and the biggest plots, had gone. Only two months later, when continuing with team colleagues an intergovernmental inquiry and returning (in those unimaginable days before small digital and mobile phone cameras) to take more notes, such information was top secret. Already it was becoming too politically sensitive. Instead there was just that glossy-brochure stuff with its soft-porn PR information highly sifted to ensure it "systematically minimizes discrepancy with policy goals," in the phrase that emerged recently in the US-led war on not poverty but supposedly terrorism.

The ruler's foreign advisor on aid (or for that matter anything else) is unlikely ever to have been a rebel (save, for example, for such a case as where for "national reconciliation" it may be precisely a—former—rebel who is chosen). Generally, advising (and development and humanitarian studies writing in academia though again with glorious exceptions) tends to be about causes without rebels. Instead she—more advisors than rulers are women—is likely to recommend a neopopulist "people-centered" approach (despite, however, ironically *not* knowing who are poor and which *people*, instead referring only to the usual "less than a dollar a day" poverty *league tables* and such).

To advisers who in an earlier life were once rulers such as government ministers, all will already be known about what a regime considers necessary for its survival and why—and how—reasons of government must in the end trump reasons of development where they differ. Rulers' advisors who are not already familiar with such requirements will soon find they must quickly learn how to handle facts and arguments about what are mostly non-aid matters. Otherwise they will soon be out of a job.

Man is dog's best friend. A poor country's former minister of public works strongly advised another poor country "*not* to go for labour-intensive approaches to physical reconstruction after a nature-sent disaster, for two reasons." He said when I asked him why, "One, too slow, two, too politically risky to mobilize any large number of poor workers over a long period." Speed, he believed, was of the essence and as much for political (of avoiding organized unrest) as practical (without timely emergency action the situation would only become worse) reasons. *Man must not bite dog.* I asked a seasoned trustee of a major NGO in the United Kingdom whether her organization's claim that "only three per cent of the contributions made to us are spent on our administration" could possibly be true. "Well," she said, "it is not in anyone's best interests to dissuade the donations from coming in, *that* is what matters most!" (In a later encounter, however, she herself volunteered that "such a number all depends on how it is measured.") *Let dog eat dog.* Blinkered if not actually blindfolded into Bosnia went a number of like-minded public administration international consultants. One reflected on what he had and hadn't done there: "For all that we knew about financial management, we knew almost nothing about Bosnia. We were . . . doing surgery before we knew anatomy" (Huddleston 1999, 149). They were trying only to transfer a model, along with "best practice" procedures to ensure against foreign-body rejection, not query it. "If management evaluations were to find that the model is perhaps not transferable after all, and that therefore there is no model . . . they would have no replication to recommend and would be seen not to have delivered on the terms of reference" (Wooldridge 1997, 15). *Mandate bites man.* Perfectly correctly according to their women and children mandates, self-referentially UNICEF, like other agencies in that sector, announces time after time, in Haiti last week, in Chile this, that "women and children are at greatest risk." Not the elderly and disabled, which, to get real, is generally more likely to be the case.

Finally *nothing bites nothing.* A UN special agency staffer comes up disingenuously with "a remarkably low dollar sum," a statement that is supposed to show that "it wouldn't cost as much in money terms as one may think to implement universal immunization," perhaps adding to drive the point home that "in fact you may be surprised to hear it is not money as such that is needed so much as political will." (In aid speak "will" surreally substitutes often for what in other sociolects is "capital.")

Tell me only what I need to tell could, however, be another byte. The commissioning agency rejects the findings of the social research into the particular cases that it has commissioned because it is malinformed, not ill informed. It peeps into the *wrong* reality, that of the track record "on the ground *over there.*" The *right* reality, that is, the reality that matters most to the agency for its resources and standing, is the domestic one *at home.* Not its record as its clients (or hosts or beneficiaries) know it, lest, if that were to "get out," it could be used to challenge that domestic standing.

"Why do objectives espoused by aid agencies apparently fail to impact on the reality of assistance delivery and why does reality not impact what objectives are professed. . . . If principles and rights are not genuinely the objectives of aid organizations, what other ends do they pursue?" are the two excellent core questions posed of international aid and aiders by Zoe Marriage in a brilliant research-based book (Marriage 2006). Personally I don't find either question too difficult to answer where, and whether in the name of cosmopolitanism or not, the northern, metropolitan, domestic must hold sway over perhaps everything foreign. No matter how close what are announced as new objectives may be to old, nothing mundane must be allowed to spoil the show, to soil the power game that fantasy and delusion can incubate and decorate stylishly. Thus inauthenticity, *not* getting real about virtuals, remains safe. "Policy goals" that are "sincere" must continue to be "resolutely pursued" by the means announced. Horrendous costs, murderous ethics, multiple purposes that to an extent are self-contradictory, and ends not being achievable anyway by the money, material, or bullets spent are set aside. Or even, as in the foundational "responsibility to protect" writing, and in fact most of its elaborations since, barely if at all even mentioned let alone assessed.

Academia and Aidemia

By "aidemia," a made-up word, I refer generically to "aid practitioners" and their world of work and wisdom. "Academia" of course is standard speak about, for example, the world of university people. Ordinarily the two would be thought of as very different bodies corporate, and institutionally in many regards so they are. Often enough while trespassing in the former from my normal habitus in the latter, I encounter regularly something close to disdain, even hostility, from, surprisingly as it was at first to me, nongovernmental aidemics particularly. Not governmental or intergovernmental. Consultants from commercial companies in "the advice business" tend strongly to keep their distance too from university-based competitors, rather more than just the ways of trade would suggest, perhaps dictate. But within each there are subworlds. Perhaps still increasing numbers of people cross over at times from one to the other. A former Department for International Development director of social development in the United Kingdom takes a university fellowship to write her reflections, a former director of development studies joins a UN special agency as a top executive, and so on and so forth at other levels. Most of the critical analysis of aid and economic development, aid and humanitarian relief, and aid and governance that has been fruitful of new positions is owed not to aidemia staffers but to academics temporarily bought in.

Indeed what can come as a kind of culture shock to such an academic is what little knowledge, and less interest, staffers in, say, a head office in capacity-building aid, may have even in human capital theory and the powerful critiques of that (not least with regard to its false promise for gender equality, where, that is, gender is framed at all). That, at least, was what emerged when, while embedded there in fact for principally another purpose, the chief of one such office asked me to undertake some informal mentoring of his subordinate staff for a week. Pretty well total ignorance of, in fact, humanitarian, development, and governance theory generally (such as is taught regularly in development studies master's degrees and the like) including, if such could be judged from her writings on postconflict aid, on the part of the office's deputy chief. Worse, there was no interest whatsoever to learn. ("I have heard of a book on development and freedom by Nobel Prize winner Amartya Sen, but I'll probably not be able to read it until leaving this position," said one staffer to me over a nice and friendly lunch.) Ah, Saint Sen!

About a professional aid practitioner, a good first question to ask in the particular case is precisely what that practitioner practices. One of my former humanitarian and development studies students now employed in a donor agency answered that question regretfully: "Mostly contract management only . . . that's as close as I can get to development here" (so later she left that aid organization for another, where, however, she found little difference). Another reported, "They said that as I was a woman, I'd work in the gender section, which is not where I want to be at all." (Later, being as well an economist, she, happily, found something closer to her professional training and interests in another agency.) A third was disappointed, not to say appalled, having notable Asian experience, to be given instead an Africa desk. In professional terms what a practitioner finds herself or himself practicing in an aid agency, large or small, appears to depend more on the vacant positions to be filled at the time than anything professionally specific (except where some sort of "parking" policy may prevail for special cases).

Academics speak truth to power, but aidemics dare not even rock the boat. Do they and don't they? In my experience that is far from the truth—and the power. In both academia and aidemia, there are many, some subtle, ways in which, in effect, power defines or even selects what truth it wants to speak and/or hear or not (cf. Sullivan 2000). In the bureaucracies of either, internal transparency and accountability in situations of deceit, incompetence, and fraud are hardly ever rewarded. Whistle-blowing is as rare (and no less penalized) in one as it is in the other. In neither are there clear social constituencies (let alone economic markets) that might be expected somehow to act even just as balancing wheels, let alone something that might actually even engender management responsibility. In both "writing to win" (say, a further contract or a prize) is scarcely unknown. Sociologically, again in both worlds, normally *who* is lying or truthing to *whom*, that is, *relationships*, count more than either content taken in abstraction.

The big systemic divide is between social research, sponsored and conducted under whichever -*emia* colors, and commissioned management consultancy. For one thing, research and consultancy teams tend to be selected differently. In consultancy, not only may the team leader be selected last but he or she may not even be consulted as to who the other team members should be. Then as the consultancy proceeds, the team leader comes to manage it, unlike as in research, partly as a matter of damage limitation. Damage to yourself. "You spend your times in places you don't want to know with people you would not choose. I [as team leader] would not choose them; they would not choose me" (Frank 1986, 232–33). (That some of my own consultancy experience is completely different in that regard relates partly to the different institutional factors such as where it is less individuals than, for example, a technical institute's consultancy wing that is commissioned [with recruiting then being in-house mainly]).

Not every team in which, in whatever role, I served were dream teams, but almost all were close to, if not fully, that, however, as things worked out on the road, and only once did I accept a consultancy to go somewhere I didn't (at first) want to go, Bhutan. My second and third assignments in that country were just like all my others elsewhere: consultancy invitations accepted with alacrity for the mode of close access they gave to a country so as to have the chance of learning up close about an aspect or two of the pattern and story of international aid in a setting that otherwise would have been next to impossible to reach. (But not such access at any price. One tender won by myself and some colleagues then at the Institute of Relief and Development in London in the 1980s, offered by Bob Geldof's LIVE AID for an evaluation of its work then to date in Africa, had to be rejected on professional ethical grounds [much though then that we needed the work]. LIVE AID refused that we should start our inquiries through interviewing its head office, saying that there was no fault on their part to be investigated, only on that of the governments concerned in Africa. Our view was that an evaluation thus denied the freedom to fully determine its own findings [in accordance after all with its Terms of Reference] was not worth doing, and it would systematically lack credibility as an independent undertaking.)

In research and thesis writing, comparing a and b across a number of bridgeable divides with regard to c and d, and so on, often is seen to have a lot to offer both the form and the content of such work. In aid consultancy, such bridgeable divides are far fewer (e.g., interagency, also intersectoral, comparison, whether of programs or outcomes, is as rare as hen's teeth). And while of course research methods must be made open to scrutiny, the hallmark of science (as well as law) being that its process is its product, at the extreme how a consultant has come to a bottom line is not what consultancy is paid to tell. Not how recommendations were arrived at so much as what the more urgent recommendations must be. Not, except in the best work, what a number of the options may be (according to statements of the pluses and negatives of each neatly compared and ranked) but only—while these days it will not be called that—the single best, the silver bullet, the true panacea.

As for whether the report by an independent consultant hired from academia to aidemia is "independent" much depends on what is meant by that relative not absolute quality. Independent from what? A school of thought (say, neoclassicism), a special public interest group, a particular organization's management? Also on whether in a particular case to be preferred is not independence but, for example, expertise in the specific sector under the spotlight or a known public standing for perhaps political probity. At all events, the overwhelming tendency prevails in this as in other consultancy: only like investigates like as, for example, where consultants hired to evaluate an INGO are drawn from the INGO world only, where that and the international governmental and intergovernmental are seen to differ culturally as well as politically.

There is, however, one commonality. In research and consultancy alike, much comes down to the precise Terms of Reference set and accepted. The only UN consultancy of my own as team leader that perhaps did fully "make the difference" that in accepting and undertaking it my team and I hoped for, on the basis of the work done, was also the only one in which the Terms of Reference required that, before we finally reached and submitted our recommendations, they must first be agreed by the government of the host country—in that case Malawi (Apthorpe, Chiviya, and Kaunda 1995).

It was astonishing at first to see that Terms of Reference requirement. It sounded very far from a "no politics please, we are experts" discourse. As things turned out, as a team and at both personal and professional levels, we were greatly favored by one of the government ministers concerned. Our mission was fully endorsed and creatively supported by one of the two, equal status, top executives in the Ministry concerned (but not the other, who so far as we could see was completely opposed to it, presumably simply not wanting *any* discussion about decentralization to become so public as well as perhaps simply being averse anyway to the idea and the word). But that is as it may be. It in no way affected, or was meant to affect, our integrity; it only made it easier and more credible for the assignment to be undertaken, including when, after we had interviewed in almost every district in the country, we went into the last "national consultation" phase that culminated in a nationwide meeting in the capital Lilongwe, chaired by that government minister and greatly facilitated by particularly one highly dedicated and effective national public servant in the Ministry, as well as by the international public servant heading the in-country office of the UNDP (as well as its chief). To that representative and thus very large public meeting we put our draft recommendations as of then for examination and fine-tuning. Next, the Ministry turned our final recommendations into a Cabinet paper, soon after which the new policy was determined and introduced. Given the difference that aid consultancy is meant to achieve, but rarely does, perhaps then that could often be normally the way to go. A certain kind of a third party boosted the inquiry and negotiation process, not a highly intrusive surgical shock event perpetrated by aliens from another planet perhaps with their own agenda.

Expatriates and Impatriates

Finally a word on a divide that may in reality be less real than one might have supposed (and hoped for): that of foreigner and national. While many foreigner-aiders are expatriates in their countries of assignment and/or employment, others are people whom in-country offices of UN organizations employ as "national" and those NGOs hire as "local" staff. Let us call them "impatriates." After allowing for certain specificities, such as what impatriates can do for the office by way of informed local networking, my impression is that some common recruitment practices in the world of international aid may transcend type of agency, type of work, category of contract, and foreigners and nationals. I refer to credentialism and that form of profiling known as "screening" (Corner 1986). In other words, only residual attention is paid to meritocratic qualifications.

Such screening's purpose is more social than technical. It looks to ensure as much likely in instant socialization into the normative ways of the organization concerned as possible. Where the limits of internal labor markets are reached, family or class background, which general educational status might signify, is heavily relied on instead. Especially perhaps in the bigger and more powerful aid organizations, which pay high salaries, as particularly impatriates may see them. So, hey, presto! Perhaps a conformity "even more Etonian than Etonian" results. The general point here is that while from such impatriate appointment the local *networking* already mentioned may gain, local *ownership* doesn't. Donors constantly write in their manifestos that "local ownership" is the very grail of an ethically responsible aid policy, to be achieved with the formative help of "local partners." "Local networking" is rather a facilitating, not constitutive, procedure and device.

The "third-rank economists from first-rank universities" pattern of recruitment to the World Bank applies *mutatis mutandis* surely also in certain other aid organizations (including the IMF and the UN), at the level of specificities (here economists on seats). Yet given that such organizations are in the first as well as the last analysis political bodies (professional only in the middle), overall it must be that nontechnocratic, political concerns should prevail particularly at the uppermost levels (Woods 2006). The overriding qualification for appointment, say, to a UN undersecretaryship in international humanitarian affairs is not meritocratic, in terms of experience and qualification in humanitarian theory and practice, but national political eligibility and reliability for such a high office, probably taking quota considerations into account as well. The national is the credential for the international; the "domestic" again.

Many years ago, the UN was found to spend little time on identification and recruitment of "experts" despite the huge percentage of the total UN budget being spent on their services (Joint Inspection Unit 1978). Perhaps that too accounts for another common practice then: extending experts' contracts beyond their initial terms. (It may have been a record that the UN project manager I succeeded in Manila while "phasing himself out" had enjoyed a period of indispensability of more than 10 years of "helping others help themselves.")

My own recruitment as a "UN expert," when nearing the end of my 18 months as director of African Research at the UN Research Institute for Social Development in one of its global projects, is, perhaps, illustrative. It went as follows. I had applied for the advertised UN job of starting a social sciences library in New York with particular reference to development. Two heads of departments—from New York—then interviewed me in Geneva (for in fact only a few more minutes than had been the case for the UNRISD appointment, when the main question put to me by its then director was about writing skills: "Writing skills are important; are you sure you know when to use a 'that' and when a 'which'?"). Then, from back in New York, they telexed that my interview had been successful and accordingly they were pleased to offer me a Community Development Research and Training assignment in Taiwan!

Quelle surprise! Neither before, during, nor for that matter after the interview in Geneva had anything whatsoever been said or hinted to me about either Taiwan or any position there. (In following up that invitation as an Africanist with some inquiry in a UN office in Geneva about East Asia, about which then I was as ignorant as can be, came among other things the answer "No, you don't need to learn to speak Chinese. Taiwan is already well 'gringoized.'" Quite wrong, as I discovered immediately on landing in Taiwan where I worked for the UN there [also in another capacity, with Amnesty International] until it "evacuated." But that is another story.) Its institutions notwithstanding, aidship depends for its intelligibility on the people who sail her, as well as the ship.

Acknowledgments

To Anne-Meike I am most grateful first for her invitation to make this nonresearch-based contribution to this collection, then for highlighting for me some areas of particular importance for it, then for allowing the scope for points to be detailed sufficiently for the purpose.

Notes

1. Thus, for example, what a major study of the campaigners for nuclear disarmament in the United Kingdom decades ago (Parkin 1968) could yield sociologically and methodologically for a study of aid workers remains still to be explored.

2. Long published work drawn on silently includes Apthorpe (1980, 1998, 2001).

References

Apthorpe, Raymond. 1980. Distant encounters of a third kind. *Bulletin of the Institute of Development Studies* 11 (3): 25–33.

———. 1998. Confessions of an aid consultant: Some personal experience of the art. In *Towards emergency humanitarian aid evaluation*, ed. Raymond Apthorpe. Canberra: Development Issues 12, National Centre for Development Studies, Australian National University.

———. 2001. Evaluations of humanitarian aid in response to the 1999 Kosovo crisis: Synthesis and meta-evaluation. In *ALNAP Annual Review 2001*, chap. 3. London: ALNAP.

———. In press. With Alice in Aidland. In *Adventures in Aidland: The anthropology of professionals in international development*, ed. David Mosse. Oxford: Berghahn.

Apthorpe, Raymond, Esau Chiviya, and Gilbert Kaunda. 1995. *Decentralization in Malawi: Local governance and development*. Lilongwe: UNDP and Ministry of Local Government and Rural Development, Government of Malawi.

Boon, James A. 1976. The birth of the idea of Bali. *Indonesia* 22:71–84.

Corner, Lorraine. 1986. Human resources development for developing countries: A survey of the major theoretical issues. In *Human resources development in Asia and the Pacific: Its social dimensions*, ST/ESCAP/472, 1–28. Bangkok: United Nations, ESCAP.

Frank, Leonard. 1986. The development game. *Granta* 20:230–43.

Gourou, Pierre. 1973. *Pour une geographie humaine*. Paris: Flammarion.

Huddleston, Mark W. 1999. Innocents abroad: Reflections from a public administration consultant in Bosnia. *Public Administration Review* 59 (2): 147–58.

Joint Inspection Unit. 1978. *Report on the role of experts in development co-operation*. Geneva: UN, Joint Inspection Unit.

Lichtheim, George. 1971. *Imperialism*. London: Penguin.

Marriage, Zoe. 2006. *Not breaking the rules, not playing the game: International assistance to countries at war*. London: C. Hurst.

Parkin, Frank. 1968. *Middle class radicalism: The social bases of the British campaign for nuclear disarmament*. Melbourne: Melbourne University Press.

Smillie, Ian. 2009. *Freedom from want: The remarkable success of BRAC, the global grassroots organization that's winning the fight against poverty*. Sterling, VA: Kumarian Press.

Sogge, David. 2002. *Give and take: What's the matter with foreign aid?* Dacca: University Press.

Sullivan, Sian. 2000. Getting the science right: Or introducing science in the first place? In *Political ecology, science, myth and power*, ed. Sian Sullivan, 15–44. London: Arnold.

Woods, Ngaire. 2006. *The globalizers: The IMF, the World Bank, and their borrowers*. Ithaca, NY: Cornell University Press.

Wooldridge, A. 1997. Management consultancy: The advice business. Special report, *Management Consultancy Survey 5*, *The Economist*, March 22.

Contributors

Raymond Apthorpe has taught social anthropology, development, and humanitarian studies at the Australian National University and has undertaken intergovernmental, governmental, and nongovernmental assignments in Africa, Asia, and the Pacific. His publications include "Reading Development Policy: On Framing, Naming, Numbering, and Coding" (1996), "Mission Possible: Six Years of WFP Emergency Food Aid in West Africa" (2001), and "With Alice in Aidland" (in press). He can be reached at raymond.apthorpe@gmail.com.

Keith Brown is an associate research professor at the Thomas J. Watson Institute for International Studies at Brown University. His collaborative work on democracy promotion includes the edited collections *Transacting Transition: The Micropolitics of Democracy Assistance in the Former Yugoslavia* (Kumarian Press, 2006) and "How (Not) to Export Civil Society" (*Southeastern Europe*, June 2009).

Sara de Jong obtained her PhD in politics from the University of Nottingham. Currently she is affiliated with Amsterdam University College and to Aletta, Institute for Women's History in the Netherlands. Her research interests include feminist theory, postcolonial theory, global citizenship theory, NGOs, critical pedagogy, and critical theory.

Anne-Meike Fechter is a senior lecturer in anthropology at the University of Sussex, Brighton, United Kingdom. Her past research focused on corporate expatriates (*Transnational Lives: Expatriates in Indonesia*, Routledge, 2007), and she is currently conducting a research project on aid workers as mobile professionals in Cambodia.

Philip Fountain is a doctoral candidate in anthropology at the Australian National University. He has carried out ethnographic fieldwork in Papua New

Guinea, Indonesia, and North America. His current research explores enacted theologies of development in Christian NGOs.

Heather Hindman is an assistant professor at the University of Texas at Austin. In past research she focused on expatriate employment structures and the mediating role played by midlevel global actors in Nepal. After a recent trip to Kathmandu, she began research on a new project on entrepreneurialism, the prospects for "Bipalis" who return to Nepal, and the effects of the nation's period of long-term provisionality.

Silke Roth is a senior lecturer in sociology at the University of Southampton. She is coeditor (with Florian Kreutzer, in German) of *Transnational Careers: Biographies, Life Conduct and Mobilities* (2006) and (with Ansgar Klein, in German) of *NGOs Between Crisis Prevention and Security Politics* (2007). She is currently working on a monograph on biographies and careers of aid workers.

Ritu Verma is a senior researcher at Out-of-the-Box Research and Action in Cape Town and a visiting research fellow at the Department of Anthropology, University of Sussex. Her interests include the sociocultural and geopolitical dimensions of access to natural resources in East Africa and the Himalayas. Her doctoral research explored the role of culture and social lives of development practitioners in shaping development disconnects.

Thomas Yarrow lectures in social anthropology at Bangor University. Through various forms of ethnographic research, he has developed regional interests in West Africa and theoretical interests in a range of areas including the anthropology of development, public culture, knowledge, elites, modernity, and space and place.

Index

Also From Kumarian Press . . .

Anthropology and Development:

Twinning Faith and Development:
Catholic Parish Partnering in the US and Haiti
Tara Hefferan

Development and Culture
Edited by Deborah Eade

Development Brokers and Translators:
The Ethnography of Aid and Agencies
Edited by David Lewis and David Mosse

Women and the Politics of Place
Edited by Wendy Harcourt and Arturo Escobar

New and Forthcoming:

Class Dynamics of Agrarian Change
Henry Bernstein

The Politics of Collective Advocacy in India:
Tools and Traps
Nandini Deo and Duncan McDuie-Ra

Dual Disasters:
Humanitarian Aid After the 2004 Tsunami
Jennifer Hyndman

Philanthropy and the Nonprofit Sector:
An Introduction
Ken Menkhaus

Visit Kumarian Press at www.kpbooks.com or call toll-free 800.232.0223 for a complete catalog.

Kumarian Press, located in Sterling, Virginia, is a forward-looking, scholarly press that promotes active international engagement and an awareness of global connectedness.